MANAGEMENT FUNCTIONS IN RECREATIONAL THERAPY

David R. Austin
Bryan P. McCormick
Marieke Van Puymbroeck

SAGAMORE
PUBLISHING

Publishers: Joseph J. Bannon and Peter L. Bannon
Sales and Marketing Manager: Misti Gilles
Director of Development and Production: Susan M. Davis
Technology Manager: Mark Atkinson
Production Coordinator: Amy S. Dagit
Graphic Designer: Marissa Willison

ISBN print edition: 978-1-57167-801-0
ISBN e-book: 978-1-57167-802-7
Library of Congress Control Number: 2016943604

Printed in the United States

SAGAMORE
P U B L I S H I N G

1807 N. Federal Dr.
Urbana, IL 61801
www.sagamorepublishing.com

Dedication

To all those who have or will serve as first-line recreational therapy managers and those who have or will practice as clinicians but appreciate the value of sound management practices.

Table of Contents

Preface

This book provides students and practitioners with perspectives on the management of recreational therapy heretofore unavailable to them. Following an introduction to management, reasons for the study of management, and understandings of the healthcare environment, in-depth coverage is given to the five basic functions of management: planning, organizing, staffing, influencing, and controlling. In addition, chapters are provided on key concepts related to the management of recreational therapy programs. Included are chapters on internship supervision, clinical supervision, volunteer management, and managing marketing.

The final chapter in the book is unique in that in contains areas of substantial importance to managers that have received little attention in the recreational therapy literature. Topics encompassed are workplace politics, the transition to first-line management, professional etiquette, how to work with your supervisor, networking concepts, stress and burnout, supporting research, and the benefits of mentoring and how to establish a mentorship program. Many of the management concepts apply to middle level managers, but the focus of our book is on first-line recreational therapy managers and the areas of management identified by the National Council for Therapeutic Recreation Certification (NCTRC).

We wished to provide a book that is readable and easy to follow. We believe we have done so by following a format for each chapter that lists objectives for the chapter, gives definitions of key terms used within the chapter, and ends with a conclusion or summary of the chapter. We also wished for the book to be as inexpensive for students as possible. Sagamore Publishing agreed and has produced the book in paperback to reduce its cost.

Thanks are extended to Joe and Peter Bannon of Sagamore Publishing, who believed in the unique contribution our book could bring to recreational therapy. And our appreciation goes to Amy Dagit for her excellent editorial assistance and Marissa Willison for her work on layout and cover design. Thanks also to Susan Davis for her continuing support.

Instructors using the book in their courses may obtain an Instructor's Guide from Sagamore Publishing at http://www.sagamorepub.com/resources. Included in the Instructor's Guide are possible learning activities for each chapter. Also available to instructors are examination questions for each chapter and PowerPoint slides that illustrate all tables and figures that appear within the book, as well as PowerPoint slides that the authors have developed to enhance the suggested learning activities found in the Instructor's Guide.

David R. Austin, Ph.D., FDRT, FALS
Bryan P. McCormick, Ph.D., CTRS, FDRT, FALS
Marieke Van Puymbroeck, Ph.D., CTRS, FDRT

About the Authors

David R. Austin, Ph.D., FDRT, FALS is Professor Emeritus of Recreational Therapy in the Department of Recreation, Park, and Tourism Studies at Indiana University Bloomington.

Bryan P. McCormick, Ph.D., CTRS, FDRT, FALS is Professor of Recreational Therapy in the Department of Recreation, Park, and Tourism Studies at Indiana University Bloomington.

Marieke Van Puymbroeck, Ph.D., CTRS, FDRT is Professor of Recreational Therapy and Coordinator of Recreational Therapy in the Department of Parks, Recreation, and Tourism Management at Clemson University.

Chapter 1

Introduction to Management

Objectives
- Provide reasons why a student preparing to become a recreational therapist should study management.
- Define the term *management.*
- Define the term *leadership.*
- Explain the relationship between leadership and management.
- List the types of power managers and leaders may employ.
- Identify leadership styles managers may adopt.
- Explain what is meant by the term *supervisor* or *first-line manager.*
- Become interested in learning about management theories, principles, and practices.

Key Terms
- **Leadership:** Involves influencing the beliefs, opinions, and actions of others.
- **Management:** The art and science of accomplishing goals through people or, simply put, getting things done through people while performing the functions of planning, organizing, staffing, influencing, and controlling.
- **Manager:** A generic term describing anyone overseeing the work of others from supervisors (also termed first-line managers) to middle managers up to senior managers.
- **Supervisor or first-line manager:** The terms *supervisor* and *first-line manager* are synonymous and refer to the first level of management in which the individual oversees those who directly deliver services. Occasionally, the term *front-line manager* is used in the management literature to refer to the first level of management.
- **Legitimate power:** A type of power bestowed on those in positions of authority, such as management personnel.
- **Authoritarian leadership:** An autocratic top-down leadership style in which managers order or direct employees (known as Theory X).
- **Participative leadership:** A leadership style that encourages employees to participate in decision making (known as Theory Y).

- **Theory Z:** A leadership theory developed by the Japanese that reflects Japanese cultural traditions and values that seem compatible with a paternalistic approach to leadership.
- **Bureaucratic leadership:** A controlling, by-the-book management approach in which managers emphasize the enforcement of policies, rules, procedures, and orders for upper management.
- **Situational leadership:** A flexible and adaptive leadership style in which managers respond to the contingencies at hand.
- **Laissez-faire leadership:** A hands-off leadership style that may be applied with strong work teams but may lend itself to misuse by incompetent or lazy managers.

Why Study Management?

The reason for students pursuing professional preparation in recreational therapy (RT) to study management may not be clear initially. Management may not seem to be a topic of concern for healthcare professionals, such as recreational therapists, who strive to help clients achieve improved health and well-being. Management may even be viewed negatively. It may seem that it only relates to students in the business school concerned with how corporations increase productivity and profits.

Yet the contention of the authors of this text is that management is integral in preparing RT professionals. First, recreational therapists at all levels can use management knowledge and skills. Management skills are valuable in many professional endeavors of recreational therapists. For example, in instances (e.g., long-term care) in which there is only a sole recreational therapist, that individual manages aide-level staff and volunteers as well as performs other functions, such planning and evaluating the program and preparing budgets for equipment and supplies. Richeson (2015) explained that recreational therapists in geriatric care are asked to perform any number of roles, one of which is a supervisor or first-line manager:

> Recreational therapists in long-term care settings often are asked to take on the role of department directors. This role includes supervisory and managerial responsibilities such as organizing multiple projects, motivating staff, coaching individual persons and teams, assessing individual skills and weaknesses, hiring and developing staff, fostering accountability and ownership, delegating responsibility, prioritizing tasks, earning trust and respect, and communicating with peers and superiors. (p. 199)

At one time, recreational therapists only had to have clinical skills, but today not only in long-term care but also in all types of settings, they may be called upon to do more. For instance, even when recreational therapists are a part of a department of recreational therapists, they may be called upon to perform management functions for a particular area of the department's services, such as supervising the aquatic therapy program or adventure therapy program.

A second reason to gain understandings of management is that recreational therapists often have opportunities to advance into supervisory positions as first-line managers. Because most organizations do not provide adequate orientation programs for new supervisors (McConnell, 2014), prior management training gained while completing bachelor's or master's degrees in RT will serve recreational therapists well by giving them the background to make career advancement possible.

Finally, equipped with knowledge of management, recreational therapists realize that good management practices are necessary to ensure a constructive environment in which to help clients achieve their goals. Well-run organizations positively affect the abilities of recreational therapists to do their job of bringing about therapeutic outcomes. With a background in management, recreational therapists will have an appreciation for and understanding of working within a system that follows sound management practices. In short, recreational therapists with knowledge of management can better grasp the big picture of an organization and understand the roles of managers within the structure so they have a comprehension of how the organization functions and how to best fit into and succeed within it.

The National Council for Therapeutic Recreation Certification (NCTRC) certainly endorses the inclusion of the organization and management of RT services as a part of the professional preparation of recreational therapists and lists a number of management tasks (e.g., personnel, intern, and volunteer supervision and management; budgeting and fiscal responsibility) as required knowledge areas for the NCTRC exam (NCTRC, 2014).

Specifically, two of the NCTRC Standards of Knowledge, Skills, and Abilities for the CTRS are to (1) "have a basic understanding of the published standards of practice for the profession of therapeutic recreation [or recreational therapy] and the influence that such standards have on the program planning process" and (2) "possess a broad understanding of organizing and managing therapeutic recreation [or recreational therapy] services including, but not limited to, the development of a written plan of operation and knowledge of external regulations, resource management, components of quality improvement, as well as basic understanding of staff/volunteer management" (NCTRC, 2014, pp. 29–30).

The NCTRC (2014) conducted a job analysis of tasks performed and areas of knowledge required of CTRSs that provides the knowledge base for therapeutic recreation/recreational therapy (TR/RT) practice and "forms the basis of the NCTRC exam content. . . ." (p. 26). Among those areas the NCTRC identifies as skills and areas of knowledge under the category of Management of TR/RT Services are the following: (a) comply with standards and regulations (e.g., government, credentialing, agency, professional); (b) conduct an initial and/or ongoing organizational needs assessment for TR/RT service delivery (e.g., populations served, internal and external resources); (c) prepare and update comprehensive TR/RT written plan of operation (e.g., programs, risk management, policies and procedures); (d) confirm that programs are consistent with agency mission and TR/RT service philosophy and goals; (e) recruit, train, educate, supervise, and evaluate professionals, paraprofessionals, and/or volunteers (e.g., plan in-service training, develop staffing schedules); (f) provide staff development and mentorship; (g) develop, implement, and/or maintain TR/RT internship program in accordance with legal requirements and professional guidelines; (h) prepare, implement, evaluate, and monitor TR/RT service annual budget; (i) support research programs or projects; (j) prepare and report quality improvement data; and (k) write summary reports of TR/RT services (NCTRC, 2014, p. 27).

Thus, students wish to study RT management for a number of reasons, including preparing to become a CTRS. In this chapter, the reader will become acquainted with management, how leadership relates to management, and leadership styles used by managers. As a result, it is hoped that the reader will gain (a) a basic understanding of what management is about and (b) an interest in learning more about management.

> "Reading a book about management isn't going to make you a good manager any more than a book about guitar will make you a good guitarist, but it can get you thinking about the most important concepts."
>
> Drew Houston

Defining Management

Various definitions of management are listed in the literature. Darr (2011) presented the following definition of management:

Management or managing has four main elements. It is (1) a process comprised of interrelated social and technical functions and activities (2) that accomplishes organizational objectives, (3) achieves these objectives through use of people and other resources, and (4) does so in a formal organizational setting. (p. 8)

Grohar-Murry and Langan (2011) wrote this when defining management:

Management is considered a discipline and a process. Management, as a process, uses both interpersonal and technical aspects through which objectives of an organization (or part of it) are accomplished efficiently and effectively by using human, physical, financial, and technical resources. The management role is dedicated to facilitating the work in the organization through one's own efforts and the efforts of others. (p. 148)

Similarly, Dunn (2002) wrote:

The term *management* has been defined in many ways, generally as a process of coordinating and integrating human, technical, and other resources to accomplish specific results. A more meaningful definition for our purposes (within healthcare management) *is the process of getting things done through and with people by directing and motivating the efforts of individuals toward common objectives.* (p. 12)

These definitions of management explain that there are a number of elements involved in management including human, technical, physical, and financial resources, and each focuses on management accomplishing the objectives of the organization through the efforts of the manager and the personnel the manager is directing and motivating. Some definitions focus exclusively on management being the accomplishment of objectives with and through people. Bleich and Kosiak (2007) defined management "as the work of any individual who guides others through a series of routines, procedures, or predefined practice guidelines" (p. 6). Even more succinct is this definition of management supplied by McConnell (2014): "Management is getting things done through people" (p. 6).

Based on the definitions of management presented, it may be concluded that a central dimension in management involves overseeing the work of others to reach the organization's goals. The emphasis on the element of managers' interactions with those with whom they work logically leads to the conclusion that management is largely a social enterprise. Torkildsen (2005) indicated as much when he wrote this: "Management—in the simple idiom of today—is getting things done with and through people, and as such management is a social process" (p. 371).

Thus, management clearly involves the social dynamic of overseeing the work of others to reach the organization's goals. Perhaps at one time this was accomplished by "bosses" who employed authoritarian management styles in which they barked orders for underlings to carry out. McConnell (2014) indicated that such a management style is not appropriate and will not work today. He wrote: "Given today's generally enlightened workforce, today's supervisors must be leaders. They are the primary source of answers, instructions, assistance, and guidance for the employees who report to them" (p. 7).

Ambrose and Gullatte (2011) provided a statement that not only defines management, but also includes the importance of the element of leadership brought out by McConnell (2014). Their statement is a good means to sum up this segment on defining management and leads to the topic of leadership and management. They wrote:

> Management is the art and science of executing or getting goals accomplished through people. The differences between leadership and management are often blended by a fine distinction. McCrimmon (2010) simplified the distinction: Managers execute, while leaders direct. Successful managers are skilled at planning, organizing, monitoring, supervising, and coordinating people and activities. On the other hand, they also are skilled at leadership—thinking strategically, challenging the status quo, envisioning future direction, and inspiring, coaching, and empowering people so that they *want* to go in that direction. (Ambrose & Gullatte, 2011, p. 2)

Leadership and Management

As Ambrose and Gullatte (2011) indicated, management and leadership are not the same even though they are related, because the best managers possess leadership qualities. Nevertheless, the terms *management* and *leadership* are sometimes used to mean the same thing (Arikian, 2010; Sullivan, 2012). As discussed in the segments that follow, the terms have separate meanings.

Management

Managers are formally appointed to their positions of authority within an organization. Thus, managers have a legitimate source of power (see Table 1.1) having been delegated authority because of their positions. In their positions, managers are expected to execute specific functions to meet their responsibility for effectively accomplishing the goals outlined for them by the organization (Marquis & Huston, 2009). The specific functions of management involve planning, staffing, organizing, influencing, and controlling. (These five aspects are discussed in detail in Chapter 4.) In short, management involves the work of managers, who have the responsibility to get things done by carrying out basic management functions with and through those with whom they work.

Leadership

Leadership involves influencing the beliefs, opinions, and actions of others or, as put by Ambrose and Gullatte (2011), "leadership is a process of persuasion and example by which one inspires and engages others in achieving a shared vision" (p. 2). Similarly, Bannon (1999) characterized leadership as the ability to influence and motivate people toward achieving identified goals. In his words, "a leader is a person who has influence with people, which causes them to listen and agree on common goals, to follow that person's advice, and to go into action toward these goals" (Bannon, 1999, p. 388). Writing about leadership in nursing, Cherry (2011) wrote: "Leadership is a combination of intrinsic personality traits, learned leadership skills, and characteristics of the situation. The function of a leader is to guide people and groups to accomplish common goals" (p. 335).

The emphasis of leaders is on interpersonal relationships through which they influence followers. They focus on gathering information, encouraging group processes, giving feedback, and empowering others (Marquis & Huston, 2009). Of course, the best leaders successfully influence the behaviors of followers, and as Cherry (2011) and Sullivan (2012) make clear in the segment that follows, the ability to influence is a key to good management.

The Relationship of Leadership and Management

It is apparent that leadership and management differ but are closely connected. Cherry (2011) and Sullivan (2012) each summed up the relationship between leadership and management. Cherry wrote:

Although leadership and management are intertwined and it is difficult to discuss one without the other, these concepts are different. Leadership is the ability to guide or influence others, whereas management is the coordination of resources (time, people, supplies) to achieve outcomes. People are led, whereas activities and things are managed. Leaders are able to motivate and inspire others, whereas managers have assigned responsibility for accomplishing the goals of an organization. A good manager should also be a good leader, but this may not always be the case. A person with good management skills may not have leadership ability. Similarly persons with leadership abilities may not have good management skills. Leadership and management skills are complementary; both can be learned and developed through experience and improving skills in one area will enhance abilities in the other. (p. 336)

Sullivan (2012) similarly wrote:

All good managers are also good leaders—the two go hand in hand. However, one may be a good manager of resources and not be much of a leader of people. Likewise, a person who is a good leader may not manage well. Both roles can be learned; skills gained can enhance either role. (p. 41)

From the accounts of Cherry (2011) and Sullivan (2012), management and leadership clearly differ. Management deals with accomplishing the organization's goals. The process of goal attainment, however, typically involves people fulfilling tasks. This is when leadership comes into play. Good managers have good leadership skills through which they influence staff to get things done efficiently and effectively.

In short, management and leadership are intertwined. Management gets things done. Leadership provides a means by which to get things done through others. The best managers have good leadership skills.

Management and leadership skills can be learned and enhanced. That is what this book is about, the development of management and leadership skills, with its focus specifically directed toward enhancing the management and leadership skills of recreational therapists.

In the remainder of this chapter, concepts basic to understanding the dynamics of leadership within management are presented. First covered are the types of power available to those in management positions. This is followed by a brief discussion of leadership styles that may be assumed by those in management positions.

Power in Management and Leadership

Yoder-Wise (2011) stated: "*Influence* is the process of using power" (p. 179). Grohar-Murry and Langan (2011) wrote: "The force needed to meet goals and get things done is power" (p. 130). Managers may rely upon a number of types of power to influence staff to achieve the organization's goals. It is important that managers understand and are able to apply the dynamics of power to influence positive outcomes from staff. For example, supervisors are given legitimate power by nature of being put in places of authority by higher level managers. Those bestowed authority as managers will also likely hold reward power and coercive power. Managers who possess good leadership qualities are likely to have referent or expert power. Referent power is gained by possessing a winning personality and being someone whom others like because of qualities of being open and friendly. Expert power is obtained by those with admired skills and abilities, such as a recreational therapist who has a reputation as being a master clinician. The most effective managers know how to exercise each type of power and do not rely exclusively on one (Friedman, 2011). Sources and examples of power are listed in Table 1.1.

Table 1.1

Sources and Examples of Power

Type	Source	Example
Legitimate	Power bestowed on those in positions of authority.	Appointed by an authority to a management position.
Connection	Power from relationships with those with influence.	Being on an interdisciplinary team made up of doctors and others of influence.
Information	Having information valuable to others.	Having knowledge of decisions made by senior managers.
Reward	Having the ability to bestow awards.	Having the authority to reward staff for their behaviors.
Coercive	Power that comes from being able to levy punishment.	The ability to use the agency's disciplinary system to alter behavior.
Expert	Power derived from the skills and knowledge possessed by the individual.	Having a high level of clinical skills as a recreational therapist.
Referent	Gained by the closeness others feel for an individual.	Being liked because of an open, friendly, winning personality.

Note. Adapted from *Therapeutic Recreation Processes and Techniques: Evidence-Based Recreational Therapy* (7th ed., p. 292), by D.R. Austin, 2013, Urbana, IL: Sagamore.

Leadership Styles

Managers may adopt a number of leadership styles. These are briefly introduced in this chapter and are covered in greater detail in Chapter 8. What follows largely draws upon McConnell's (2014) presentation of leadership styles. Although the expression *leadership styles* is employed in the literature, these approaches could be termed management styles because they are adopted by managers and some rely on directing employees rather than on leading them.

Authoritarian Leadership (Theory X)

McConnell (2014) described the controlling nature of authoritarian leadership style, which minimizes the degree of involvement by subordinates:

> Leaders who use this style are often described as task-oriented, paternalistic, or autocratic. They "run a tight ship," and they order or direct their employees. This style is also referred to as top-down or "I" (the leader comes first) management (also referred to as Theory X). (p. 211)

Participative Leadership (Theory Y)

McConnell (2014) described participative leadership as follows:

Participative leaders believe that people want to work and are willing to assume responsibility. They believe that, if treated properly, people can be trusted and will put forth their best efforts. Participative leaders motivate by means of internal factors (for example, task satisfaction, self-esteem, recognition, and praise). They explain why things must be done, listen to what employees have to say, and respect their opinions. They delegate wisely and effectively. (p. 212)

Theory Z Leadership

Ironically, the third leadership style as presented by McConnell (2014) is not related to authoritarian leadership (also referred to as Theory X) and participative leadership (referred to as Theory Y). McConnell explained Theory Z leadership as follows:

Unrelated to Theory X and Theory Y, Theory Z was labeled as such primarily to distinguish it from authoritarian leadership. Originated by the Japanese, Theory Z is characterized by employee participation and egalitarianism. It features guaranteed employment, maximum employee input, and strong reliance on team mechanisms such as quality circles. (p. 213)

Bureaucratic Leadership

McConnell (2014) described bureaucratic leadership (perhaps better termed bureaucratic management because the manager directs rather than influences) as follows:

Terms descriptive of this style include rules-oriented, by-the-book management, and "they" management (essentially impersonal). Bureaucratic managers act as monitors or police. They enforce policies, rules, procedures, and orders from upper management. They tend to be buck-passers who take little or no responsibility for directives and who often experience near-paralysis of thought and action when encountering a situation for which no rule exists. (p. 213)

"Leadership styles have evolved in the past few decades. The biggest shift has been a move from the old-school traits that we have traditionally been taught to value, such as authoritativeness, strategic thinking, and bottom-line decision-making, to a greater emphasis on humility, vulnerability, transparency, selflessness, and authenticity."

(T. Spaulding, 2015, p. 54)

Situational Leadership

McConnell (2014) coined the phrase "different strokes for different folks leadership" to describe situational leadership because this leadership style is flexible and adaptive as it is based on the contingencies at hand.

Here is how McConnell (2014) described situational leadership:

> As the name suggests, flexible leaders adapt their approach to the specific situations and to the particular needs of different members of the team. As employees gain experience and confidence, the leadership style changes from highly directive to supportive (from task-related to people-related). For example, two new employees may start work on the same date. If one has had previous experience and the other has had none, different directive styles are needed. A show-and-tell approach is required for the novice, but the same may not be appropriate for the experienced person. (pp. 213–214)

Laissez-Faire Leadership

McConnell (2014) used terms such as "hands-off," "fence-straddling," and "absentee" to describe laissez-faire leadership. He wrote: "Laissez-faire managers avoid giving orders, solving problems, or making decisions. They are physically evasive and are sometimes nowhere to be found when needed. Verbally, they are often masters of double-talk" (p. 214).

Which Leadership Style to Apply

From the review of the various leadership styles, it is apparent that no single leadership style is appropriate for all situations. But knowing the options available will help the recreational therapist select from the available styles to fit the situation. It is probable that recreational therapists will have a primary leadership style but will modify their usual style to meet the situation. Many in healthcare have favored participative management as an approach. For example, Muller (1995) wrote: "The need and demand for the highest-quality management of all health care delivery activities requires a participative management approach" (p. 15). Furthermore, many RT managers likely will generally employ a participative management style because of the humanistic and optimistic perspective that they tend to embrace. This style fits well when working with skilled and educated professionals who enjoy being part of a collaborative in which they are involved in decision making. Yet a firm, autocratic style will be required in some instances, such as when dealing with safety or regulatory issues or when supervising unskilled staff who are not well prepared to participate in decision making and who would probably not be comfortable doing so (Dunn, 2002; Zimmerman, 2002). Because of its flexible nature, situational leadership is well suited to both instances when a collaborative, collegial approach is called for as well as when a more directive approach is needed. Thus, it would seem situational leadership may have application in RT.

The astute manager will be able to use any of the leadership styles or a mixture of them when needed. Dunn (1998) concluded: "Employing the appropriate style will largely determine the degree to which the leader can influence others in the performance of a task. This is what leading is all about" (p. 351).

Supervisor or First-Line Manager

Whichever leadership styles recreational therapists put into practice will most likely be employed when taking on the role of a supervisor or first-line manager because most management positions open to recreational therapists are supervisory in nature. The terms *supervisor* and *first-line manager* are synonymous and refer to the first level of management in which the individual oversees those who directly deliver services. A typical position is supervisor of an RT department. Larger RT departments may have supervisors who provide the direct supervision of staff and who report to a departmental director. In these instances, those in supervisory positions would be considered to be first-line managers and the director would likely be considered to be a middle manager. The primary focus of this text will remain on supervisors or first-line managers.

Dunn (2016) indicated three essential skills are necessary for supervisors or first-line managers. First, the good supervisor or first-line manager must understand the clinical and technical work performed within the service area (e.g., RT unit or department). Second, the supervisor or first-line manager needs to possess human relations skills to perceive how to work well with staff and how to motivate them. Third, the supervisor or first-line manager needs the conceptual skills to comprehend the big picture of how all the parts of the organization work together, to grasp how to coordinate them.

Cadwell (2006) contrasted the differences between staff and first-line managers. These are listed in Table 1.2.

Table 1.2
Differences Between Staff and First-Line Managers

Staff

• Focus on their specific job skills	• Work a specified number of hours
• Contribute to the department's success	• Receive information from others
• Do the work	• Are personally motivated and satisfied
• Work on specific priorities	• Are effective team members
• Are most concerned about the quality of their own work	• Have a good attitude, but can "get away" with having a bad attitude from time to time

First-Line Managers

• Focus on supervising staff	• Are willing to work overtime and on a scheduled day off if needed
• Contribute to the entire organization's success	• Share information with others
• Ensure work gets done	• Motivate and develop other employees
• Are involved with multiple priorities	• Are effective team builders
• Are concerned about the quality of the entire team's work	• Maintain a positive attitude even when circumstances would make it easy to be negative

Note. Adapted from *First-Line Supervision* (5th ed., p. 3), by C. M. Cadwell, 2006, New York, NY: American Management Association.

Summary

The purpose of the chapter was to introduce students studying RT to concepts of management and the need for them to gain understandings of management theories and principles. After a presentation on why RT students should study management, discussion followed on the terms *management* and *leadership* and their relationship to one another. Coverage was then given to the types of power managers may employ. Next, there was an extensive review of a number of leadership styles managers may adopt. The chapter concluded with a discussion of possible application of leadership styles by recreational therapists and an explanation that most management positions open to recreational therapists will be supervisory or first-line management positions.

As a result of this chapter, the authors of this text hope that RT students will understand that management involves more than what they may have considered to be the mundane functions of management (i.e., planning, organizing, staffing, influencing, and controlling) and that it has an important social component as well. The authors of this text desire that this initial chapter will "whet the appetites" of RT students to learn more about management.

References

Ambrose, D., & Gullatte, M. M. (2011). Inspiring self and others to leadership. In M. M. Gullatte (Ed.), *Nursing management principles and practice* (2nd ed., pp. 1–19). Pittsburgh, PA: Oncology Nursing Society.

Arikian, V. (2010). Leadership and management in nursing practice. In M. Klainberg & K. M. Dirschel (Eds.), *Today's nursing leaders: Managing, succeeding, excelling* (pp. 77–88). Boston, MA: Jones & Bartlett.

Austin, D. R. (2013). *Therapeutic recreation processes and techniques: Evidence-based recreational therapy* (7th ed.). Urbana, IL: Sagamore.

Bannon, J. (1999). *911 management.* Urbana, IL: Sagamore.

Bleich, M. R., & Kosiak, C. P. (2007). Managing, leading, and following. In P. S. Yoder-Wise (Ed.), *Leading and managing in nursing* (4th ed., pp. 3–25). St. Louis, MO: Mosby Elsevier.

Cadwell, C. M. (2005). *First-line supervision* (5th ed.). New York, NY: American Management Association.

Cherry, B. (2011). Nursing leadership and management. In B. Cherry & S. R. Jacob (Eds.), *Contemporary nursing: Issues, trends, & management* (pp. 333–363). St. Louis, MO: Elsevier Mosby.

Darr, K. (2011). Introduction to management and leadership concepts, principles, and practices. In R. E. Burke & L. H. Friedman (Eds.), *Essentials of management and leadership in public health* (pp. 7–24). Sudbury, MA: Jones & Bartlett Learning.

Dunn, R. T. (2016). *Dunn & Haimann's healthcare management* (10th ed.). Chicago, IL: Health Administration Press.

Dunn, R. T. (1998). *Haimann's supervisory management for healthcare organizations* (6th ed.). Boston, MA: WCB/McGraw-Hill.

Dunn, R. T. (2002). *Haimann's supervisory management for healthcare organizations* (7th ed.). Chicago, IL: Health Administration Press.

Friedman, L. H. (2011). Changing role of public health managers and leaders. In R. E. Burke & L. H. Friedman (Eds.), *Essentials of management and leadership in public health* (pp. 149–158). Sudbury, MA: Jones & Bartlett Learning.

Grohar-Murry, M. E., & Langan, J. (2011). *Leadership and management in nursing* (4th ed.). Upper Saddle River, NJ: Pearson Health Science.

Marquis, B. L., & Huston, C. J. (2009). *Leadership roles and management functions in nursing: Theory and application* (6th ed.). Philadelphia, PA: Wolters Kluwer/ Lippincott Williams & Wilkins.

McConnell, C. R. (2014). *Umiker's management skills for the new health care supervisor* (6th ed.). Burlington, MA: Jones & Bartlett Learning.

McCrimmon, M. (2010). How managers differ from leaders. Retrieved from http:// www.leadersdirect.com/whats-a-manager

Muller, M. (1995). Participative management in health care services. *Curationis, 18*(1), 15–21.

National Council for Therapeutic Recreation Certification. (2014). Certification standards part II: NCTRC exam information. Retrieved from http://www.nctrc. org/documents/1NewAp.pdf

Richeson, N. E. (2015). Geriatric practice. In D. R. Austin, M. E. Crawford, B. P. McCormick, & M. Van Puymbroeck (Eds.), *Recreational therapy: An introduction* (4th ed., pp. 193–209). Urbana, IL: Sagamore.

Spaulding, T. (2015). *The heart-led leader.* New York, NY: Crown Business.

Sullivan, E. J. (2012). *Effective leadership and management in nursing* (8th ed.). Boston, MA: Pearson.

Torkildsen, G. (2005). *Leisure and recreation management* (5th ed.). New York, NY: Routledge.

Yoder-Wise, P. S. (2011). *Leading and managing in nursing* (5th ed.). St. Louis, MO: Elsevier Mosby.

Zimmerman, P. G. (2002). *Nursing management secrets.* Philadelphia, PA: Hanley & Belfus.

Chapter 2

Recreational Therapy and Management

Objectives
- List the four levels of management.
- Differentiate between the terms *human relations skills, conceptual skills,* and *technical skills.*
- State what is meant by clinical skills.
- Give examples of management skills.
- State the purposes of clinical supervision.
- Argue for or against the notion that clinical supervision should not be provided by the first-line manager.
- List skills recreational therapists possess that transfer to management.
- List pluses and minuses of becoming a first-line manager.

Key Terms
- **Levels of management:** Management levels typically are first-line managers, middle managers, senior managers, and the chief executive officer.
- **First-line manager or supervisor:** The terms *first-line manager* and *supervisor* are synonymous and refer to the lowest level of management in which the individual oversees those who directly deliver services. Sometimes, the term *front-line manager* is used in the literature to describe the manager who oversees staff who deliver direct services.
- **Human relations skills:** Understanding supervisees and being able to lead them, as well as to deal with clients, the public, team members in the workplace, and personality conflicts.
- **Conceptual skills:** Having the cognitive ability to examine how factors interact in a given situation to foresee the consequences of actions. Problem solving is the primary conceptual skill required of first-line managers.
- **Technical skills:** Having to do with the clinical skills and managerial skills required of first-line managers.
- **Clinical supervision:** A program that serves the dual purpose of helping the supervisee develop and maintain clinical skills and of protecting client welfare.

In Chapter 1, a general picture of management was provided by defining the term, discussing the relationship between management and leadership, and presenting leadership styles that managers may apply. Chapter 2 looks at the levels of management and how recreational therapists fit into and function within these levels. The primary emphasis is on the functioning of first-line managers.

Levels of Management

Five levels of employees are typically found within health and human service agencies in which recreational therapists are employed. These are shown in Figure 2.1. The initial level is the nonsupervisory level into which entry-level recreational therapists are generally hired. The next level is first-line managers or supervisors. First-line managers or supervisors report to middle managers, who are at the next level of management. In turn, middle managers report to senior managers. Organizations also tend to have a chief executive officer (CEO) to whom senior managers report. The degree of responsibility and authority grows as individuals move up the managerial ladder from first-line managers, to middle managers, to senior managers, and ultimately to CEO.

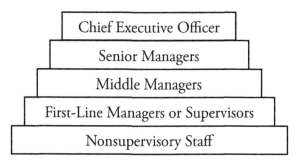

Figure 2.1. Levels of employees.

Human Relations Skills, Conceptual Skills, Technical Skills, and Levels of Management

All levels of management require human relations skills, conceptual skills, and technical skills. *Human relations skills* have to do with understanding supervisees and being able to motivate and lead them. Human relations also includes dealing with clients and the public as well as working with teams and dealing with personality conflicts. *Conceptual skills* involve the mental ability to examine how factors interact in a given situation to foresee the consequences of actions. *Technical skills* have to do with clinical skills and managerial skills.

Managers employ human relations skills at all levels, although those with whom they interact will differ. For example, first-line managers will primarily deal with those they supervise and with clients. In contrast, CEOs will largely deal with senior managers, boards, and CEOs of other organizations.

Technical and conceptual skills are applied in different proportions depending on where the manager is along the management ladder. Technical skills are predominantly the responsibility of first-line managers. The first-line manager must possess high-level clinical skills[1] to supervise providers of direct client services. The first-line manager also has to develop managerial skills (e.g., budgeting and program planning and evaluation). The first-line manager needs to use conceptual skills primarily to problem solve.

In comparison, middle and senior managers are not required to use technical skills to the degree of first-line managers. Because of their levels of responsibility and authority, it is incumbent upon middle and senior managers, however, to have well-honed conceptual skills because they are regularly called upon to make decisions (or decide not to make decisions) and to comprehend the possible consequences of their decisions (or lack of decisions). CEOs and senior managers must also demonstrate the ability to create visions for their organizations and to develop long-range plans (Burke & Friedman, 2011; Hurd, Barcelona, & Meldrum, 2008).

As mentioned in Chapter 1, the majority of management positions open to recreational therapists are supervisory or first-line management positions. The primary focus of this chapter is on the supervisor or first-line manager rather than on higher levels of management.

First-Line Management Position

From the review of the human relations, technical, and conceptual skills required of first-line managers, it should be clear that the role of being a supervisor is difficult and demanding. Cadwell (2006) indicated the following about assuming the role of supervisor: "Now you're the one who has worry about things that don't get done. Your responsibility goes beyond just putting in your time. You are responsible for results—your own results as well as those of your employees" (p. 1).

It is particularly incumbent on supervisors to have the human relations skills to oversee the staff they supervise daily. The technical skills that supervisors have to demonstrate are no less important. Supervisors who oversee the clinical work of therapists must possess high levels of clinical skills and be able to set up mechanisms (e.g., staff training, clinical supervision programs) to help their staff continue to update and increase their levels of clinical skills in areas such as client assessment, clinical reasoning, and outcome measurement.

First-line managers will also likely have to consult with staff on how to handle difficult cases, unless a clinical supervisor (different from the first-line manager) is provided to assist staff. No individual can be expected to have the clinical skills to perform as a first-line manager or as a clinical supervisor without first gaining the education and a great deal of clinical experience. More detailed information on the role of the clinical supervisor is provided later in this chapter.

---

[1] Clinical skills are competencies connected with the provision of client services by recreational therapists who follow the RT process of assessment, planning, implementation, and evaluation to bring about health-related outcomes.

Of course, technical skills in management are likewise required of first-line managers. These supervisors need to have skills in every area of management functioning including planning, staffing, organizing, influencing, and controlling. Information on these management functions is provided throughout this text. Dunn (2002) articulated the arduous task that awaits supervisors:

> The supervisor must be a good boss, a good manager, and a team leader of the employees who work in this unit. This includes having the technical, professional, and clinical competence to run the department smoothly and see that the employees carry out their assignments successfully. (p. 6)

In addition to performing responsibilities with their employees, supervisors must maintain a good relationship with their superior. In the case of a supervisor of a recreational therapy (RT) department, the middle manager likely holds a title such as chief of therapy services, rehabilitation services director, or activity therapy coordinator.

McConnell (2014) captured well the relationship of the supervisor with the higher level manager:

> If you have been promoted for the ranks, you already know something about the person who is now your immediate boss. You know whether he or she prefers to communicate verbally or in writing. You have learned how to interpret the boss's body language, when to stay out of the way, and what pleases or displeases this manager. If you are new to the department, you need to learn these things as soon as you can.
>
> Good supervisors help their managers control their time by handling trifles themselves. They give the managers all necessary information, even when the news is bad. They don't run to their managers with problems asking for help, they do their homework and offer recommended solutions. They admit their mistakes and do not make the same mistake twice. (p. 13)

The supervisor additionally needs to establish and maintain good working relationships with colleagues who are supervisors of other units and other leaders within the organization, such as the volunteer director. Building rapport with peers and leaders within the organization pays off when a time arises to ask for their help or advice.

Perhaps the most challenging part of the job of the supervisor is being "the person in the middle," the connecting link, between higher management and staff. In this role, the supervisor must assume responsibility for communicating the employees' concerns to higher level managers while carrying out the goals and policies imposed by senior managers. It is a formidable task to represent the supervisor's staff but also carry out the responsibilities of a first-line manager, who must implement directives from above and oversee staff to ensure the work gets done (Dunn, 2002).

The best way to encapsulate the role of the first-line manager is perhaps to list the activities performed by first-line managers as Cadwell (2006) has in his book *First-Line Supervision*:

- Focus on supervising people.
- Contribute to the entire organization's success.

- Ensure work gets done.
- Be involved with multiple priorities.
- Be concerned about the quality of the team's work.
- Be willing to work overtime and on a scheduled day off, knowing there may not be extra pay.
- Share information with others.
- Motivate and develop other employees.
- Be an effective team builder.
- Maintain a positive attitude even when circumstances would make it easy to be negative. (p. 4)

Clinical Supervision

The term *clinical supervision* has been introduced to describe a possible task of the first-line manager or a function that is assigned to an experienced clinician. In the following section, the nature of clinical supervision will be discussed and distinctions will be made between clinical supervision and managerial or administrative supervision.

Aasheim (2011) wrote, "Effective [clinical] supervision serves the dual purpose of protecting client welfare and helping the supervisee develop and maintain clinical skills" (p. 30). Furthermore, Aasheim stated that clinical supervision "is intended to protect the welfare of the supervisee's clients above all else" (p. 6). Thus, clinical supervision has two purposes. First, clinical supervision allows the agency to deliver quality clinical services to clients. Second, clinical supervision permits clinicians to gain and refine clinical practice skills to grow as helping professionals.

The first purpose has to do with accountability by ensuring the clinical program of the organization is conducted as intended. Clinical supervisors protect the integrity of the agency's clinical program by helping to ensure that supervisees competently carry out the therapeutic intents of the program. The second purpose of clinical supervision concerns the continuing development of the clinical skills possessed by all therapists in an organization. Austin (2013) wrote:

> The supervisor helps the supervisee to acquire and refine clinical practice skills and to grow as a professional. This supervision is an ongoing process that begins during initial field placements and never ends, because even the master clinician always has more to learn. (p. 388)

Morton-Cooper and Palmer (2000) emphasized the continuing nature of clinical supervision: "Clinical supervision should continue throughout professional life" (p. 149). Thus, although clinical supervision is supplied to students completing their university internships, it is not exclusively provided to interns, because all engaged in clinical practice need clinical supervision throughout their careers.

Clinical Supervision Defined

Perhaps the following definitions drawn from the literature on clinical supervision will be helpful to understanding the nature of clinical supervision. Austin (2013) wrote:

Clinical supervision then may be defined as a joint relationship in which the supervisor assists the supervisee to develop himself or herself in order to deliver the highest possible level of clinical service while promoting accountability in the agency's clinical program. (p. 388)

Williamson, an early advocate for clinical supervision, in 1961 wrote the following about clinical supervision:

Supervision is a dynamic enabling process by which individual workers who have direct responsibility for carrying out some part of the agency's program plans are helped to make the best use of knowledge and skills, and to improve their abilities so that they do their jobs more effectively and with increasing satisfaction to themselves and the agency. (p. 19)

Thus, the primary focus of the clinical supervisor is the behavior of supervisees as they interact with clients and staff. Austin (2013) amplified on this thrust:

Skills related to the achievement of client objectives remain at the heart of clinical supervision. On occasion, however, clinical supervision involves issues related to teamwork or to maintaining positive relationships in working with other staff in order to conduct a successful clinical program. (p. 390)

Clinical Supervision and Managerial Supervision

Some first-line managers are given the responsibilities of providing clinical supervision and managerial supervision for members of their staff. Many authorities, however, believe that the two functions of clinical supervision and managerial supervision (sometimes referred to as administrative supervision) are distinct and separate. For example, Corey, Haynes, Moulton, and Muratori (2010) stated: "*Clinical supervision* focuses on the work of the supervisee in proving services to clients." They also stated, "*Administrative supervision* focuses on the issues surrounding the supervisee's role and responsibilities in the organization as an employee: personnel matters, timekeeping, documentation, and so forth" (Corey et al., 2010, p. 3).

Bond and Holland (1998) wrote, "Management supervision and clinical supervision are different functions and should not be undertaken by the same person" and "any embodiment of clinical supervision within management will be liable to cause confusion and mistrust and lead to mixed messages about its aims and potential" (p. 18). Aasheim (2011) elaborated on this view:

These supervisors who are both managerial and clinical supervisors are in a dual relationship with their supervisee/employee. In these cases, agency or administrative needs may take precedence above the clinical focus and supervisee development, and the supervisor's role may be in direct opposition. For instance, clinical supervisors often make great efforts to ensure the supervisee feels safe and comfortable to discuss time of professional incompetence and needed development. However, many supervisees may find it difficult to divulge professional weaknesses to their direct manager who has great control and influence over their ability to be promoted, given a raise or bonus, approved for vacation time, and the like. (p. 100)

Similarly, Austin (2013) voiced his concern about the dangers of the first-line manager providing clinical supervision:

> It is my belief that administrative supervision and clinical supervision should be kept distinct and separate. The authoritative nature of administrative supervision (with administrative power) simply gets in the way of establishing the cooperative, helping relationship that must exist as a part of clinical supervision. In many respects, the process of clinical supervision parallels the therapist-to-client relationship. The [clinical] supervisor must remain attentive to helping the supervisee meet his or her needs while maintaining a supportive atmosphere. The supervisee must feel free to be open and honest in his or her communications with the supervisor. While many agencies have supervisees receiving both their administrative and clinical supervision from the same individual, I would urge managers to give every consideration to keeping the two types of supervision separate. (p. 392)

All clinicians clearly need and deserve to receive clinical supervision, and the job of the first-line manager is to see that clinical supervision is provided, to protect the integrity of the clinical program and to advance the skills of clinicians. As has been indicated, clinical supervision can be given by either the first-line manager or a designated clinical supervisor. It seems to the authors of this text that ideally clinical supervision should be given not by the first-line manager but by a senior clinician, because of the reasons provided in the review of clinical supervision and managerial supervision. Incidentally, clinical supervisors do not exclusively perform in the role of clinical supervisor. Like most first-line managers, clinical supervisors still fulfill their role as recreational therapist by providing direct client services.

Recreational Therapists in Nonsupervisory Positions

Being a supervisor is rewarding for individuals who enjoy having an increased salary, career advancement, and the satisfaction of seeing a program prosper under their direction. Because of the demanding and challenging role that first-line managers must assume, or because they are still in the process of honing their clinical skills (which typically takes several years), some recreational therapists do not wish to assume supervisory positions. Other recreational therapists gain a great deal of satisfaction from working directly with clients and therefore prefer to serve as clinicians rather than to take on first-line management responsibilities. In still other instances, a single recreational therapist is employed at a facility or by an agency to provide direct client services. Therefore, the lone recreational therapist does not have the opportunity to assume formal supervisory responsibilities. Thus, for any number of reasons, many recreational therapists serve as clinicians rather than assume management positions.

Need for Clinicians to Gain Management Knowledge and Skills

To reiterate on the introduction to Chapter 1, there are several reasons for students in RT to learn about management functions, even if they perceive themselves as assuming roles as clinicians. For instance, recreational therapists who do not desire to become first-line managers or who have not even contemplated assuming formal supervisory positions at some time may wish to take on supervisory responsibilities. Unfortunately, most organizations do not provide adequate orientation programs for new supervisors

(McConnell, 2014), so it behooves all recreational therapists to gain basic management knowledge and skills so they have some preparation to become first-line managers should they desire to assume such a role in the future. Even if clinicians never end up taking on management responsibilities, with a background in management they will have an appreciation for and understanding of working within a system that follows sound management practices. Having knowledge of management, recreational therapists can better understand the roles and functions of managers so they comprehend how the organization works and how to best fit into and succeed within it.

Sole recreational therapists in a facility or agency will also be well served by having management skills because they will have to engage in management activities even though they are not formally identified as managers. For instance, they will likely have to supervise aide-level staff and volunteers. They will have to do program planning and evaluation. They will probably have to request and monitor a budget for their program. They are apt to have to recruit and train volunteers. Thus, the sole recreational therapist may be called up to undertake many management functions.

As indicated in Chapter 1, the National Council for Therapeutic Recreation Certification (NCTRC) endorses the inclusion of the organization and management of RT services as a part of the professional preparation of recreational therapists and lists a number of management tasks (e.g., personnel, intern, and volunteer supervision and management; budgeting and fiscal responsibility) as required knowledge areas for the NCTRC exam (NCTRC, 2014).

Many Therapists' Skills Transfer to Management

To perform management functions, recreational therapists need to learn new processes and skills. Certainly, almost all recreational therapists enter the profession thinking they will not assume managerial positions. The professional preparation of recreational therapists does and should primarily focus on the development of clinical skills. Students may not realize that many of the clinical skills they learn transfer well to the roles of first-line managers. Skills typically held by therapists that translate into management processes and skills include the following:

- First-line managers must possess technical skills including managerial skills and clinical skills. Because supervisors have to be well versed in clinical practice, most apparent in the list of skills that recreational therapists may transfer into first-line management are the clinical skills developed through education and experience.
- A cornerstone in the practice of RT is the RT process also known as the APIE process. It is a problem-solving process used in working with clients that is easily transferable to first-line management for which supervisors use the steps in the APIE process of assessment, planning, implementation, and evaluation in their major conceptual skill of having to solve problems.
- Communications skills necessary for therapeutic communication with clients are easily used by first-line managers in exercising human relations skills, such as leading staff, working with teams, and dealing with personality conflicts.
- A skill recreational therapists possess is how to motivate clients. This skill can be transferred into management. First-line managers need to motivate their

employees, and in knowing how people are influenced by the types of power available, recreational therapists may apply this skill in first-line management.

- The skills recreational therapists possess to empower clients are useful in empowering employees, for example, by employing a participative leadership style as a first-line manager.

- Good recreational therapists have to become adept at being flexible as they work with client groups. Likewise, first-line managers, who must adapt to ever changing situations, need flexibility.

- Recreational therapists are generally liked by their clients, but a skill that successful recreational therapists ultimately develop is not to strive to be liked but rather to be respected. Likewise, first-line managers have to learn that they too need most of all to be respected.

- Recreational therapists value and strive to gain feedback from clients about their satisfaction with their clinical program. First-line managers must also regularly gain feedback from their staff.

- Modeling behaviors for clients is a skill that recreational therapists employ. Similarly, teaching by example is a skill that first-line managers employ with their employees.

- Treating clients with dignity and respect is a skill to which recreational therapists subscribe. Likewise, first-line managers need to treat staff with dignity and respect.

- Recreational therapists value being a part of a profession, join their professional associations, attend professional meetings, and continually update and improve their skills. These skills translate well to first-line managers, who also need to demonstrate professional behaviors and grow in their roles.

- Competent recreational therapists maintain high ethical and moral standards. First-line managers should be models of integrity.

Do You Want to Be a First-Line Manager?

A legitimate question for recreational therapists to ask is whether they have a desire to become first-line managers. Hopefully, as a result of reading this chapter, the reader will now have an understanding of what is involved in first-line management and can begin to analyze the pluses and minuses connected with assuming a supervisory role within RT.

Summary

To handle assignments, first-line managers of RT units must have technical, professional, and clinical competence. In addition, they must maintain good relationships with their staffs as well as those in higher management and other managers in comparable positions.

Clinical supervision was described and a distinction made between clinical supervision and managerial or administrative supervision. It was explained that authorities have made a case for keeping clinical supervision and managerial supervision distinct and separate.

The need for recreational therapists to gain management knowledge and skills was discussed and therapists' skills that transfer to management functions were presented. The chapter concluded by asking readers to analyze for themselves the pluses and minuses of assuming a supervisory role in RT.

References

Aasheim, L. (2011). *Practical clinical supervision for counselors: An experiential guide.* New York, NY: Springer.

Austin, D. R. (2013). *Therapeutic recreation processes and techniques: Evidence-based recreational therapy* (7th ed.). Urbana, IL: Sagamore.

Bond, M., & Holland, S. (1998). *Skills of clinical supervision for nurses: A practical guide for supervisees, clinical supervisors, and managers.* Philadelphia, PA: Open University Press.

Burke, R. E., & Friedman, L. H. (2011). *Essentials of management and leadership in public health.* Sadbury, MA: Jones & Bartlett Learning.

Cadwell, C. M. (2006). *First-line supervision* (5th ed.). New York, NY: American Management Association.

Corey, G., Haynes, R., Moulton, P., & Muratori, M. (2010). *Clinical supervision in the helping professions* (2nd ed.). Alexandria, VA: American Counseling Association.

Dunn, R. T. (2002). *Haimann's supervisory management for healthcare organizations.* (7th ed.). Chicago, IL: Health Administration Press.

Hurd, A. R., Barcelona, R. J., & Meldrum, J. T. (2008). *Leisure services management.* Champaign, IL: Human Kinetics.

McConnell, C. R. (2014). *Umiker's management skills for the new health care supervisor* (6th ed.). Burlington, MA: Jones & Bartlett Learning.

Morton-Cooper, A., & Palmer, A. (2000). *Mentoring, preceptorship, and clinical supervision* (2nd ed.). London, England: Blackwell Science.

National Council for Therapeutic Recreation Certification. (2014). Certification standards part II: NCTRC exam information. Retrieved from http://www.nctrc.org/documents/1NewAp.pdf

Williamson, M. (1961). *Supervision: New patterns and processes.* New York, NY: Association Press.

Chapter 3

Understanding the Healthcare Environment

Objectives

- Identify themes in healthcare policy.
- Explain how the U.S. approach differs from that of other countries.
- Identify key developments influencing U.S. healthcare access, quality, and cost.
- Distinguish between Medicare and Medicaid.
- Distinguish between the nature of health services and the settings of health services.
- Describe public and private insurance mechanisms.
- Identify key payers in public and private healthcare financing.
- Identify the effects of the Affordable Care Act of 2010 on healthcare and RT.

Key Terms

- **Affordable Care Act of 2010 (ACA):** Also known as Obamacare, this act is recognized as the most important piece of healthcare legislation since the creation of Medicare and Medicaid. This act established individual and employer mandates for insurance, insurance exchanges and subsidies for direct-purchase insurance, and changes in public payment for health services as well as in structures of care.
- **Direct-purchase insurance:** Insurance policies purchased as an individual from a private insurer.
- **Employer-based insurance:** Insurance provided as a benefit to employees in which employees' costs are substantially subsidized by the employer.
- **Health insurance:** An arrangement made by an individual, group, or employer with a private company or government entity in which financial responsibility for covering health services is either completely or partially transferred from the care recipient to the insurer.
- **Medicare:** Created under the Social Security Amendment of 1965, Medicare is a federally administered health insurance program to serve older adults and some people with long-term disabilities. It is the largest federally funded health insurance program and the single largest payer for health services.

- **Medicaid:** Created under the Social Security Amendment of 1965, Medicaid is a jointly funded program by the federal government and state governments. Medicaid was initially designed to provide health insurance for citizens living in poverty who had certain health conditions. Under the ACA, Medicaid has been expanded in most states to cover all people below, at, or near the poverty level regardless of health condition.

The purpose of this chapter is to introduce readers to the policies, issues, and practices within the present U.S. healthcare environment. Granted, not all recreational therapists work within healthcare. Yet historically and presently a majority of recreational therapists work within a practice setting in which financing is largely a function of the public or private health insurance industry. In the most current profile of the employment sectors of recreational therapists, 38% work in hospitals, 19% work in skilled nursing facilities, 11% work in residential/transitional services, and 4% work in outpatient or day treatment settings (National Council for Therapeutic Recreation Certification, 2014). Thus, almost 75% of recreational therapists work in the healthcare environment. An understanding of this environment and of the factors that have driven change in this environment remains critically important, particularly to those with management responsibilities.

Key Themes in Healthcare Policy

Understanding healthcare policy is critical to understanding how health services are organized and delivered within a society. In addition, healthcare policy identifies basic assumptions about the view of health services by societies. For example, societies in Canada and Northern Europe assume that all citizens should have access to the *same level of health services.* This is accomplished either through universal health insurance (e.g., Canada) or through the provision of health services by the national government (e.g., the United Kingdom's National Health Service). Other societies, such as those in the United States, have historically assumed that all citizens should have access to some *minimum level of health services.* This is accomplished through programs such as Medicare, serving the retired, older adults, and people with disabilities (in some cases), as well as Medicaid, serving the needs of individuals who are economically disadvantaged. The assumption in the United States is that those not in the groups covered by Medicare or Medicaid have access to health services through out-of-pocket payment or through employer-based health insurance plans. Recently, the United States made a shift in its approach to health services through the Patient Protection and Affordable Care Act of 2010 (ACA). The intent of the ACA is to ensure that all Americans have at least some minimal level of insurance coverage. The details of the ACA and its implications for U.S. health services are described later in this chapter.

"Start with an end in mind."

Stephen R. Covey

Regardless of a society's approach to health services, three key elements can typically be identified in all health policies. These themes relate to people's abilities to obtain health services, characterized by *access*; the degree to which services are effective, safe, and coordinated, characterized by *quality*; and *cost* at the individual level and the societal level. Each is explored in greater detail in the following sections.

Access

On the surface, access references little more than the ability to obtain health services. At the same time, a number of factors either improve or interfere with access to health services. The present system of health services seems natural with its hospital-based system of services, but this has only been the case in the United States for the past 100 years (Sparer, 2011). Prior to the end of the First World War (1918), most health services were provided in homes by family members who were at times supported by an assortment of trained and untrained service providers. Services were typically paid for directly or "out of pocket."

The few hospitals that existed through the 19th century were public hospitals or clinics organized by local governments to serve the needs of the poor, older adults, and individuals with disabilities. Although these public hospitals and clinics provided access to health services, they have been characterized as providing "poor quality care and were avoided by people who had any alternative" (Sparer, 2011, p. 26). In the 20th century, a number of changes began the evolution to the current system of services. First, changes in medical education resulted in increasing acceptance of its scientific basis, thus placing medical doctors as the principal providers of medical care. Second, a relatively rapid growth occurred in the number of hospitals in the United States from less than 200 in 1873, to nearly 7,000 by 1930 (Anas, Law, Rosenblatt, & Wing, 1990). Another development was the passage of the Hill–Burton Act in 1946 that provided federal aid to states for construction of hospitals. This legislation supported the creation of hospitals in areas where people had historically had little access to modern medicine and its increasing technological advances.

With the increasing centralization of and the professionalization of services within hospitals, the costs of services also began to rise. Although not as acute a problem in the early 20th century as it would become by the later half, rising costs led to another hallmark of the U.S. healthcare system: private health insurance. With rising costs, access not only involved the availability of health services, but also the ability to pay for those services. By most accounts, private health insurance was born through the creation of prepaid hospital plans modeled upon a plan created at Baylor University Hospital in Dallas, Texas, in 1929. Because of the effects of the Great Depression, a number of Baylor University employees were found to be delinquent in their payments for services. The hospital created one of the first payment plans in which employees could access up to 21 days of services per year by paying the hospital $6/month (Starr, 1982). This model was eventually adopted by hospitals across the United States that affiliated under the symbol of the Blue Cross. By 1930, a similar system of payments to physicians had begun to develop that was affiliated under the symbol of the Blue Shield (Cunningham & Cunningham, 1997).

By the time of the Second World War, a number of factors contributed to further expansion of the private health insurance system in the United States. With the onset of the war, the U.S. government instituted wage and price controls; however, employer-sponsored health insurance was excluded from these controls. This created a situation in which employers could not offer high wages to attract the best employees, but could offer employer-sponsored health insurance as a benefit to attract employees. In addition, the federal government exempted health insurance premiums paid by employers from federal income tax. As a result of these factors, a large number of Americans now had access to health services through employer-sponsored health insurance. Yet as this became the norm, and as health services costs continued to rise, those who did not have access to health insurance through employment found it increasingly difficult to afford, and thus access, care. Those excluded were mainly older adults, the poor, and people with disabilities.

Medicare and Medicaid. The passage of the Social Security Amendments of 1965 (PL 89-97) sought to afford access to many unable to afford healthcare because of a lack of employment. Cited at the time as "the most far-reaching social security legislation to be enacted since the original Social Security Act" (Cohen & Ball, 1965, p. 3), this act resulted in the creation of Medicare and Medicaid. Specifically, Medicare was created as a federally administered program principally to support older adults, and Medicaid was created as a cofunded federal and state program principally to support those in poverty. Thus, the act created the first public health insurance model in the United States for segments of the population who could not access health services through out-of-pocket payment or employer-sponsored health insurance. Yet segments of the U.S. population were still unable to access health services because of the inability to pay. More than 80% of the uninsured were those in families with part-time or full-time workers, typically who were self-employed or employed by a small business (Sparer, 2011). In 1997, the state Children's Health Insurance Program (CHIP) was passed as a state-administered program to provide additional access to children of the "working poor," mainly through expansions of Medicaid services. By 2005, more than 4 million children were enrolled in the program (Sparer, 2011).

Patient Protection and Affordable Care Act. The most recent major event in access to health services in the United States was the passage of the Patient Protection and Affordable Care Act of 2010 (ACA). This legislation bring about a number of actions, but principal among them was to reduce the number of uninsured in the United States. However, unlike previous legislation that created the government as insurer, this act focused on mandating individual and employer-sponsored health insurance. Federal funding was to be used to subsidize insurance premiums for those with incomes within 400% of the poverty level and to fund expansion of state Medicaid coverage. At the time of this writing (Fall 2015), many of the intended outcomes of the ACA have been enacted, but other provisions have been challenged in the U.S. Supreme Court, leaving the final effect of this legislation on access to health services uncertain.

Quality

As noted by Sparer (2011), the quality of health services has been suspect for a considerable part of U.S. history. Although perhaps difficult to fathom today, early medicine had little interest in scientific knowledge. Instead, "theories based on what was thought to be rational wisdom combined with experience were the essentials of medical knowledge" (Breslaw, 2012, p. 5). This reliance on tradition derived from experience persisted well into the 1900s. In a review of one of the most commonly used textbooks of medical education (*Cecil Textbook of Medicine*, 1927), Beeson (1980) found that only about 6% of the interventions were considered effective in 1980. The concerns about medical education in the beginning of the 20th century prompted the American Medical Association to approach the Carnegie Foundation to commission a review. In this review, Flexner (1910) cited multiple problems with medical education, including low admission standards, few opportunities for clinical experience, and poor laboratory facilities. The result of this report was a closure of most for-profit medical schools and a reorganization of remaining ones to the model of Johns Hopkins Medical School (Ludmerer, 2011). The Johns Hopkins model required among other requisites, a baccalaureate degree for entrance, medical science as a part of training, and training under qualified clinical faculty.

Another policy approach that has evolved related to the quality of services is the regulation of health professionals through licensure. As licensing is exclusively the domain of states, this approach to improving quality has developed over different times in different states. The first medical profession to be governed by licensure was physicians. Although there were efforts in colonial America to regulate the practice of physicians, the first modern licensing authority was created in Texas in 1873, and by 1900 almost all states had established licensing boards (Melnick, Dillon, & Swanson, 2002). These early licensing boards created a range of ways of examining applicants' capacity to practice medicine, and as a result there was virtually no reciprocity for physicians to practice from one state to another. In fact, not until the early 1990s was a uniform medical licensing examination adopted by all U.S. states (Melnick et al., 2002). Other allied health professions followed suit in the following century. For example, by 1959 there were practice acts regulating physical therapy practice in 46 states (Johnson & Abrams, 2005), and by 2014 there were licensure laws governing occupational therapy practice in all 50 states (Willmarth, 2015).

Challenges to quality services more recently have been identified as a growing complexity of science and technology, a rise in chronic conditions, a system of delivery of health services that is poorly organized, and barriers to embracing information technology (Institute of Medicine, 2001). Thus, although much of the 20th century approach to the quality of healthcare was focused on improving the quality of care through improving the training and regulation of those providing services, the decades since the creation of Medicare in 1965 have seen a change to evaluating quality as an outcome of healthcare services. Furthermore, quality has come to be seen as multidimensional, encompassing not only the effectiveness of care, but also patient safety, timeliness, patient centeredness, care coordination, efficiency, health system infrastructure, and access to healthcare (Agency for Healthcare Research and Quality, 2013).

Cost

The third major theme in healthcare policy is cost, or at times cost control. As noted in the Access section, cost has become a major element in access to health services. The

U.S. system has evolved from the recipient of services paying the provider directly out of pocket, to the recipient of services paying only a small fraction of the cost of services directly. For example, in 1960 out-of-pocket expenses accounted for more than 55% of healthcare expenditures, and since then there has been a steady decline, and by 2010 just over 13% of healthcare expenditures were paid directly by consumers (see Figure 3.1). This is not to imply that the actual dollar amount paid directly by consumers for healthcare has decreased; in fact, the opposite has occurred.

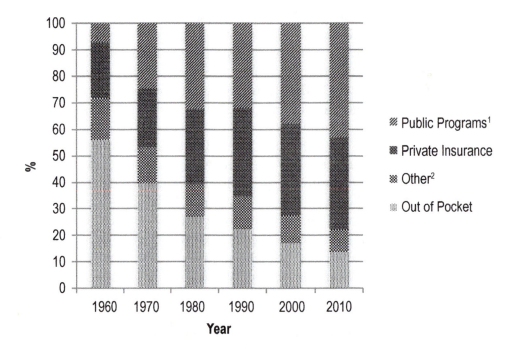

[1] Includes Medicare, Medicaid, CHIP, U.S. Department of Defense, and Veterans' Administration.
[2] Includes worksite health; workers' compensation; maternal and child health; vocational rehabilitation; school health; and other federal, state, and local programs.

Figure 3.1. Personal healthcare percentage of expenditures by source, 1960–2010. Adapted from *National Health Expenditures by Type of Service and Source of Funds, CY 1960–2013*, by Centers for Medicare and Medicaid Services, 2013 (http://www.cms.gov/Research-Statistics-Data-and-Systems/Statistics-Trends-and-Reports/NationalHealthExpendData/NationalHealthAccountsHistorical.html).

Increasing costs. From 1960 to 1970, out-of-pocket expenditures almost doubled from $13.1 billion to $25 billion (Centers for Medicare and Medicaid Services, 2013). This pattern of approximately doubling each decade continued through the year 2000, at which point the rate of increase declined to about 50%. Out-of-pocket expenditures declined in percentage while increasing in actual dollars because of a rapid growth in private and public health insurance expenditures (see Figure 3.2). For example, within five years of their creation, Medicare and Medicaid accounted for $7.3 billion and $5.0 billion in expenditures, respectively. However, by 1990 Medicare expenditures had increased by more than 1500% ($107 billion) and Medicaid had increased by more than 1300% ($70 billion). This led to a focus on cost containment for much of the 1990s that dramatically changed the way healthcare services were purchased.

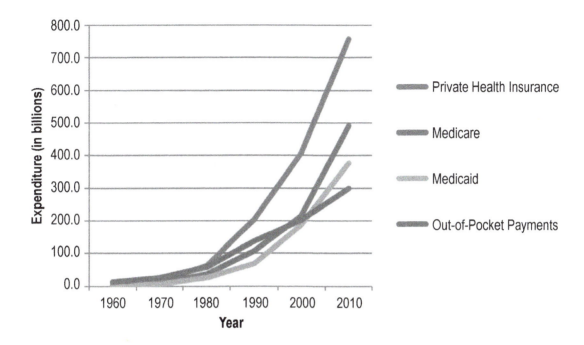

Figure 3.2. U.S. healthcare dollar expenditures by source (in billions), 1960–2010.

Cost containment measures. Initiatives in the 1970s controlled rising healthcare expenditures in the Medicare and Medicaid programs, but these programs were mainly focused on controlling the use of unnecessary services and were largely ineffective (Mueller, 1993). Not until the Tax Equity and Fiscal Responsibility Act of 1982 and the Social Security Amendments of 1983 were steps taken to control costs through controlling payments. The result of these pieces of legislation was that the model of payment for hospital care under Medicare was no longer based on a fee-for-service model in which healthcare providers delivered services to their patients and then sent a bill for those services. Instead, a prospective payment system (PPS) was set up, in which the administrative agency supervising the Medicare program set rates in advance (prospectively) on a cost-per-case basis. This initial PPS tied payments to patient groups based on similar diagnoses known as diagnosis related groups (DRGs). Hospitals were now encouraged to provide care as cost effectively as possible because their payments were no longer tied to the amount of services provided, but to the payment associated with the DRG. This model was seen to be effective in controlling costs, and Medicare subsequently adopted the PPS for physicians' payments as well. The PPS was initially only applied in short-stay hospitals, but by 2003 all healthcare services under Medicare were based on a PPS (Mayes, 2014).

The various PPS appeared to contain healthcare costs in a number of areas of health services; however, there was an unintended consequence. Because the PPS only covered Medicare beneficiaries, healthcare providers could charge higher rates to their patients with private insurance to make up for revenues lost through the Medicare PPS. This came to be known as cost-shifting and led to escalating costs in the private health insurance sector that affected employers and their workers (Mayes, 2014). The result was that much of the private health insurance sector adopted various forms of managed care to control costs. The adoption of managed care slowed the rate of growth in healthcare costs in the short term, but by the early 2000s rampant healthcare cost inflation was again the norm.

Most recently, cost containment efforts have been seen in the passage of the Patient Protection and Affordable Care Act of 2010 (ACA). A number of approaches appear within the ACA (Oberlander, 2011). The first approach is the creation of Accountable Care Organizations (ACOs) and medical home concepts that have sought to control costs by changing the organization of health services to maximize efficiencies in health services (Pauly, 2011). Another approach is the creation of health insurance exchanges intended to insure large numbers of people, thus creating savings through reductions in administrative costs, promoting competition among insurers and concentrating purchasing power. Although not set to go into effect until 2018, a third approach is to institute a tax on insurance plans that are high cost and providing extensive health services coverage. The idea behind this as a cost containment measure is that if these "Cadillac plans" are taxed, then overly generous plans will be scaled back, patients will use less medical care, and spending will decline (Oberlander, 2011).

Although the long-term effectiveness of these cost control measures is unknown and there is some debate about how much they will really address rising costs, cost remains a major issue in U.S. healthcare. In an international comparison of 11 countries in 2014, the U.S. healthcare system was rated at the most costly in the world with annual per person spending of $8,508 (Commonwealth Fund, 2014). The next highest country in expenditures was Norway with an annual spending of $5,669/person. The biggest difference was that Norway's overall healthcare system was ranked 2nd best, whereas the U.S. healthcare system overall was ranked 11th, or worst.

Organization of U.S. Healthcare

Although the term *healthcare* is frequently used in reference to the system of physicians, hospitals, and allied health services, this system is more accurately identified as the medical care system. To understand the system of care in the United States, the nature of services and the settings in which these services occur must be considered.

Nature of Services

Traditionally, medical services are organized along the lines of primary, secondary, and tertiary care (Cacace & Nolte, 2011). This organizational structure represents the nature of services and the ways in which medical care recipients access services. Thus, *primary care* is the element of the medical care system that most clients access first. Most primary care is provided in the offices of primary care physicians (PCP), and clients refer themselves to such care. Primary care has become increasingly important in a medical care system that is seeking to control costs because services at this level are the most general and thus the least costly. Thus, PCPs have increasingly become the gatekeepers to more costly specialty services of secondary and tertiary care.

Secondary care is a more specialized form of care typically provided in local hospitals and outpatient centers (Cacace & Nolte, 2011). Services such as routine surgeries, diagnostic laboratory services, inpatient rehabilitation (including mental health), and pediatric rehabilitation are typical of the secondary care sector (McCormick, 2002). These services are provided to fewer people (compared to primary care) because of less demand, but they typically involve a larger number of health professionals and technology. As a result, secondary care services are more costly than primary care services. This is also the sector in which the majority of nationally certified recreational therapists practice (National Council for Therapeutic Recreation Certification, 2014).

Finally, *tertiary care* is the most complex and costly of all medical care sectors. These providers are highly specialized and typically work at regional centers specializing in areas such as trauma, organ transplant, cardiac specialty, burns, and pediatrics. Such tertiary care providers typically perform the most complex medical procedures with the most advanced technologies, making it the most costly sector.

Settings for Services

Although prior to the middle of the 20th century the majority of medical care occurred in the homes of service recipients, changes in policy, as already noted, have moved most medical services to physicians' offices, hospitals, and other medical care facilities. At present, most of U.S. medical care occurs in ambulatory settings, inpatient settings, or home settings.

In *ambulatory settings,* clients or patients receive services and do not remain in the facility overnight. As implied in the name of such settings, most clients walk in (ambulate) and walk out on the date of services. Primary care services are the prime example of ambulatory settings. This would typically also include laboratory and most diagnostic services as well. Another example of an ambulatory setting is outpatient services. Although these services are often housed in a hospital setting, services are provided without an overnight stay. Other examples of ambulatory settings include urgent and some emergency care, community mental health services, adult day services, and day treatment programs.

In *inpatient settings,* clients or patients remain in a facility overnight, thus receiving 24-hour care. In many inpatient settings, clients remain for multiple nights. Community hospitals are the main example of this type of facility, and they include most hospitals other than federal hospitals, psychiatric hospitals, and long-term care facilities (American Hospital Association, 2015). As Figure 3.3 shows, community hospitals including not-for-profit, for-profit, and state and local government facilities account for approximately 88% of all hospitals. Although the number of hospitals in the United States grew steadily from the Second World War through the mid-1970s, there was subsequently a steady decline in the number of hospitals from 1975 to 2005 (Jonas, Goldsteen, & Goldsteen, 2007).

Within the inpatient setting, there are further distinctions. For example, in acute care settings, the nature of illness or injury is relatively severe, requiring immediate and highly intensive medical services. Acute care settings typically have the shortest length of stay and are technology and staff intensive. Examples of acute care settings include intensive care units, crisis units, and emergency departments. In contrast, in postacute care settings, there is typically a lower need for the intensity of services provided in the acute care setting. As implied by the name, postacute care settings most often receive clients after stabilization in an acute care setting. Postacute care settings include inpatient rehabilitation facilities and inpatient psychiatric facilities, as well as surgical recovery centers, brain injury care centers, and hospice care. The length of stay in the acute setting is typically multiple days, but in the postacute setting the length of stay is typically multiple weeks. The final distinction within the inpatient setting is extended care, when, as implied by the title, clients spend the greatest length of time with the lowest intensity of services. Extended care settings include skilled nursing facilities and specialized units for those with Alzheimer's or dementia, as well as state hospitals for those with mental illness or developmental centers for persons with developmental disabilities. In addition, residential services, such as group homes, are considered within this sector of the inpatient setting because residents typically have 24-hour supervision and are living in an environment owned by a health or human service provider.

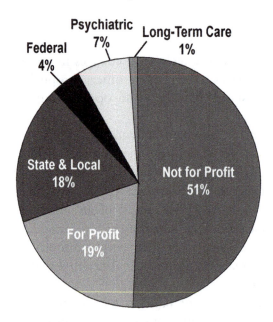

Figure 3.3. Registered hospitals in the United States, 2014. Adapted from "Fast Facts on US Hospitals," by American Hospital Association, 2015 (http://www.aha.org/research/rc/stat-studies/fast-facts.shtml).

Home care is the final setting of services. As noted previously, although this began as the principal location for most medical care services, it significantly declined with the advent of the modern hospital (Jonas et al., 2007). There has been some resurgence of home-based primary care; however, at present most home care is focused on supporting older adults to remain in their homes and communities. Based on the most recent data available from the Centers for Medicare and Medicaid Services (2015), in 2013 home care accounted for 3% of personal healthcare expenditures, compared to 6% for nursing care and continuing care facilities and 38% for hospitals. The role of recreational therapy (RT) in home care is not well documented. For example, the National Council for Therapeutic Recreation Certification (2014) does not list home care within the primary sectors of employment for recreational therapists. Examples of RT in home care include its use in managing depression among older adults (Johnson, 1999) and managing chronic health conditions (Craig, Wilder, Sable, & Gravink, 2013).

Future Organization of Medical Service

The current organization of medical services has evolved mainly over the last century. The Flexner report of 1910 began a transformation of medical training and medical care in the United States that saw an increasingly scientific and technological approach to medical services and located much of that technology in hospitals. At the same time, this focus on ever increasing scientific knowledge created an array of medical specialties with accompanying highly specialized practices. Thus, there is a "system" in which multiple specialists may interact with a single patient across all nature and settings of services. The result has been poorly coordinated care (Shih et al., 2008).

The organization of medical services in the future is likely to see more emphasis on the transitions across settings and services. This is also likely to mean fewer physicians practicing independently or in a small practice. Evidence of this change is already seen in the 32% increase in hospital employment of physicians from 2000 to 2010 (Kirchoff, 2013). One way for hospitals to better coordinate care is through the acquisition of primary and specialty care practices. This type of arrangement is known as vertical integration (from primary through tertiary) and is frequently seen in larger healthcare systems.

Another likely evolution is an emphasis on medical services out of the inpatient setting. With hospitals accounting for almost one third of all health expenditures in the United States (Centers for Medicare and Medicaid Services, 2013), this remains an area in which cost containment is likely. The system reforms of the 1980s and 1990s resulted in dramatically reduced lengths of stay as one means to reduce hospital costs, and further reductions in this area seem unlikely. Instead, the current focus of healthcare reforms has been on reducing or eliminating unnecessary admissions as well as readmissions. Thus, an increasing focus on home and community-based services to keep people from needing hospitalization as well as to support them posthospitalization is likely.

Financing Healthcare

A key characteristics of the U.S. system of health and medical care is its complexity and multiple stakeholders. This is no less true of the system of payment for services. As noted previously, initially health services were paid directly by the recipient of those services to the service provider. As care moved out of homes and PCPs moved to hospitals and other specialized care settings, the cost of services steadily increased. Thus, the ability for people to pay directly for their care became more difficult. The result has been that, at present, few people pay for the entire cost of care directly. Instead, it is financed by a third party. These third parties include insurance companies as well as state and federal governments. Thus, understanding the financing of healthcare services requires basic understanding of insurance, the major payers, and the payment systems involved.

Insurance Basics

As noted previously, health insurance in the United States began as a hospital payment system that expanded as an employment benefit (Starr, 1982). The basic logic behind insurance is that when the resources of a group of people are pooled, the financial risk of any member of that group—in terms of having to pay individually for expensive medical services—is greatly reduced. In addition, the ability to predict the number and cost of medical services for the group is greatly increased through a phenomenon known as the *law of large numbers.* Statistically speaking, the greater the population examined, the greater the accuracy of predicting certain outcomes. For example, the number of automobile accidents (and their attendant injuries) in a given city can be predicted with some accuracy based on the history of accidents in that city. These estimates cannot indicate which individuals will experience an accident, simply the total number likely to occur. The same is true for illness, injury, and disability. It is possible to estimate the number of people in a group who will experience a stroke in a given period, and if the average cost of treatment for this same group is known, an insurer can predict the total cost for stroke for the entire group. This cost, plus administrative cost, as well as profit if the company is a for-profit insurer, is then spread out over the entire group for the period of *coverage.* This derives from the fact that all members of the group are now covered for their individual financial risk as a result of their payment into the group's pooled resources. Insurance works because the majority of people paying into the pool will never need to use their insurance coverage; however, those that do will have the resources of the entire group to pay for that care.

Two principles. This entire system works on two other principles. The first is that people only seek medical services for medical need, or there is no *moral hazard.* Why would this be a problem? It seems odd to seek healthcare when a person does not need the services. The problem is most often seen in members of a population who are particularly socially isolated. For these people, a visit to the emergency room results in a great deal of social contact and concern—something they may need desperately—but at significant cost of medical facilities and personnel for a nonmedical need. One way to minimize moral hazard is by having patients pay some portion of their own care out of pocket in the form of *copayments* and/or *deductibles.* The logic goes that if someone has to pay at least something for seeking medical care, this person will be less likely to seek this care when it is unnecessary. The second principle is that the group being insured represents a broad spectrum of the population. This prevents insurers from experiencing what is referred to as a *death spiral.* What if the group insured had a large number of people who had higher than average risk for using health insurance? This would increase the cost of insuring the group, driving up each individual's payment (known as a premium). Likely, the healthiest members of this group would not want to pay these higher prices and might discontinue their insurance with the company. The result would be an even greater concentration of those most ill in the group (the overall number of the group would decline, but those most ill would make up a greater percentage of the total group), thus further increasing the cost of insuring the group and driving out more of the healthiest members. Such a cycle could collapse the insurance system for this group. Thus, insurers are interested in keeping the groups they insure broad in makeup and populated with relatively healthy people.

Effects of the ACA. The ACA of 2010 has changed a couple of factors that were driving some of the insurance concepts in U.S. healthcare. First, it prevented insurers from using *preexisting condition* clauses. These clauses frequently prevented people with existing health conditions from obtaining insurance or significantly increased the cost of insurance for those people. Insurers used this to minimize the number of ill people in their pool. It also contributed to the death spiral phenomenon because those with existing health conditions knew that they would need healthcare services and thus were less likely to change insurers (and often jobs) because they could be prevented from getting insurance from another carrier. Thus, they were more likely to stay in the death spiral pool because they could not risk losing coverage. The second factor is the *individual mandate* that requires all people to obtain health coverage. As already noted, the larger the pool being covered, the better the ability to estimate costs of coverage and the less any one individual must pay for that coverage.

Public Financing

In many industrialized nations, the government is the sole entity financing health services, but in the United States it is simply the largest provider of healthcare financing. This has an interesting effect on the rest of the system. One of the main effects is that regulations developed to administer the major public financing systems are frequently adopted by private financing organizations. Public financing occurs through a number of systems developed to support specific segments of the U.S. population. The two largest public financing systems are Medicare and Medicaid.

Medicare. The Medicare system was created under the Social Security Amendments of 1965, which was one of the most significant pieces of healthcare legislation in U.S. history (Knickman, 2015). At that point in U.S. history, healthcare was frequently financed through insurance as a part of employment. It became apparent that adults in retirement were losing access to healthcare because of the loss of employment-based insurance. The Medicare program was set up principally to provide health insurance benefits to retirees. The program is funded by payroll taxes and administered through the federal government by the Centers for Medicare and Medicaid Services. The Medicare program also provides health insurance to people with certain long-term health conditions and disabilities, but 78% of Medicare dollars go to adults over the age of 65 (Neuman, Cubanski, & Damico, 2015). Medicare is the largest single purchaser of health services in the United States, accounting for 20% of healthcare financing in 2013 (Dangremond, 2015).

Medicare is made up of different parts, with some being covered as a benefit and others requiring a premium. *Medicare Part A* covers inpatient hospital stays, and all beneficiaries automatically receive Part A coverage. In contrast, *Medicare Part B* covers outpatient care (mainly physicians' costs) and requires that beneficiaries pay a monthly premium. Although it receives less attention than other parts of the Medicare program, *Medicare Part C* provides provisions for private health insurance companies to provide Medicare benefits through managed care plans. Finally, *Medicare Part D* is the newest part of the Medicare program and was passed into law in 2003 to provide prescription drug benefits to Medicare beneficiaries. Like Part B, Part D benefits require a monthly premium.

Medicaid. Medicaid was also created as a part of the Social Security Amendments of 1965. As with Medicare, it was designed to support a segment of the population that did not have access to health services because these people had no employer-based insurance. In contrast to Medicare, Medicaid is funded through federal and state taxes, but administered at the state level. This has resulted in Medicaid services varying from state to state. Until the passage of the ACA, Medicaid was available to people living below the poverty level who also had a qualifying medical condition or need (Kominski, 2013). The ACA changed the qualifications for Medicaid by establishing eligibility solely on income level. This essentially expanded Medicaid coverage to anyone with an income up to 138% of the federal poverty level (Kominski, 2013). State mandate for Medicaid expansion was one part of the ACA found to be unconstitutional in 2012 and as a result became voluntary on the part of states. Thus, the ACA provided the federal government the authority to provide significant financial incentives to states to expand their Medicaid coverage; it was voluntary on behalf of the states to adopt expansion.

Additional public programs. Although Medicare and Medicaid make up the largest part of public healthcare financing, 10% of public financing goes to finance specific beneficiaries (Centers for Medicare and Medicaid Services, 2014). Programs to support active duty and honorably discharged military personnel and their families (Department of Defense and Veterans Health Administration) are included in this portion of the public healthcare dollar. Notably, the Veterans Administration operates the largest single vertically integrated health system in the United States (Knickman, 2015) and is among the largest employers of recreational therapists. In addition, the *Indian Health Service* provides health insurance for federally recognized Native American tribes as well as their descendants. Finally, *Workers' Compensation* provides public health insurance for people who are injured in the course of their employment. Although administered by each state, funding for the program is provided by the federal government through payroll taxes.

Private Financing

The majority of Americans access healthcare through private financing of healthcare services. This includes direct payments by individuals for health services and payments made by private insurance companies.

Direct payments by individuals. In 2012, direct payment by individuals for health services totaled $328.8 billion, or about $1,047/person. Although perhaps sounding like an incredible amount, it represented only 12% of all spending on health services (Centers for Medicare and Medicaid Services, 2013). Considering the financing of healthcare services overall, few people pay the entirety of their costs for health services.

Employer-based insurance. As noted previously, health insura. employer-based hospital prepayment plans during the Great Depressic Second World War, they became an employer-sponsored benefit to att because there was a freeze on wages. As of 2014, employment-based healtl. has been the main source for healthcare financing, accounting for more tl.   ɔ% of the U.S. population (Smith & Medalia, 2015). As Figure 3.4 shows, the overall proportion of the U.S. population covered by any form of health insurance (private and public) has increased over the past two decades, but the proportion obtaining healthcare financing through employment-based plans has decreased. The benefit of employer-based insurance is that although employees typically pay some portion of their insurance costs, the employer pays the majority.

Direct-purchase insurance. The direct-purchase insurance sector of private healthcare financing has historically been the smallest segment of healthcare financing. One reason this segment has been so small is that the individual has to bear the entire cost of health insurance. In contrast, public insurance (e.g., Medicare Parts B and D) and employer-based insurance subsidize insurance premiums so individuals pay only a fraction of their costs. Thus, historically direct-purchase insurance has been costly. As Figure 3.4 shows, this phenomenon has changed since the enactment of the ACA in 2010. Although the proportion of the U.S. population accessing health financing through direct-purchase insurance has hovered around 8%–9%, beginning in 2010 this figure steadily increased, reaching 14% by 2014. Two elements of the ACA appear to be driving this increase. First, the ACA mandates that individuals have health insurance or pay a fine. This *individual mandate* has encouraged many who had not previously been insured to seek insurance coverage. Second, the ACA has created *insurance exchanges*. These exchanges encourage private insurers to offer different levels of healthcare service coverage (bronze, silver, gold, platinum). In addition, under the ACA these plans are subsidized such that in 2015 an average single adult (21 years old, nonsmoker) making $20,000/year (160% of federal poverty level) would pay $84/ month out of pocket for a silver-level policy that without subsidy would cost $216/ month ($132 in subsidy). Although the ultimate effect of the insurance exchanges is on the proportion of the U.S. population directly purchasing health insurance, some have argued that this could lead to the end of employer-based health insurance (Pilzer & Lindquist, 2015).

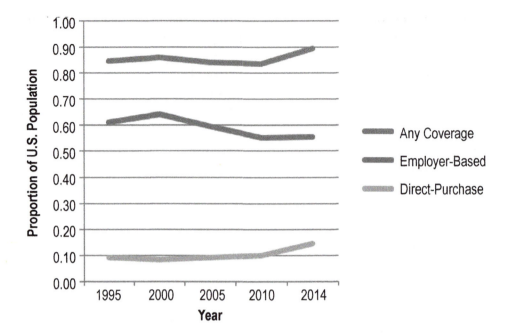

Figure 3.4. Proportion of U.S. population with private health insurance. Adapted from "Health Insurance Coverage: 1995," "Health Insurance Coverage: 2000," "Income, Poverty, and Health Insurance Coverage in the United States: 2005" "Income, Poverty, and Health Insurance Coverage in the United States: 2010," and "Health Insurance in the United States: 2014," by U.S. Census Bureau, 1996, 2002, 2006, 2011, 2015 (https://www.census.gov/hhes/www/hlthins/publications/reports.html).

Payment Systems

So far this chapter has considered how healthcare is allocated and organized as well as how it is financed. The remaining part of the puzzle is the payment system. This system has evolved as healthcare services have become more complex, technological, and costly. In addition, because of the increasing cost of care, the insurance system has developed such that the consumer (first party) rarely pays the entire cost of care to the provider (second party), but instead an insurer (third party) pays on behalf of the consumer. This system is known as a third-party payment system, and this system has driven changes in health services payments.

Fee for Service

Like many other services, healthcare was once a service in which a consumer received services from a provider. The provider presented a bill (fee) for those services, and the consumer paid for those services. Most economic transactions work in this way, and it is known as a fee-for-service system (FFS). This has also been characterized as a cost-based payment system in which payments are based on the established costs of providing that service. This was the principal approach to health services payments through the early 1980s. Although payers would sometimes negotiate "allowable costs," providers by and large set costs. One problem that arose for public insurers was that the costs of care were growing rapidly and were becoming difficult to sustain.

Prospective Payment

The Tax Equity and Fiscal Responsibility Act of 1982 and the Social Security Amendments of 1983 created a different system of payment for some segments of the public insurers. Instead of providing payment for billed costs, insurers set payments in advance, or prospectively. This system came to be known as the prospective payment system (PPS) and meant that, based on a *case grouping method*, providers were paid a fixed sum[1] to provide services for a consumer within a specified group. The first case grouping method was termed diagnosis related groups (DRGs), in which consumers with the same diagnosis were in a single group and the payment to treat any consumer with that diagnosis was the same for all providers. This payment system encouraged providers to provide care as efficiently as possible because the payment was set in advance. If a provider incurred more cost than the payment to treat a consumer, the provider bore the additional costs. If the provider could provide services for less than the payment, the provider kept the surplus. One outcome of the PPS was to shorten hospital stays in short-term general hospitals—the first setting in which the DRG system was applied.

Capitation

The FFS and PPS are both directly tied to health conditions and the expenses incurred to treat those conditions, but capitation represents a bit of a departure. Capitation to some extent derives from the insurance concept of the law of large numbers. Under capitation, a health service provider agrees to cover all medical care costs for a group of people for a payment—per head—of those covered. Hence, capitation literally means payment per head of insured. Under this system, payment is not tied to services for any one individual. In this system, the healthcare provider assumes financial risk for the entire group, and thus, there are incentives to keep people healthy. As with the PPS, if the provider can provide care for the group at less cost than the capitation rate, the provider keeps the surplus. This works on the law of large numbers because if the covered group is large enough, the number and nature of healthcare needs is predictable. Thus, the per-head costs are predictable as well.

New Developments in U.S. Healthcare

The Patient Protection and Affordable Care Act of 2010, also known as the ACA and Obamacare, was one of the most sweeping pieces of healthcare reform legislation in U.S. history since the Social Security Amendments of 1965 that created Medicare and Medicaid (Kominski, 2013). The ACA has undergone multiple legal challenges up to the level of the U.S. Supreme Court, which has principally supported the constitutionality of the law. The law has sought to address all three of the key policy areas including access, quality in terms of health outcomes, and cost containment. The act has resulted in a number of new initiatives and funding approaches. For example, Accountable Care Organizations (ACOs) have evolved as a means to manage the overall care and the overall cost of health services for a covered group. Characterized as

---

[1] Conceptually, this was a lump sum. In reality, there were variations to the payment to account for variables such as regional cost variation and hospital type.

a new form of managed care (Knickman, 2015), ACOs assume responsibility for all levels of necessary care and are funded based on health services consumer outcomes paid via a capitation model. For example, a consumer treated by an ACO who is readmitted within a given period for the same condition will negatively affect funding for the ACO because this is seen as a poor outcome of health services. ACOs receive payment for quality and effectiveness of care, in contrast to FFS payment systems that were based on volume of care. In addition, payment systems are likely to move further from an FFS model in which the volume of services is rewarded to one in which value or outcomes are rewarded (Knickman, 2015). This change will result in less concern for reimbursement for specific health services and greater concern for the value of services provided under increasingly bundled or capitated payment systems. Ensuring that RT services are covered and that RT can be demonstrated to be important to health outcomes and value will be the main concerns of the future in an evolving U.S. healthcare system.

Conclusion

Although all recreational therapists do not work in healthcare settings, a majority are employed in some sector of the healthcare industry. In the United States, this system of care is relatively complex and has evolved rapidly over just the past 100 years. RT managers are in an important position to ensure that their services are developed and provided to contribute to the health and function of their clients in ways that meet the needs of multiple stakeholders. As such, managers must understand the nature and settings of healthcare services as well as the public and private insurance-based system of payment for those services. With the passing of the Patient Protection and Affordable Care Act of 2010 (ACA 2010), further reform has been seen that has sought to increase access, improve quality, and manage costs. Although the future of the ACA is as yet unclear, healthcare reform will be one of the factors affecting the management functions of future RT managers.

References

Agency for Healthcare Research and Quality. (2013). *2010 national healthcare quality report*. Rockville, MD: Author.

American Hospital Association. (2015, January). Fast facts on US hospitals. Retrieved September 17, 2015, from http://www.aha.org/research/rc/stat-studies/fast-facts.shtml

Anas, G., Law, S., Rosenblatt, R., & Wing, K. (1990). *American health law*. Boston, MA: Little, Brown.

Beeson, P. (1980). Changes in medical therapy during the last half century. *Medicine, 59*, 79–99.

Breslaw, E. G. (2012). *Lotions, potions, pills, and magic: Health care in early America*. New York: New York University Press.

Cacace, M., & Nolte, E. (2011). Healthcare services: Strategy, direction, and delivery. In K. Walshe & J. Smith (Eds.), *Healthcare management* (2nd ed., pp. 145–168). Maidenhead, Great Britain: McGraw-Hill Education.

Centers for Medicare and Medicaid Services. (2013). *National health expenditures by type of service and source of funds*. Retrieved from http://www.cms.gov/Research-Statistics-Data-and-Systems/Statistics-Trends-and-Reports/NationalHealthExpendData/NationalHealthAccountsHistorical.html

Centers for Medicare and Medicaid Services. (2014). *The nation's health care dollar: Where it came from, where it went*. Retrieved from https://www.cms.gov/Research-Statistics-Data-and-Systems/Statistics-Trends-and-Reports/NationalHealthExpendData/Downloads/PieChartSourcesExpenditures2013.pdf

Centers for Medicare and Medicaid Services. (2015). *NHE fact sheet*. Retrieved from https://www.cms.gov/Research-Statistics-Data-and-Systems/Statistics-Trends-and-Reports/NationalHealthExpendData/NHE-Fact-Sheet.html

Cohen, W. J., & Ball, R. M. (1965). Social security amendments of 1965: Summary and legislative history. *Social Security Bulletin, 1965, 3*–21.

Commonwealth Fund. (2014). *Mirror mirror on the wall, 2014 update: How the U.S. health care system compares internationally*. Retrieved from http://www.commonwealthfund.org/publications/fund-reports/2014/jun/mirror-mirror

Craig, P. J., Wilder, A., Sable, J. R., & Gravink, J. (2013). Promoting access, transition, and health: A community-based approach to managing chronic health conditions. *Annual in Therapeutic Recreation, 21*, 45.

Cunningham, R., III, & Cunningham, R. M., Jr. (1997). *The Blues: A history of the Blue Cross and Blue Shield system*. DeKalb: Northern Illinois University Press.

Dangremond, C. K. (2015). A visual overview of health care delivery in the United States. In J. R. Knickman & A. R. Kovner (Eds.), *Health care delivery in the United States* (11th ed., pp. 13–27). New York, NY: Springer.

Flexner, A. (1910). *Medical education in the United States and Canada*. New York, NY: Carnegie Foundation.

Institute of Medicine. (2001). *Crossing the quality chasm: A new health system for the 21st century*. Washington, DC: National Academies Press.

Johnson, C. D. (1999). Therapeutic recreation treats depression in the elderly. *Home Health Care Services Quarterly, 18*(2), 79–90.

Johnson, M. P., & Abrams, S. L. (2005). Historical perspectives of autonomy within the medical profession: Considerations for 21st century physical therapy practice. *The Journal of Orthopaedic and Sports Physical Therapy, 35*, 628–636.

Jonas, S., Goldsteen, R. L., & Goldsteen, K. (2007). *Introduction to the U.S. health care system* (6th ed.). New York, NY: Springer.

Kirchoff, S. M. (2013). *Physician practices: Background, organization, and market consolidation* (CRS Report R42880). Retrieved from Federation of American Scientists website: http://fas.org/sgp/crs/misc/R42880.pdf

Knickman, J. R. (2015). Health care financing. In J. R. Knickman & A. R. Kovner (Eds.), *Health care delivery in the United States* (11th ed., pp. 231–252). New York, NY: Springer.

Kominski, G. F. (2013). The patient protection and affordable care act of 2010. In G. F. Kominski (Ed.), *Changing the U.S. health care system: Key issues in health services policy and management* (4th ed., pp. 3–31). Somerset, NJ: John Wiley & Sons.

Ludmerer, K. M. (2011). Abraham Flexner and medical education. *Perspectives in Biology and Medicine, 54,* 8–16.

Mayes, B. R. (2014). Strategies for health care cost containment (1980s–present). In T. R. Oliver (Ed.), *US health care and health care policy* (pp. 227–240). Thousand Oaks, CA: CQ Press.

McCormick, B. P. (2002). Healthcare in America: An overview. In D. R. Austin, J. Dattilo, & B. P. McCormick (Eds.), *Conceptual foundations for therapeutic recreation* (pp. 185–206). State College, PA: Venture.

Melnick, D. E., Dillon, G. F., & Swanson, D. B. (2002). Medical licensing examinations in the United States. *Journal of Dental Education, 66,* 595–599.

Mueller, K. J. (1993). *Healthcare policy in the United States.* Lincoln: University of Nebraska Press.

National Council for Therapeutic Recreation Certification. (2014). *CTRS professional profile* [Brochure]. Retrieved from http://nctrc.org/wp-content/uploads/2015/02/MM2-ctrs-professional-profile-brochure.pdf

Neuman, P., Cubanski, J., & Damico, A. (2015). Medicare per capita spending by age and service: New data highlights oldest beneficiaries. *Health Affairs, 34,* 335–339.

Oberlander, J. (2011). Throwing darts: Americans' elusive search for health care cost control. *Journal of Health Politics, Policy, & Law, 36,* 477–484.

Pauly, M. V. (2011). Patient Protection and Affordable Care Act cost-containment choices: The case for incentive-based approaches. *Journal of Health Politics, Policy, & Law, 36,* 591–596.

Pilzer, P. Z., & Lindquist, R. (2015). *The end of employer-provided health insurance.* Hoboken, NJ: Wiley.

Shih, A., Davis, K., Schoenbaum, S. C., Gauthier, A., Nuzum, R., & McCarthy, D. (2008). *Organizing the U.S. health care delivery system for high performance.* Retrieved from The Commonwealth Fund website: http://www.commonwealthfund.org/publications/fund-reports/2008/aug/organizing-the-u-s--health-care-delivery-system-for-high-performance

Smith, J., & Medalia, C. (2015). *Health insurance coverage in the United States: 2014* (P60-253). Washington, DC: U.S. Census Bureau.

Sparer, M. S. (2011). Health policy and health reform. In A. R. Kovner & J. R. Knickman (Eds.), *Health care delivery in the United States* (10th ed., pp. 25–45). New York, NY: Springer.

Starr, P. (1982). *The social transformation of American medicine.* New York, NY: Basic Books.

U.S. Census Bureau. (1996). *Health insurance coverage: 1995.* Retrieved from https://www.census.gov/hhes/www/hlthins/publications/reports.html

U.S. Census Bureau. (2002). *Health insurance coverage: 2001.* Retrieved from https://www.census.gov/hhes/www/hlthins/publications/reports.html

U.S. Census Bureau. (2006). *Income, poverty, and health insurance coverage in the United States: 2005.* Retrieved from https://www.census.gov/hhes/www/hlthins/publications/reports.html

U.S. Census Bureau. (2011). *Income, poverty, and health insurance coverage in the United States: 2010*. Retrieved from https://www.census.gov/hhes/www/hlthins/publications/reports.html

U.S. Census Bureau. (2015). *Health insurance in the United States: 2014*. Retrieved from https://www.census.gov/hhes/www/hlthins/publications/reports.html

Willmarth, C. (2015). 2015 state legislative forecast. *OT Practice, 20*(2), 6.

Chapter 4

Basic Management Functions

Objectives

- Name the five management functions.
- Define the term *planning*.
- Describe how planning is a continuous process.
- Outline the steps involved in the planning process.
- Define the term *organizing*.
- List elements that the manager can use to augment authority.
- Describe what is meant by unity of control.
- Describe what is meant by span of control.
- Define the term *staffing*.
- Outline the five steps in staffing.
- Describe what is meant by clinical supervision.
- Define the term *influencing*.
- List dimensions involved in the influencing function.
- Define the term *controlling*.
- Describe the close relationship between planning and controlling.
- Explain why it is said that the five management functions blend together to form an overall system.

Key Terms

- **Management process:** The management process pertains to the five interacting management functions of planning, organizing, staffing, influencing, and controlling.
- **Planning:** Planning is the first management function and involves stipulating the actions intended to reach specific goals. Plans are sometimes referred to as blueprints for the future.
- **Organizing:** Organizing is the process of establishing a formal structure through which work gets done.
- **Staffing:** Staffing involves the recruitment and selection of qualified staff to fill the various positions needed based on the organization of duties to achieve the plan.
- **Influencing:** Influencing involves the supervisor eliciting action from staff to reach the organization's objectives.
- **Controlling:** Controlling involves follow-up and correction to ensure plans are carried out and goals and objectives are being achieved.

The focus of this chapter is on the five functions managers perform. Sometimes these functions are referred to as the management process because they are interacting functions (Clark, 2009). Within the management literature, the titles given to management functions vary (e.g., using the term *directing* rather than *influencing*) and occasionally authors may subsume the function of staffing under organizing, so they list only four management functions rather than the five most commonly found in the literature. Within this chapter, the five management functions traditionally found in the literature will be described and Dunn's (2002) terms for these five functions will be adopted because they seem to be the most descriptive of each of the functions. These are planning, staffing, organizing, influencing, and controlling.

The explanations of each management function described in this chapter are meant only to serve to introduce the functions managers perform or what managers do. The following chapters in this text will cover in detail the performance of each management function by first-line managers in recreational therapy (RT).

Planning

Cherry (2011) warned: "*Without effective planning, the management process will fail*" (p. 344). Planning is certainly fundamental to management. Therefore, it is considered to be the first management function (McConnell, 2014). Dunn (1998) wrote: "Planning, the first management function, determines in advance what should be done in the future" (p. 16).

Nevertheless, although planning is the first management function, it does not end with initial efforts by managers, as Dunn (2002) stated:

Planning must come before any of the other management functions. Even after the initial plans are laid out and the manager proceeds with the other management functions, the function of planning continues in revising the course of actions and choosing different alternatives as the need arises. Therefore, although planning is the first function a manager must tackle, it does not end at the initiation of the other functions. The manager continues to plan while performing the organizing, staffing, influencing, and controlling functions. (p. 17)

Planning Defined

McConnell (2014) provided the following definition of planning:

Planning is the projection of actions intended to reach specific goals. In other words, a plan is a blueprint for the future; it is the expression of what we wish to accomplish or the best prediction of what might occur in the future. Planning begins with the questions of *what* and *why*, then focuses on the *how, when, who,* and *where*. (p. 32)

Thus, planning is accomplished as a means to reach goals and objectives established by the organization or a unit within the organization. The result of planning activities is a plan that provides direction for accomplishing desired ends. McConnell (2014) indicated that the plan itself provides a "blueprint" to follow in reaching goals and objectives by addressing what needs to be accomplished and why, along with how and when it will be accomplished and by whom and where it will be carried out.

Although there are various types of plans (e.g., strategic plans, operational plans for units), McConnell (2014) indicated: "Daily work planning, the simplest, most elementary form of planning in the working world, frequently proves to be the form of planning most immediately beneficial to the individual supervisor" (p. 34).

> "The best way to predict your future is to create it."
>
> Abraham Lincoln

Steps Involved in Planning

Cherry (2011) clearly articulated the steps involved in developing any plan:
- Identifying the goals and objectives to be achieved
- Identifying the resources (e.g., people, supplies, and equipment) needed
- Determining action steps to take
- Establishing a timeline for the action steps and goal achievement (p. 344)

Elements Involved in Planning

Cherry (2011) explained that the manager must understand elements involved in planning including (a) the mission statement and philosophy of the organization, (b) the strategic plan of the organization, (c) the goals and objectives for the organization, and (d) the operational plan for the individual unit (p. 344).

The *mission statement* for any organization or for a unit within an organization (e.g., the RT department) is provided in a brief paragraph and is the foundation on which to build any plan because it states the purpose of the organization or unit and the reason for its existence. Or, as Zimmerman (2002) wrote, "an organizational mission statement reflects the organization's core value. It gives direction for goals and objectives. A purpose is the reason for an organization's existence. The terms *mission* and *purpose* are often used interchangeably" (p. 12).

Organizations sometimes also have a *vision statement*. It is a sentence that states "where the organization wants to go and what it will look like when it gets there. It is an image of a desired future" (Zimmerman, 2002, p. 12). The vision statement "should be clear, exciting, and should leave broad latitude for the pursuit of new opportunities" (McConnell, 2014, p. 34). Individual departments or units then create their own mission and/or vision statements based on those of the organization.

The statement of *philosophy* for the organization flows out of the mission statement. Philosophical statements address fundamental beliefs and values of organizations and provide a basis for action. O'Malley and Androwich (2008) wrote about the philosophy of an organization: "It is, in essence, a value statement of the principles and beliefs that direct the organization's behavior" (p. 227). In turn, departmental or unit philosophical statements reflect the organization's philosophy and provide fundamental beliefs about its specific area of practice, such as RT (Marquis & Huston, 2009).

Strategic planning is a written document prepared by upper management in organizations to offer a long-range perspective (e.g., 3–5 years). Purposes of strategic plans include identifying strategies to respond to anticipated changes affecting the organization; dedicating resources to key areas or new programs; streamlining services by eliminating duplication, waste, and underused services; and establishing timelines for achieving goals.

Goals and objectives reflect the actions that need to occur to achieve the strategic plan. Typically, goals for the overall organization are formulated as a part of the strategic plan, and goals for a particular unit (e.g., RT department) are established to support the overall goals of the organization. Goals and objectives offer managers a road map for planning. Or, as McConnell (2014) stated, the goals and objectives help direct planning. In contrast to mission statements that are typically open ended, goals state specific ends. They are made even more specific by listing objectives that fall under or subdivide each goal. Objectives are behavioral in content and are specific, realistic, measurable, and achievable statements that when reached serve as indicators that a goal has been achieved.

The *operational plan* is completed for a unit or department and is apt to be the responsibility of the first-line manager, such as the supervisor of RT. It is more short range than the strategic plan of the overall organization, and its concern is with the regular activities of the unit. Concerns include the numbers and types of clients to be served; the qualifications and abilities of staff; the types of supplies, equipment, and other resources required; the allocation of resources (e.g., staff, supplies, time) within budgetary restraints; and other activities, such as staff development, compliance with standards and regulations, and quality improvement and client safety projects (Cherry, 2011).

Organizing

Organizing Defined

The second management function is organizing. As defined by McConnell (2014), "organizing is the process of gearing up to implement decisions that result from the planning process; in other words, it is the establishment of the structure in which work gets done" (p. 39).

Organizing at the Organizational and Unit Levels

Organizing has to do with setting up the framework for an organization or unit within an organization. Descriptions of organizing at organizational and unit levels follow.

Organizational level. Cherry (2011) explained:

At the organizational level, organizing is necessary to establish a formal structure that defines the lines of authority, communication, and decision making within an organization. The formal organizational structure helps define roles and responsibilities of each level of management. The organizational chart provides a visual picture of the organization and identifies lines of communication and authority. . . . Organizing also involves developing policies and procedures to help outline how work will be done and establishing position qualifications and job descriptions to define who will do the work. (p. 346)

Unit or departmental level. At the unit level, or departmental level, Cherry (2011) indicated that organizing involves establishing work activities to meet the organization's goals effectively and efficiently. This involves (a) using resources (people, supplies, time) wisely, (b) assigning duties and responsibilities appropriately, (c) coordinating activities with other departments, and (d) effectively communicating with subordinates and supervisors to ensure a smooth workflow (Cherry, 2011, p. 346).

Authority

Supervisors or first-line managers use the authority assigned to them by their positions according to their place in the organizational hierarchy. Typically, their place in the hierarchy is indicated by where they are on the organizational chart. The first-line manager of an RT department or unit would be at the top of the organizational chart for the department or unit and would be in an equal place on the overall organizational chart with other department or unit heads.

Having authority is necessary to accomplishing work through personnel management (e.g., assigning subordinates), fiscal management (e.g., approving purchases of supplies or equipment), and procedural management (e.g., formulating policies and enforcing them). Managers should not be given responsibilities without being allocated the authority to fulfill their responsibilities. Therefore, authority is passed down the hierarchy to the point it needs to be exercised (McConnell, 2014).

Unity of command and span of control. The terms *unity of command* and *span of control* are used to describe types of authority under the organizing function. At one time, the principle of *unity of command* related to each employee reporting to only one supervisor. Because of new management practices, such as matrix management, the concept has come to mean that the employee responsible for completing a task has to be accountable to a specific individual. Typically, the unity of command for the first-line manager involves assigning responsibilities to staff and having them be accountable to a specific person (e.g., aquatics supervisor). The term *span of control* has to do with the number of staff who report to a single supervisor. Ideally, first-line managers should not supervise too large a number of employees, or they could become overworked. Of course, there is a danger of supervisors micromanaging should they be put in charge of supervising too few employees (McConnell, 2014).

Staffing

The third management function is staffing. Once the organizing function of designing the structure has been completed, the manager has to find staff to fulfill the responsibilities that have to be carried out. The staffing function is the process of providing and maintaining staff for the unit. Staffing is a critical management function because it takes well-selected and well-prepared individuals assigned to appropriate positions to offer a quality program of services.

Staffing Defined

Dunn (2002) stated:

Staffing represents the manager's responsibility to recruit and select employees to ensure qualified employees to fill the various positions needed based on the organization of duties to achieve the plan, while at the same time remaining within the budgeted labor amount for the department. (p. 18)

Steps in the Staffing Function

Cherry (2011) described five steps in staffing, modeled from Marquis and Huston (2009):
1. Determine the number and type of staff needed based on goals and budget requirements.
2. Recruit, interview, select, and assign personnel based on job description requirements and performance standards.
3. Get new employees off to a good start by offering excellent orientation, training, and socialization programs.
4. Implement an ongoing staff-development program to ensure employees at all levels have opportunities to develop personally and professionally and to enhance knowledge and skill levels.
5. Implement creative and flexible scheduling based on patient care needs, employee needs, and organizational productivity requirements. (Cherry, 2011, pp. 346–347)

Clinical Supervision: An Ongoing Program for Staff

The authors of this text wish to emphasize the fourth step in staffing particularly: "Implement an ongoing staff-development program to ensure employees at all levels have opportunities to develop personally and professionally and to enhance knowledge and skill levels" (Cherry, 2011, p. 347). A supervisor should never assign an employee to a task and then let the individual learn by trial and error. Every staff member needs to be provided necessary training (McConnell, 2014). In the case of recreational therapists, every therapist should receive clinical supervision.

As noted in Chapter 2, clinical supervision has two purposes. First, clinical supervision permits clinicians to gain and refine clinical practice skills to grow as helping professionals. Second, it allows the agency to deliver quality clinical services to clients. Thus, within clinical supervision the clinical supervisor assists supervisees to develop themselves to deliver the highest possible level of clinical service and promotes accountability in the agency's clinical program (Austin, 2013). It is the first-line manager's responsibility to design and carry out an ongoing staff-development program to enhance the knowledge and skill levels of the supervisees.

As indicated in Chapter 2, clinical supervision can be given by either the first-line manager or a designated clinical supervisor. The opinion of the authors of this text is that clinical supervision should be given not by the first-line manager but by a senior clinician. But whether supervision is given by a senior clinician or the first-line manager, it is critical that a clinical supervision program be conducted for recreational therapists.

Influencing

It is not sufficient for the manager to plan, organize, and staff. The manager must also engage in the fourth management function of influencing staff. The function of influencing is sometimes referred to in the literature as coordinating, leading, directing, or motivating (Dunn, 2002; McConnell, 2014).

Influencing Defined

Dunn (2002) defined the influencing function as one in which "the supervisor evokes actions from others to accomplish organizational objectives" (p. 383). Furthermore, Dunn (2002) stated: "Influencing is the process around which all performance revolves; it is the essence of all operations" (p. 18).

The Manager's Role

The manager's role is to maintain the smooth functioning of the unit and take corrective actions when employees do not carry out their assignments as specified. But influencing is more than giving out assignments and supervising staff to see they get done. Influencing involves building an effective workforce and providing an environment that inspires staff to perform at their best. There are many dimensions involved in influencing, including the following:

- Coaching
- Giving directives
- Role modeling
- Implementing change
- Creating a motivating climate
- Maintaining morale
- Relating to peers
- Employing leadership styles
- Communicating
- Giving feedback
- Delegating
- Managing conflict

All of these dimensions involved in influencing must become major components of what the first-line managers does. They are discussed in Chapter 8, which covers each in detail.

Controlling

The fifth, and final, management function is known as controlling. Controlling has to do with monitoring the performance of the organization or unit to determine whether the goals and objectives stated in the organizational or unit plan are being carried out and if deviations occur what corrections need to be made in performance or, alternatively, if the goals and objectives of the original plan need to be modified.

Defining Controlling

McConnell (2014) stated: "The simplest and perhaps most appropriate definition of controlling is follow-up and correction" (p. 47). Dunn (2002) offered a more extensive definition:

> Controlling is the function that ensures that plans are followed, that actual performance matches the plan, and that objectives are achieved. A more comprehensive definition of controlling includes determining whether the plans are carried out, if progress is being made toward objectives, and whether other actions must be taken to correct deviations and shortcomings. Again, this relates to the importance of planning as the primary function of the manager. A supervisor could not check on whether work was proceeding properly if there were no plans to check against. Controlling also includes taking corrective action if objectives are not being met, and revising the plans and objectives if circumstances require it. (p. 19)

Thus, a close relationship exists between the planning and controlling functions. The plan sets forth goals and objectives and methods for achieving them. Controlling involves measuring performance against the planned goals and objectives of the unit or organization. Therefore, the managerial function of controlling involves measuring actual performance against the planned goals and objectives. Controlling is often thought of as a budgeting function to make sure that finances are in line with the planned budget. Controlling not only involves managers meeting financial criteria, but also includes controlling processes, procedures, and policies related to service delivery. So, as McConnell's definition indicated, controlling has to do with follow-up of the implementation of the plan of any organization or unit. Cherry (2011) wrote about controlling in terms of practices related to service delivery.

Considerations in Controlling

As Cherry (2011) indicated, controlling has the purpose of ensuring that healthcare staff accomplish goals and objectives while they maintain a high level of performance. She suggested that to monitor staff performance that performance standards need to be established and a performance appraisal systems needs to be set up.

> "I like work. It fascinates me. I can sit and look at it for hours."
>
> Jerome K. Jerome

Another concern in controlling is establishing a risk management program to minimize risks to clients, staff, volunteers, and visitors. Maintaining standards of care is a control to ensure high-quality services are provided to clients. Performance standards are based on written policies and procedures of the organization or unit and on standards of practice (e.g., the standards of practice of the American Therapeutic

Recreation Association). A final element in the controlling function is budget planning and monitoring.

Potential Pitfalls

Perhaps a good way to end this chapter on basic management functions is to present a series of potential management pitfalls that relate to all management functions. Dunn (1998) provided a list of potential pitfalls for managers. These appear in Table 4.1.

Table 4.1
Management Blunders to Avoid

1. *Failure to communicate.* Well-informed employees are the key to a healthy, upbeat workplace. When you notice problems, act. By talking about little things, rumors are prevented and gossip is silenced.
2. *Failure to delegate.* By delegating, employees have an opportunity to solve problems and grow professionally.
3. *Taking things personally.* Turning a work-related issue into a personal one can trigger animosity. Keeping professional objectivity and decorum is important.
4. *Failure to motivate.* Important motivators, besides the paycheck, are benefits, opportunities for professional growth, friendships on the job, and opportunities to broaden one's knowledge.
5. *Treating everyone the same.* No two employees possess the same skills, temperaments, or experiences. Some need a fixed routine; others demonstrate creativity. Treat each employee accordingly.
6. *Failure to demonstrate loyalty.* Loyalty is a two-way street. Demonstrate loyalty for paying attention to employees' personal needs.
7. *Failure to obtain information.* Incorrect or incomplete information leads to poor decisions. By keeping several information channels open, unpleasant surprises are minimized.
8. *Failure to plan ahead.* Mismatched priorities, poor schedules, and ineffective allocation of time result from poor planning. Set clear goals and objectives.
9. *Forgetting to say, "Thank you."* A word of praise for a job well done affirms an employee's value and boosts morale.
10. *Failure to set priorities.* Employees should understand what is expected of them.

Note. From *Haimann's Supervisory Management for Healthcare Organizations* (6th ed., pp. 485–486), by R. T. Dunn, 1998, Boston, MA: WCB/McGraw-Hill.

Conclusion

Five managerial functions have been reviewed in this chapter: planning, organizing, staffing, influencing, and controlling. Each management function was presented separately, but it should be acknowledged that in actual practice the functions tend to blend together. Dunn (2002) articulated this well:

> Although the five management functions can be separated theoretically, in the daily job of the manager these activities are inseparable. Again, each function blends into the other, and each affects the performance of the others. The output of one provides the input for another, all as elements in a system. (p. 19)

References

Austin, D. R. (2013). *Therapeutic recreation processes and techniques: Evidence-based recreational therapy* (7th ed.). Urbana, IL: Sagamore.

Cherry, B. (2011). Nursing leadership and management (pp. 333–363). In B. Cherry & S. R. Jacob (Eds.), *Contemporary nursing: Issues, trends, & management.* St. Louis, MO: Elsevier Mosby.

Clark, C. C. (2009). *Creative nursing leadership & management.* Boston, MA: Jones & Bartlett.

Dunn, R. T. (1998). *Haimann's supervisory management for healthcare organizations* (6th ed.). Boston, MA: WCB/McGraw-Hill.

Dunn, R. T. (2002). *Haimann's supervisory management for healthcare organizations* (7th ed.). Chicago, IL: Health Administration Press.

Marquis, B. L., & Huston, C. J. (2009). *Leadership roles and management functions in nursing* (6th ed.). Philadelphia, PA: Wolters Kluwer Health/Lippincott Williams & Wilkins.

McConnell, C. R. (2014). *Umiker's management skills for the new health care supervisor* (6th ed.). Burlington, MA: Jones & Bartlett Learning.

O'Malley, A. A., & Androwich, I. M. (2008). Strategic planning and organizing patient care (pp. 225–245). In P. Kelly (Ed.), *Nursing leadership & management* (2nd ed.). Clifton Park, NY: Thomson/Delmar Learning.

Zimmerman, P. G. (2002). *Nursing management secrets.* Philadelphia, PA: Hanley & Belfus.

Chapter 5
Planning

Objectives
- Define the term *planning*.
- Identify the need for mission and vision statements when planning.
- Describe the need for unit or departmental philosophy, goals, and objectives.
- Describe tasks involved in program planning for an RT unit or department.
- Explain the importance of timelines in planning.
- Explain differences between strategic planning and operational planning.
- Describe the purpose of the ATRA Standards of Practice.
- Describe the need for protocol development for treatment interventions.
- Explain fiscal planning while including the concepts of the balance sheet, income statement, cash flow, and operating budget.
- Explain determining costs using the concepts of indirect costs, cost centers, revenue centers, and apportionment.
- Explain the CCR and ABC methods of cost allocation.
- Be able to calculate a realistic charge for a unit of RT service.
- Identify principal steps in operational budget planning.

Key Terms
- **Planning:** Planning is the management responsibility that requires looking at the future and making plans to meet current and anticipated needs. Planning focuses on meeting the goals and objectives of an organization, or a unit within the organization. Plans are sometimes referred to as blueprints for the future.
- **Mission statement:** States the purpose for the existence of the organization or unit.
- **Operational planning:** Planning that addresses the current and near future. Operational plans typically focus on activities of a department or unit for a single fiscal year.
- **Vision statement:** States the long-term, ultimate goal for the organization or unit.
- **Philosophy:** An organization's fundamental beliefs and values on which all services or programming is based.

- **Standards of Practice:** Refers to the ATRA *Standards for the Practice of Recreational Therapy and Self-Assessment Guide* (2013) that explains the standards required for competent practice.
- **Strategic planning:** Planning focused on the longer term. Strategic plans typically provide general directions for organizations for the coming 3 to 5 years.
- **Protocols:** A written description of how a program will be conducted that includes key elements such as the title, purpose, expected outcomes, techniques or interventions employed, staff requirements, and evaluation methods.
- **Balance sheet:** Presents what an organization owns as well as what it owes to others.
- **Income statement:** Lists an organization's revenues and expenses as well as the resulting net income or loss for the budget period.
- **Cash flow statement:** Reports the cash available from operating activities, investments, or other financial activities.
- **Operating budget:** Also known as the operating statement, the operating budget shows revenues and expenses for services.
- **Indirect costs:** Nonoperating costs sometimes referred to as overhead and include ongoing fixed costs (e.g., utilities) that are typically allocated to departments that generate charges.
- **Cost centers:** Departments within organizations that do not generate charges.
- **Revenue centers:** Departments within organizations that generate charges.
- **Apportionment:** The process of allocating costs associated with cost centers that do not generate revenues.
- **Activity based costing (ABC):** A method that uses both direct service and product costs as well as cost drivers to allocate indirect costs accurately.
- **Full-time equivalent (FTE):** One FTE represents a single full-time employee.
- **Cost to charge ratio (CCR):** A ratio of the cost divided by the charges.

Planning is the first management function. As such, it is fundamental to management. Planning involves developing an initial plan, but continues and evolves as revisions are made to meet emerging needs.

McConnell (2014) defined planning as follows:

Planning is the projection of actions intended to reach specific goals. In other words, a plan is a blueprint for the future; it is the expression of what we wish to accomplish or the best prediction of what might occur in the future. Planning begins with the questions of what and why, then focuses on the how, when, who, and where. (p. 32)

The planning process is the mean for the organization to accomplish its goals and objectives. Cherry (2011) identified steps in planning, beginning with the identification of goals and objectives:

- Identifying the goals and objectives to be achieved.
- Identifying the resources (e.g., people, supplies, and equipment) needed.
- Determining action steps to take.
- Establishing a timeline for the action steps and goal achievement. (p. 344)

To accomplish the steps involved in planning, the manager must first stipulate the organization's goals and objectives. To derive a clear listing of goals and objectives, the manager must first understand the mission, vision, and philosophy of the organization because the goals and objectives must flow out of the organization's stated mission, vision, and philosophy.

Decision Making in Planning

Decision making and planning in the management of recreational therapy (RT) must be consistent with the mission, vision, philosophy, and goals and objectives of the unit and organization (Cherry, 2011). Therefore, first, it is important to understand these key concepts.

Mission Statement

A *mission statement* identifies the purpose for the existence of the organization or unit and influences the vision, philosophy, and goals and objectives of the unit or organization. The mission statement also provides structure for all planning that occurs for the organization or unit. It is important that the employees, family members, or patients receiving services and the community know and support the mission statement. For these reasons, the mission statement should be broad enough to provide information about the facility, but narrow enough to distinguish the agency from similar agencies. Mission statements from well-known healthcare organizations are shown in Table 5.1.

Table 5.1
Organizational Healthcare Mission Statements

The Shepherd Center (Atlanta, Georgia)
Shepherd Center's mission is to help people with a temporary or permanent disability caused by injury or disease, rebuild their lives with hope, independence and dignity, advocating for their full inclusion in all aspects of community life while promoting safety and injury prevention.

The Mayo Clinic (Arizona, Florida, Minnesota)
To inspire hope and contribute to health and well-being by providing the best care to every patient through integrated clinical practice, education and research.

Note. Shepherd Center mission statement from "History and Mission," by Shepherd Center, n.d.-a (http://www.shepherd.org/about/history-and-mission). Mayo Clinic mission statement from "About Mayo Clinic Health System," by Mayo Clinic, n.d. (http://mayoclinichealthsystem.org/about-us/mission-and-values).

The mission statements in Table 5.1 have a *structure* (provide service type), show a *process* (describe how it happens), and identify *outcomes*. For example, in the Shepherd Center mission statement, the structure is rebuilding; the process is with hope, independence, and dignity; and the outcomes are full inclusion in all aspects of community life, safety, and injury prevention.

RT departments (and other departments with large systems) may also have specific mission statements. What are the structure, process, and outcomes in the departmental mission statements in Table 5.2?

Table 5.2
Recreational Therapy Department Mission Statements

The Shepherd Center (Atlanta, Georgia)
Shepherd Center's Recreation Therapy Department's mission is to help people with a temporary or permanent disability caused by injury or disease to lead healthy and active lifestyles as independently as possible through the use of recreation activities, providing education, skill development, and community reintegration opportunities.

VA Palo Alto Health Care System (California)
To provide clinical and holistic services which improve functional levels, promote optimal wellness, facilitate community reintegration, and enhance quality of life.

Note. Shepherd Center department mission statement from "Recreation Therapy," by Shepherd Center, n.d.-b (https://www.shepherd.org/resources/therapeutic-recreation). VA Palo Alto Health Care System department mission statement from "Recreation Therapy Service," by VA Palo Alto Health Care System, n.d. (http://www.paloalto.va.gov/services/rectherapy/).

Vision Statements

Vision statements are also important to the planning function. The vision statement for an organization or unit focuses on the future, looking ahead to where the agency or unit wants to be as a long-term, aspirational goal. The vision statement provides a statement of a destination or goal that is better than the current status. The vision needs to be consistent with the mission, but also provide an opportunity to look ahead for better provision of services. The vision statement for the Mayo Clinic is provided in Table 5.3. Does the mission statement in Table 5.1 identify something greater than the services provided today?

Table 5.3
Organization Vision Statements

The Mayo Clinic (Arizona, Florida, Minnesota)
Mayo Clinic will provide an unparalleled experience as the most trusted partner for health care.

Note. From "About Mayo Clinic Health System," by Mayo Clinic, n.d. (http://mayoclinichealthsystem.org/about-us/mission-and-values).

Departments within organizations may also have a vision statement. These vision statements provide the long-term focus for the unit while remaining consistent with the unit mission. Two examples of departmental vision statements are shown in Table 5.4.

Table 5.4
Organization Vision Statements

VA Palo Alto Health Care System (California)
To be the benchmark of excellence and value in Recreation Therapy / Creative Arts Therapy.

Capital Health (Canada)
To be leaders in Therapeutic Recreation Practice.

Note. VA Palo Alto Health Care System vision statement from "Recreation Therapy Service," by VA Palo Alto Health Care System, n.d. (http://www.paloalto.va.gov/services/rectherapy/). Capital Health vision statement from "Mission, Vision, & Values," by Capital Health, n.d. (http://www.cdha.nshealth.ca/recreation-therapy/mission-vision-values).

It is evident from the examples that mission and vision statements do not have to be wordy, convoluted statements. These statements should be straightforward and direct. Mission and vision statements act as guides for employees and administrators, but also play a part in marketing services to the community. Thus, if they are jargon-laden, it will be hard for those outside the organization to understand.

Philosophy

When it comes to management issues, an organization bases all its services on its fundamental beliefs and values. The organization or unit's *philosophy* plays a substantial part in the services offered and the manner in which they are offered and potentially may affect the long-term outcome. The philosophy provides the climate in which the mission and vision will be addressed. Philosophies are sometimes called value statements, likely because they are expressing the values of the organization. Example philosophical statements at the organizational level are provided in Table 5.5.

Table 5.5
Organizational Philosophies

VA Palo Alto Health Care System (California)
The health and safety of our patients, employees, and community is our top priority. We put Veterans first regardless of their individual backgrounds, beliefs, cultures, and religion. Our service advocates or encourages Veterans to participate in the highest level of their care possible.

Rocky Mountain Multiple Sclerosis Center (Colorado)
The needs of the patient come first.

Note. VA Palo Alto Health Care System philosophy from "Recreation Therapy Service," by VA Palo Alto Health Care System, n.d. (http://www.paloalto.va.gov/services/rectherapy/). Rocky Mountain Multiple Sclerosis Center philosophy from "MS Awareness Month," by Rocky Mountain Multiple Sclerosis Center, n.d. (http://www.mscenter.org/get-involved/events/ms-awareness-month).

Philosophies, when applied to the departmental or unit level, indicate the theoretical perspective of the agency, or which service-delivery model it uses as a basis for service provision. Table 5.6 contains the RT department–specific philosophy for the California State Hospital, Atascadero.

Table 5.6
Departmental or Recreational Therapy–Specific Philosophy

California Department of State Hospitals: Atascadero
Our Philosophy of Recreation Therapy is to utilize various recreational activities as interventions that promote change, wellness and independence in the areas of physical, emotional, cognitive and social impairments. Goal-directed interventions are taught to aid in overcoming barriers associated with mental illness, substance abuse, cognitive deficits and physical limitations; as well, goal-directed interventions teach, encourage and improve quality of life through positive leisure and recreation participation. Involvement in a variety of therapeutic groups and supplemental activities is encouraged with the goal to teach transferable skills when integrating back into a community setting.

Note. From "Philosophy and Treatment Goals of the Recreational Therapy Program," by California Department of State Hospitals, n.d. (http://www.dsh.ca.gov/Atascadero/Internships/Recreational_Therapy_Internship.aspx).

Developing Goals and Objectives

After the mission, vision, and philosophy have been developed for the organization and department, the next step is to develop the goals and objectives that provide distal (long-term) and proximal (short-term) targets toward which to direct the activity of the organization or unit. In many ways, these goals and objectives are similar to the those that students in RT programs have learned to develop. Goals are broad and provide the direction toward which the organization wants to move, and objectives are the specific actions required to achieve the goals. However, goals and objectives in the management process are not patient specific. Goals for one organization and one RT program are shown in Table 5.7.

Table 5.7
Organization and Recreational Therapy Department Goals

Rocky Mountain Multiple Sclerosis Center (Colorado)
We are committed to providing innovative, specialized, comprehensive and interdisciplinary care to treat, support and rehabilitate people living with MS.

We are committed to providing services that support individuals and families with MS throughout the entire MS life cycle.

We are committed to educating people diagnosed with MS, their families, healthcare professionals, and the general public about multiple sclerosis.

We are committed to building the body of knowledge about MS, leading the way in MS research, developing new, effective treatments, and finding the cure for MS.

Table 5.7 (cont.)

California Department of State Hospitals: Atascadero Recreational Therapy Department

The focus of treatment is addressed and implemented through a variety of therapeutic activities within structured groups. These areas include; Psychiatric, Social, Dangerousness, Substance Abuse, Legal, Health and Wellness, Leisure and Recreation, Education, Occupation and Community Integration. Some examples of treatment goals include:

- Improve problem solving skills and frustration tolerance through a variety of recreation activities
- Develop leisure skills through positive leisure education and experiences
- Develop an awareness of physical fitness, health and wellness benefits
- Improve social anxiety, cooperation, and sense of personal responsibility through involvement in organized group activities
- Increase self-esteem through creative opportunities in the area of art and music
- Develop coping strategies to better manage symptoms of mental illness
- Reduce stress and anxiety through recreational pursuits

Note. Rocky Mountain Multiple Sclerosis Center goals from "About," by Rocky Mountain Multiple Sclerosis Center, n.d. (http://www.mscenter.org/about-us).California Department of State Hospitals goals from "Recreational Therapy Treatment Goals," by California Department of State Hospitals, n.d. (http://www.dsh.ca.gov/Atascadero/Internships/Recreational_Therapy_Internship.aspx).

Many agencies do not provide objectives for their organizations online, but example objectives are provided in Table 5.8 based on the first goal from each organization in Table 5.7.

Table 5.8

Examples of Objectives (authors' examples, not agency's examples)

Rocky Mountain Multiple Sclerosis Center (Colorado)

We are committed to providing innovative, specialized, comprehensive and interdisciplinary care to treat, support and rehabilitate people living with MS.

Objective 1: Rehabilitative services will be provided 7 days per week to improve functional skills of clients.

California Department of State Hospitals: Atascadero Recreational Therapy Department

Improve problem solving skills and frustration tolerance through a variety of recreation activities

Objective 1: The recreational therapy program will provide 2 interventions per week that focus on increasing problem-solving skills.

Relationships of Vision, Mission, Philosophy, Goals, and Objectives

From the descriptions and examples of visions, missions, philosophy, goals, and objectives, it should be evident that the vision leads to the mission, and the mission to the philosophy, and the philosophy to the goals and objectives. Said another way, the goals and objectives allow the vision, mission, and philosophy to be achieved.

Goals provide general direction toward sought outcomes. Objectives are the narrowest and most specific elements included in planning as they further define and support goals. In fact, a good way to measure goal achievement is that several objectives related to a goal have been reached. Thus, objectives provide specific and measurable statements of sought goals. The acronym SMART is often found in the literature as a means to describe well-formulated objectives that are Specific, Measurable, Attainable, Relevant, and Timelined (Austin, 2013).

Program Development

Developing a comprehensive program for an RT department or unit involves skills similar to what recreational therapists employ every day in developing goals and objectives in planning for individual clients, but the focus is on applying the concepts to the overall program. Therefore, as with individual treatment planning, the identified goals and objectives for the RT unit form the basis for developing the overall program. Of course, all goals and objectives need to tie back to the vision, mission, and philosophy set for the unit, which reflect the needs of the client population to be served. Goals for an RT program, for example, might include providing programs to assist clients to achieve functional improvements and to cope with chronic conditions, as well as to build strengths through interventions to increase personal awareness; develop interpersonal or social skills; develop leisure skills; decrease stress; decrease depression; improve physical fitness; improve mental functioning; and develop feelings of positive self-regard, self-efficacy, perceived control, pleasure, and enjoyment (Austin, 2015).

The following is a way to conceptualize program planning for an RT unit:
- Identify goals and objectives.
- Indicate what tasks need to be carried out to achieve the goals.
- Decide who will be responsible for each task related to each program.
- Determine needed resources (funding, people, materials), or what is needed to complete each task.
- Identify success criteria or how you will identify your success and how you will track progress.
- Establish timelines or a time frame by which to start and complete the tasks.

Timelines for Action Steps and Goal Achievement

It is important to precisely create a timetable for completing each task or achieving each goal. For example, when should a specific intervention program be implemented, such as a summer adventure therapy program, and when should it conclude?

It is also important to track the progress made toward achieving each task. A means to track progress is to set specific due dates or milestones for completing steps along the way. Such tracking will allow the manager to stay focused on the plan as well as allow for making corrections if necessary or for celebrating achievements. Free online calendars offer a means to keep track of progress and specific dates and to share this information with others, such as the RT staff.

"I love deadlines. I like the whooshing sound they make as they fly by."

Douglas Adams

Staff Involvement

It is also important to involve all members of the RT unit in the overall program planning. Their involvement will help ensure that nothing is overlooked and will increase the probability that staff will be more dedicated to carrying it out fully. Of course, once staff are invested, the manager needs to keep them informed about what is occurring during the planning process so they know their input has not been ignored. Before the plan is finalized, it is a good idea to distribute it to staff so they are clear on their responsibilities and the timelines established and can provide feedback before the plan is put into place.

Operational and Strategic Planning

What do the terms *strategic planning* and *operational planning* refer to? It is important to understand the differences between strategic planning and operational planning.

In general terms, strategic planning determines an organization's overall direction. Strategic plans typically encompass the long term or the coming 3 to 5 years. The operational plan determines what a department or unit within an organization is doing day by day and month by month. Operational plans typically focus on a single fiscal year.

Strategic Planning

Strategic planning refers to a formal process, founded on the enduring purpose of the organization and accomplished by higher level managers, for deciding a relatively small number of key decisions that an organization sets to thrive over the long term. Thus, it results in the documentation of a relatively small set of extensive goals for the organization to pursue over the next few years. The goals are general in nature, but the strategic plan provides a means to direct personnel in the organization toward the intended directions. The strategic planning process allows high-level management the opportunity to reexamine the established directions for the organization by asking questions, such as the following: Do we need to alter our priorities? Have the needs of our clients changed? Can we streamline services by eliminating duplication, waste, and underused services? Do our current personnel have the capacity and commitment to achieve our goals?

Operational Planning

In contrast to strategic planning, operational planning is tactical in nature and is for the short term. A highly detailed plan is produced at the department or unit level to achieve the goals and objectives. Thus, operational planning specifies concrete short-term objectives for a specific functional area within an overall organization, such as the RT department or unit. Concerns for operational plans include the numbers and types of clients to be served; the qualifications and abilities of staff; the types of supplies, equipment, and other resources required; the allocation of resources (e.g., staff, supplies, time) within budgetary restraints; and other activities, such as staff development, compliance with standards and regulations, and quality improvement and safety projects (Cherry, 2011).

Operational planning is typically accomplished within the annual planning cycle, although it may occur more frequently within RT departments or units that organize their actions around summer and winter programs. Finally, rather than being done by high-level management, operational planning is the responsibility of the department or unit manager.

Differences Between Strategic Planning and Operational Planning

Table 5.9 outlines differences between strategic planning and operational planning.

Table 5.9
Differences Between Strategic and Operational Planning

	Strategic planning	Operational planning
Authority	Top-Level Managers	Department or Unit Manager
Time Span	A Few Years (e.g., 3–5)	Typically Annually
Meaning	Organization's Vision	Achieving Goals and Objectives
Scope	Entire Organization	Department or Unit

Operational and Strategic Planning Are Linked

Despite the obvious distinctions between operational and strategic planning, they are linked and inform and support one another to realize the effective management of the organization. The operational plan contains the fine points for executing the strategic plan every day. For example, the strategic plan may outline the resource allocation needed to achieve the overall goals of the organization. The manager can compare the operational and strategic plans to determine if the department or unit is using resource allocations effectively to reach the objectives of the strategic plan (Brown & Media, 2016; Root & Media, 2016; Surbhi, 2015).

Conclusion to Discussion of Operational and Strategic Planning

From the discussion of operational and strategic planning, it should be evident that the RT department or unit deals with operational planning rather than strategic planning. Strategic planning is done by high-level managers to set directions for the overall organization. Operational planning is left to department- or unit-level managers. Thus, RT managers, working with their staff, are responsible for developing the operational plan for their department or unit.

A Tool for Planning: Standards of Practice

When planning the operations of an RT department or unit, the manager has a tool that can greatly help when developing this plan: the American Therapeutic Recreation Association (ATRA, 2013) Standards of Practice (SOP; more properly known as the *Standards for the Practice of Recreational Therapy and Self-Assessment Guide*, the most current version of the SOP). These standards guide the manager in determining what needs to be a part of the departmental practice and provide checklists and audits to use to evaluate the departmental progress toward using these standards.

The ATRA SOP provide guidance for providing RT in all settings and help to improve the quality and consistency of RT practices (Barrett & Smith, 2013). The ATRA SOP use the Centers for Medicare and Medicaid Services (2012) *active treatment* definition, which is treatment "provided under an individualized treatment or diagnostic plan; reasonably expected to improve the patient's condition for the purpose of diagnosis; and supervised and evaluated by a physician" (Section 30.2.2.1, para. 1). Active treatment defines and differentiates RT from diversional or activity programs. Recreational therapists implement active treatment that is goal directed and focused on improving function.

The ATRA SOP use a now familiar approach: structure criteria, process criteria, and outcome criteria for each standard. As Barrett and Smith (2013) defined,

- *Structure criteria*: Define and measure parameter of practice (e.g., facilities or resources).
- *Process criteria*: Define and measure provision of service (e.g., practitioner–patient/client interaction, intervention strategies).
- *Outcome criteria*: Define and measure achievement or change in patient's/ client's condition (e.g., improved functional level, health, independence, satisfaction). (p. 4)

The following 12 standards are included in the 2013 version of the ATRA SOP:
1. Assessment
2. Treatment planning
3. Plan implementation
4. Re-assessment and evaluation
5. Discharge and transition planning
6. Prevention, safety planning, and risk management
7. Ethical conduct
8. Written plan of operation
9. Staff qualifications and competency assessment
10. Quality improvement
11. Resource management
12. Program evaluation and research

In the SOP, each standard has a definition; a rationale for why this standard is relevant to RT practices; and the structure, process, and outcome criteria. The second part of the SOP is the self-assessment guide. The self-assessment guide provides the conscientious manager assessments to use in the following areas:
1. *Management audit*: Evaluates the written plan of operations (WPO) and ensures that all 12 standards are incorporated into the WPO.
2. *Documentation audit*: Evaluates the written documentation by the staff recreational therapists.
3. *Outcomes audit*: Assesses patient outcomes related to treatment provided during recreational therapy. This section also includes a patient satisfaction questionnaire that can be used to evaluate the patient's evaluation of his or her treatment.

4. *Competency assessment:* Evaluates the competency of the staff providing recreational therapy.
5. *Clinical performance appraisal:* Evaluates performance of the therapist. A form is provided to evaluate the performance of interns and those with clinical positions.

The ATRA SOP (2013) enhance the provision of RT at the facility and help to ensure that it is being written and documented correctly. The audits are also a well-developed tool to help managers evaluate the strength of the WPO, documentation, patient outcomes, and the competency of staff and interns.

The SOP remain the central focus of RT departments or units during planning. Nevertheless, the RT manager needs to consider organization-wide standards of accrediting bodies, such as the Joint Commission and the Commission on Accreditation of Rehabilitation Facilities (CARF International), that may apply to elements within the RT service. Additionally, the manager needs to consider state or federal standards related to the provision of services.

Protocols

Another important component of planning in RT is having intervention protocols that provide guidance for a variety of interventions. An example format for program protocols is provided in Table 5.10. These protocols should exist in a notebook or electronic medium at the facility so all staff have access to them.

Table 5.10
Program Protocol Format

Program Title:

Time and Place of Program:

Target Population/Size of Group:

Client Referral Criteria:

Contraindicated Criteria:

General Program Purpose:

Program Description:

Problems or Deficits the Program Might Address:

Interventions or Facilitation Techniques to Be Employed:

Staff Program Responsibilities:

Training Requirements for Staff:

Risk Management Considerations:

Expected Program Outcomes:

Program Evaluation Methods/Frequency:

Note. From *Therapeutic Recreation Processes and Techniques: Evidence-Based Recreational Therapy* (7th ed., p. 192), by D. R. Austin, 2013, Urbana, IL: Sagamore.

Fiscal Planning and Budgeting

Fiscal planning is as important as any other planning. It involves planning financial resources to ensure an organization can accomplish its mission, meet its goals, and work toward achieving its vision. In general, organizations have a variety of financial planning documents; however, most organizations have three principal accounting statements (Eldenburg, Schafer, & Zulauf, 2010). First, the financial position statement or *balance sheet* presents what an organization owns as well as what it owes to others. This statement may include capital holdings, such as buildings or equipment, and liabilities, such as outstanding loan balances. Second, an operating statement or *income statement* lists the organization's revenues and expenses as well as the resulting net income or loss for a budget period. Finally, organizations use *cash flow statements* to report cash available from operating activities, investments, or other financial activities. Of these three financial planning documents, RT managers are most likely to be directly involved in developing operating statements (also known as operating budgets) of the revenues and expenses for their services. Zeiler (2011) noted that the financial planning process should include managers at all levels of the organization. Two principal activities in financial planning for developing operating budgets are determining costs through cost accounting and determining charges that translate to revenues (Nowicki, 2008).

Determining Costs

Costs are used in planning to provide information on the amount of resources needed to provide a given product or service. Such information gives managers guidance on the resources needed to provide a service and information on services that may consume a great deal of resources. Managers can use this information to identify and manage costs, examine the profitability of a service, and determine charges needed to provide the service.

The total cost of a service is not always readily apparent, because it includes operating costs associated with producing a service and nonoperating costs that support the service. For example, providing 1 hour of RT service would obviously include the time of the recreational therapist and supplies used in providing the service (direct costs); however, in most organizations the time of additional personnel (e.g., human resources and accounting) is not directly tied to providing RT services, as well as other nonoperating costs, such as utilities and loan payments. These nonoperating costs, sometimes termed *indirect costs* and sometimes identified as *overhead,* are typically allocated to departments that generate charges (Nowicki, 2008). A further complication is that some departments or cost centers, such as housekeeping, do not generate revenues and also provide services to other cost centers, such as accounting and human resources, that do not generate revenues. Thus, although all units within an organization are considered *cost centers*, only those that generate charges are considered *revenue centers*. The process of allocating costs associated with cost centers that do not generate revenues is known as apportionment (Nowicki, 2008). Although it is a relatively complicated process, apportionment seeks to allocate indirect costs equitably to revenue centers.

Once indirect costs are identified, costs for products or services can be identified in a number of ways. Zeiler (2011) noted that currently the most widely used approach in healthcare is Activity Based Costing (ABC). The ABC method uses direct service and product costs as well as *cost drivers* to accurately allocate indirect costs associated with products. An example of a common cost driver is the full-time equivalent (FTE). One FTE represents a single full-time employee, and departments with more employees consume more human resources services than do departments with fewer employees. Another example of how the ABC method more appropriately allocates indirect costs can be seen in two common forms of RT interventions. Community reintegration activities are common RT interventions and typically involve the use of a facility's vehicle fleet. In addition to the fuel and maintenance direct costs associated, these vehicles depreciate over time and must be replaced. Although the indirect cost of vehicle depreciation could be bundled into a facility- or service-wide indirect cost unit, on-site RT interventions do not typically involve facility vehicles, so it would be inappropriate for indirect costs associated with vehicles to be included in costs for one-on-one RT interventions. Similarly, aquatic interventions are commonly used in areas such as rehabilitation. The indirect costs associated with care and maintenance of aquatic facilities would be inappropriate to apply to therapeutic procedures that do not use those facilities.

Setting Charges

Passmore (2010) recommended the process of setting charges be done by the facility's fiscal officer, who is likely to have the most accurate information on direct and indirect costs. Although there are examples of establishing costs as a basis for setting charges (e.g., Carter, Van Andel, & Robb, 2003; Passmore, 2010), these models are built on a cost to charge ratio (CCR) that although simple to develop and apply is considered to be less accurate than other approaches, such as the ABC method (Zelman, McCue, & Glick, 2009). Considering that a variety of programming activities are often provided in an RT service, it is possible to set a charge for all RT services using CCR or set charges according to differing costs using the ABC approach (Nowicki, 2008). Both approaches are presented in the sections that follow.

Identifying activities. One place to begin with calculating charges is to identify the services provided by the RT department or service. The current procedural terminology (CPT*) codes from the American Medical Association (2015; see Table 5.11) can be used to ensure that the RT activities or interventions are consistent with other services. The advantage of using these codes is that they represent a standard terminology for all health professionals.

Table 5.11

CPT® Codes Suggested for Recreational Therapy Procedures

Code	Therapeutic procedure
97110	Therapeutic procedure, 1 or more areas, each 15 minutes; therapeutic exercises to develop strength and endurance, range of motion and flexibility.
97112	Neuromuscular reeducation of movement, balance, coordination, kinesthetic sense, posture, and/or proprioception for sitting and/or standing activities.
97113	Aquatic therapy with therapeutic exercise.
97150	Therapeutic activities, direct (one-on-one) patient contact (use of dynamic activities to improve functional performance), each 15 minutes.
97530	Therapeutic activities, direct (one-on-one) patient contact (use of dynamic activities to improve functional performance), each 15 minutes.
97532	Development of cognitive skills to improve attention, memory, problem solving (includes compensatory training), direct (one-on-one) patient contact, each 15 minutes.
97533	Sensory integrative techniques to enhance sensory processing and promote adaptive responses to environmental demands, direct (one-on-one) patient contact, each 15 minutes.
97535	Self-care/home management training (e.g., activities of daily living (ADL) and compensatory training, meal preparation, safety procedures and instructions in use of assistive technology devices/adaptive equipment) direct one-on-one contact, each 25 minutes.
97537	Community/work reintegration training (e.g., shopping, transportation, money management, avocational activities and/or work environment/modification analysis, work task analysis, use of assistive technology device/adaptive equipment), direct one-on-one contact, each 15 minutes.

Note. From *Current Professional Terminology (CPT®)* (pp. 656–657), by American Medical Association, 2015.

Cost to charge ratio (CCR). Assuming that an RT service provides three types of program activities listed in Table 5.12, with their associated CPT® codes, the manager can begin to assemble costs. Staffing and supplies (direct costs) and indirect costs to the three program activities are shown in Table 5.12 for later comparison; however, to use CCR the manager need only identify totals (D1–D6) in Table 5.12. To calculate overall costs for all RT services using CCR, the manager first calculates the total direct costs from the personnel costs and supply costs (D2 + D3 = D4). The manager then identifies the indirect rate as a percentage of direct costs. Carter et al. (2003) used a figure of 40% for what they termed overhead, and that same value is used here to identify the indirect costs associated with direct costs of $303,490 (D4). The manager then translates the percentage into a proportion (40% = 0.40) and then multiplies this by the direct costs (D4), and the result is $121,396 (D5). The manager can now identify total cost by adding total direct costs (D4) to indirect costs (D5), resulting in total costs of $424,885 (D6). The final step in the CCR process is then to divide the total costs ($424,885) in D6 by the total volume of services provided (24,960) in D1. The result is a value of $17.02/unit of RT services. This then provides the basis for the charges. In most cases, this amount would be rounded down to $17.00/unit (15 minutes) charge for all RT services.

Table 5.12
Cost to Charge Ratio (CCR) Model

	1	2	3	4	5	6
				Direct	Indirect	Total
Procedures (activities)	Volume[a]	Staff cost[b]	Supplies	costs	(40%)	cost
A. Aquatic Therapy (CPT 97113)	9360	$108405	$760	$109165	$43666	
B. Community Reintegration Training (CPT 97537)	4680	$54203	$5460	$59663	$23865	
C. Cognitive Rehabilitation (CPT 97532)	10920	$126473	$8190	$134663	$53865	
D. Total	24960	$289080	$14410	$303490	$121396	$424885

Cost per Unit of Patient Care = Total Costs of Care (D6)/Units of Care Provided (D1) = $424,885.00/24960 = **$17.02** (rounded to **$17.00**)

[a] Volume is based on .25-hour (15-minute) units. [b] Based on 5 staff plus benefit rate of 31.4% (U.S. Bureau of Labor Statistics, 2016) and allocated based on proportion of total volume of services provided.

Activity Based Costing (ABC). In contrast, the ABC approach assumes that indirect costs should not be equally allocated to all activities, because they are frequently identified as directly tied to certain activities. As noted, aspects such as the maintenance of aquatic facilities are appropriately allocated to activities that use the facilities and not appropriately allocated to those that do not. The same program activities, volumes, and direct costs are presented in Table 5.13 as in the CCR model in Table 5.12. The difference is that certain indirect costs directly attributable to program activities are carved out of the total indirect costs. Thus, only the community reintegration program has indirect costs allocated from the motor pool (identified in costs per mile, B5) and only the aquatic therapy program has costs allocated from the maintenance of the aquatic facility (A6). In addition, other indirect costs (column 7) remain, such as record keeping, billing, personnel, and maintenance, that are best allocated based on the volume of care (Zelman et al., 2009). The process is then to remove costs that can be allocated to activities from the total indirect costs, allocate those indirect costs to associated activities (A6, B5), and then distribute remaining indirect costs based on volume of services (A7, B7, C7). This then allows the manager to identify the total indirect costs (A8, B8, C8) with each activity by summing allocated and other indirect costs for each activity. The manager now follows the same general process of CCR by creating total costs as the sum of direct costs (column 4) and indirect costs (column 8); however, these total costs are now associated with each activity (A9, B9, C9). From here, the manager can now establish a basis for charges by dividing the activity total cost (A9, B9, C9) by its associated volume of services (A1, B1, C1) to come up with activity-specific charges (A10, B10, C10).

Table 5.13
Activity Based Costing (ABC) Model

Procedures (activities)	1 Volume[a]	2 Staff cost[b]	3 Supplies	4 Direct costs	5 Vehicle miles[c]	6 Therapy pool[d]	7 Other indirect[e]	8 Total indirect	9 Total cost	10 Activity unit cost
A. Aquatic Therapy (CPT 97113)	9360	$108405	$760	$109165	0	$53271	$25038	$78309	$187474	$20.03
B. Community Reintegration Training (CPT 97537)	4680	$54203	$5460	$59663	$1357	0	$12519	$13876	$73539	$15.71
C. Cognitive Rehabilitation (CPT 97532)	10920	$126473	$8190	$134663	0	0	$29211	$29211	$163873	$15.01
D. Total	24960	$289080	$14410	$303490	$1357	$53271	$66768	$121396	$424886	

In ABC, cost per unit of service is subsequently calculated by summing direct costs (column 4) plus total indirect costs (column 8) and dividing by the total volume of services (column 1). This results in the following costs:

- Aquatic Therapy = [$109,165 (A4) + $78,309 (A8)] / 9360 (A1) = $20.03 (rounded down to $20.00)
- Community Reintegration = [$59,663 (B4) + $13,876 (B8)] / 4680 (A1) = $15.71 (rounded up $15.75 to account for rounding down in other rates)
- Cognitive Rehabilitation = [$134,663 (C4) + 29,211 (C8)] / 10920 (C1) = $15.01 (rounded down to $15.00)

[a]Volume is based on 15-minute units. [b]Based on 5 staff using median RT salary plus benefit rate of 31.4% (U.S. Bureau of Labor Statistics) and allocated based on proportion of total volume of services provided. [c]Vehicle maintenance based on estimated annual 2,600 miles vehicle use and estimated maintenance cost at $0.522/mile. [d]Annual therapy pool maintenance costs estimated at $15.41/sq ft for 24' x 32' therapy pool ("The Decision Matrix," 2008). [e]Other indirect costs, such as medical records, billing, personnel, and general utilities, allocated based on service volume.

The differences between the approaches are best seen in comparison to the results. A comparison of the approaches is provided in Table 5.14. In this table, the total volume of services (D1), total direct costs (D2), and total indirect costs (D3) are identical in the CCR and ABC models. The difference is in how the indirect costs are allocated to the activities. Under CCR, indirect costs are a simple percentage of direct costs, resulting in a consistent rate for all RT services (column 4), whereas with the ABC model, identifiable indirect costs are allocated to different activities, resulting in varying charges for different activities. The reason that ABC is a more accurate basis for setting charges can be seen in the differences in column 4. Under the CCR model, clients in the community reintegration program and cognitive rehabilitation program are being overcharged to account for the costs of aquatic therapy and that clients in aquatic therapy are being undercharged.

Table 5.14

Cost to Charge Ratio (CCR) Versus Activity Based Costing (ABC) Models

Procedures (activities)	1 Volume	2 Direct costs[a]	3 Total indirect CCR[b]	3 Total indirect ABC	4 Unit cost CCR	4 Unit cost ABC
A. Aquatic Therapy (CPT 97113)	9360	$109165	$43666	$78309	$17.00	$20.00
B. Community Reintegration Training (CPT 97537)	4680	$59663	$23865	$13876	$17.00	$15.75
C. Cognitive Rehabilitation (CPT 97532)	10920	$134663	$53865	$29211	$17.00	$15.00
D. Totals	24960	$303490	$121396			

[a]Staffing and supplies costs combined in this table. [b]Under CCR, indirect costs are calculated as 40% of direct costs.

Overall, setting charges may be complicated; however, recreational therapists should know and be able to identify the basis for service charges (Passmore, 2010). The example here, while theoretical, is founded on realistic estimates of costs that are publicly available. In addition, in the above example, the entire costs of a therapy pool are allocated to RT services. In most agencies that use a therapy pool, other therapies would also likely be using the pool, thus maximizing its use, and thus, the indirect cost would be spread over all services provided, not just RT services. Finally, depreciation costs (costs associated with planned replacement of facilities and equipment) are not included in this example and would likely result in a higher rate for services. Recreational therapists should work with their financial officers to develop charges that are accurate. In addition, the more accurately recreational therapists can identify costs, the better they will be able to manage overall budgets.

Operational Budget Planning

Most health and human service agencies engage in a comprehensive budgeting process (Dunn, 2007). This process involves developing unit-level budgets that are consolidated into an overall budget. Supervisory managers in RT are likely to be involved in or responsible for developing their unit's budget. The operating budget identifies the estimated revenues and expenses associated with the unit, typically for 12 months. These budgets include estimates of patient and nonpatient revenue as well as expenses (Dunn, 2007). As presented, patient revenue is typically forecast based on charges and volumes. Additionally, nonpatient revenue comes from, for example, appropriations (publicly funded agencies), charitable contributions, and grants (Carter, Smith, & O'Morrow, 2014). For most health and human service agencies, the greatest expense category is personnel. Other major categories are materials and supplies as well as indirect costs, such as depreciation, interest on debt, and insurance.

Baker and Baker (2014) identified that constructing an operating budget begins with identifying the format and scope of the operating budget. Typically, facility or organizational templates provide the basis for format, and the manager must consider scope in relation to other organizational budgets. In most organizations, a *line-item budget* format is used. In such a budget, each different category or expense is listed on a separate line. In addition, these budgets typically also include columns for previous budget years (Carter et al., 2014). The manager should consider the budget scope because if the manager's budget represents a single budget segment that will subsequently be consolidated into a larger budget, some item detail may be lost through consolidation.

Next, the manager has to gather budget information. Key sources of information for budget construction include forecasts for operating revenue, staffing, and other expenses; however, these forecasts are based upon assumptions and subsequent computation. Examination of assumptions should begin with a review of institutional and unit strategies and objectives. For example, do objectives indicate a change in levels of revenues and/or costs? Are there new or restructured programs or facilities projected for the next budget period? These assumptions aid the manager in determining what adjustments they must make to their current budget plan. Finally, the manager develops computations based on the identified assumptions to generate forecasts. One challenge in developing computations is that they must be comparable across departments. This may present challenges in forecasting staffing when one unit provides 24-hour care, with staff eligible for overtime, and another unit only provides services during business hours with salaried staff (not eligible for overtime). Baker and Baker (2014) suggested that identifying staffing needs in terms of annualized FTEs is one approach to developing comparable metrics across units in such a situation. An FTE represents the cost of productive and nonproductive (vacation, sick, holiday, continuing education) time for one full-time employee for 1 year. Overall, the operational budget represents a best estimate of the plan for the use of financial resources, both revenues and costs, for the coming budget period. Like operational and strategic planning, fiscal planning and budgeting provide a basis against which managers can evaluate performance.

Summary

Planning is the first management function. It provides a blueprint for the future of an organization or unit within an organization by (a) identifying goals and objectives, (b) identifying needed resources, (c) determining action steps to take to achieve the goals, and (d) establishing a timeline for accomplishments.

RT department or unit plans need to coincide with those of the overall organization. They include the elements of mission, vision, and philosophy that lead to establishing goals and objectives. Central to planning in RT are the ATRA SOP.

Fiscal planning and budgeting are as important as other planning. An assurance of having financial resources to meet the planned goals and objectives is critical to successful delivery of quality services.

References

American Medical Association. (2015). *Current professional terminology (CPT®)*. Chicago, IL: Author.

American Therapeutic Recreation Association. (2013). *Standards for the practice of recreational therapy and self-assessment guide*. Hattiesburg, MS: Author.

Austin, D. R. (2013). *Therapeutic recreation processes and techniques: Evidence-based recreational therapy* (7th ed.). Urbana, IL: Sagamore.

Austin, D. R. (2015). Introduction and overview. In D. R. Austin, M. E. Crawford, B. P. McCormick, & M. Van Puymbroeck (Eds.), *Recreational therapy: An introduciton* (4th ed., pp. 3–30). Urbana, IL: Sagamore.

Baker, J. J., & Baker, R. W. (2014). *Health care finance: Basic tools for nonfinancial managers* (4th ed.). Burlington, MA: Jones & Bartlett Learning.

Barrett, J., & Smith, M. (2013, October). *Standards for the practice of recreational therapy and self-assessment guide*. Paper presented at the American Therapeutic Recreation Association Annual Conference, Phoenix, AZ.

Brown, C., & Media, D. (2016). Differences between a strategic plan & an operations plan. Retrieved from http://smallbusiness.chron.com/differences-between-strategic-plan-operations-plan-10634.html

California Department of State Hospitals. (n.d.). Recreational therapy treatment goals. Retrieved from http://www.dsh.ca.gov/Atascadero/Internships/Recreational_Therapy_Internship.aspx

Capital Health. (n.d.). Mission, vision, & values. Retrieved from http://www.cdha.nshealth.ca/recreation-therapy/mission-vision-values

Carter, M. J., Smith, C. G., & O' Morrow, G. S. (2014). *Effective management in therapeutic recreation* (3rd ed.). State College, PA: Venture.

Carter, M. J., Van Andel, G. E., & Robb, G. M. (2003). *Therapeutic recreation: A practical approach* (3rd ed.). Prospect Heights, IL: Waveland.

Centers for Medicare and Medicaid Services. (2012). *Medicare benefit policy manual* (Publication 100-02). Retrieved May 20, 2015, from http://www.cms.gov/regulations-and-guidance

Cherry, B. (2011). Nursing leadership and management. In B. Cherry & S. R. Jacob (Eds.), *Contemporary nursing: Issues, trends, & management* (pp. 333–363). St. Louis, MO: Elsevier Mosby.

The decision matrix. (2008, June). *Aquatic Therapist, 2008,* 21–24. Retrieved May 8, 2016, from http://www.aquaticnet.com/design_matrix_designing_therapy_pools_for_aquatic_therapy.pdf

Dunn, R. T. (2007). *Haimann's healthcare management* (8th ed.). Chicago, IL: Health Administration Press.

Eldenburg, L. G., Schafer, E. L., & Zulauf, D. J. (2010). Financial management of organized healthcare delivery systems. In L. F. Wolper (Ed.), *Health care administration* (5th ed.). Sudbury, MA: Jones & Bartlett Learning.

Mayo Clinic. (n.d.). About Mayo Clinic Health System. Retrieved from http://mayoclinichealthsystem.org/about-us/mission-and-values

McConnell, C. R. (2014). *Umiker's management skills for the new health care supervisor* (6th ed.). Burlington, MA: Jones & Bartlett Learning.

Nowicki, M. (2008). *The financial management of hospitals and healthcare organizations* (4th ed.). Chicago, IL: Health Administration Press.

Passmore, T. (2010). *Coverage of recreational therapy: Rules and regulations* (2nd ed.). Hattiesburg, MS: American Therapeutic Recreation Association.

Rocky Mountain Multiple Sclerosis Center. (n.d.). About. Retrieved from http://www.mscenter.org/about-us

Root, G. N., & Media, D. (2016). Links between strategic & operational plans. Retrieved from http://smallbusiness.chon.com/links-between-operational-plans-17407.html

Shepherd Center. (n.d.-a). History and mission. Retrieved from http://www.shepherd.org/about/history-and-mission

Shepherd Center. (n.d.-b). Recreation therapy. Retrieved from https://www.shepherd.org/resources/therapeutic-recreation

Surbhi, S. (2015). Difference between stratetic planning and operational planning. Retrieved from http://keydifferences.com/difference-between-strategic-planning-and-operational-planning.html

U.S. Bureau of Labor Statistics. (2016). Employer costs for employee compensation [Economic news release]. Retrieved May 8, 2016, from http://www.bls.gov/news.release/ecec.nr0.htm

VA Palo Alto Health Care System. (n.d.). Recreation therapy service. Retrieved from http://www.paloalto.va.gov/services/rectherapy/

Zeiler, K. (2011). Managing costs and revenues. In S. Buchbinder & N. Shanks (Eds.), *Introduction to health care management* (2nd ed., pp. 183–209). Sudbury, MA: Jones & Bartlett Learning.

Zelman, W. N., McCue, M. J., & Glick, N. D. (2009). *Financial management of health care organizations: An introduction to fundamental tools, concepts, and applications* (3rd ed.). San Francisco, CA: Jossey-Bass.

Chapter 6
Organizing

Objectives

- Define the term *organizing*.
- Describe two levels of organizing.
- Identify key factors that influence organizing.
- Identify types of available resources the manager employs to get results.
- Explain the five steps the first-line manager needs to take in organizing an RT unit.
- Define the term *authority*.
- Explain how managers enhance their authority.
- Identify techniques for effective time management.
- Explain what is meant by span of control.
- Explain what is meant by chain of command.
- Describe organizational structures found in healthcare organizations.
- Describe what is meant by informal organizational structures, sometimes referred to as informal social networks.
- Explain the importance of managers working in cooperation with informal social networks.

Key Terms

- **Organizing:** The process of establishing a formal structure through which work gets done.
- **Resources:** Human, physical, and financial entities needed to accomplish the ends sought by organizations and units within organizations.
- **Authority:** The right to direct others given to an individual for being in an authorized position, such as a manager.
- **Organizational chart:** A visual representation of the organization that identifies lines of communication and authority.
- **Span of control:** The number of staff who report to a single individual.
- **Chain of command:** The hierarchy depicted in organizational charts.
- **Organizational structures:** Frameworks indicating hierarchical arrangements of lines of authority, communication channels, and duties within an organization, typically illustrated by an organizational chart.

- **Informal organizations:** Informal organizations, sometimes termed informal social networks, are made up of employees brought together through friendships or mutual interests to form unofficial interactive structures through which they bond together to receive psychological and emotional satisfaction.

Organizing is the second management function. As defined by McConnell (2014), "organizing is the process of gearing up to implement decisions that result from the planning process; in order words, it is the establishing of the structure in which the work gets done" (p. 39). McConnell went on to explain:

Organizing involves delineating tasks and establishing a framework of authority and responsibility for the people who will perform these tasks; that is, building the aforementioned structures. It further involves analyzing the workload, distributing it among employees, and coordinating the activities so that work proceeds smoothly. (p. 39)

Simply put, organizing is the process of assigning people and other resources to accomplish identified ends through the delineation of responsibilities and authority by means of an organizational structure. In short, it is the means to get things done.

Two Levels of Organizing

Organizing occurs on two levels. One is the overall organizational level (e.g., hospital or long-term care facility). The other is the departmental or unit level (e.g., recreational therapy unit) headed by a first-line manager.

Organizational Level

Cherry (2014) wrote about the organizational level:

At the organizational level, organizing is necessary to establish a formal structure that defines the lines of authority, communication, and decision making within an organization. The formal organizational structure helps define roles and responsibilities of each level of management. The organizational chart provides a visual picture of the organization and identified lines of communication and authority. (p. 296)

Departmental or Unit Level

The responsibility of the first-line manager is to determine how to organize the work that needs to be done to reach the departmental or unit goals efficiently and effectively. The goals of the department or unit reflect its mission, vision, and philosophy. Organizing at the departmental or unit level involves the following:
- Using resources (i.e., staff, supplies, time) wisely
- Assigning duties and responsibilities appropriately
- Coordinating activities with other departments
- Effectively communicating with subordinates and superiors to ensure a smooth workflow (Cherry, 2014, p. 296)

"Doing nothing is very hard to do . . . you never know when you're finished."

Leslie Nelsen

Key Factors Influencing Organizing

To be most effective, the organizational structure needs to be congruent with the mission, vision, and philosophy of the overall organization and the specific department or unit. The mission, vision, and philosophy statements are covered in Chapter 5, so these are only briefly reviewed here to reflect their places in organizing within recreational therapy (RT) units.

Mission

The mission statement provides the reason or purpose for the existence of the entity. It identifies the clients to be served as well as the types of services to be provided. Defining the services to be offered has direct implications for the resources needed and the design of the organizational structure. An example for an RT unit might read: "The mission of the unit is to employ the recreational therapy process of assessment, planning, implementation, and evaluation in the provision of recreation and leisure activities that serve as clinical interventions to enhance the health and wellness of clients seeking healthcare services so they may enjoy the highest quality of life available to them."

Vision

The vision is a purposeful statement that identifies the desired future. A vision statement for an RT unit might read: "To be the premier recreational therapy unit in the Midwest."

Philosophy

The philosophy of an RT unit reflects its fundamental values and beliefs and offers a climate in which the mission and vision are carried out. Examples of *values* that might direct RT services, as presented by Austin (2013), include the following:

(a) valuing the therapeutic role in helping clients to reach optimal levels of health; (b) desiring that clients maintain as much autonomy and control as possible over their lives; (c) valuing the importance of the therapist–client relationship in fostering change; (d) valuing a strength-based approach to health enhancement; (e) valuing fun, enjoyment, and pleasure as important aspects in therapy; (f) viewing clients and what is happening to them, rather than the activity, as the focus of practice; (g) valuing recreational therapy as a purposeful and goal-directed enterprise; (h) valuing every client as a person of worth who should be treated with dignity and respect; and (i) valuing the therapist's responsibility to deliver competent and ethical care. (p. 197)

Austin (2013) drew on a list of *beliefs* first set forth by Brill and Levine (2002), to list the following beliefs for RT:

(a) humans are social animals who have a need to interact with other human beings; (b) both the welfare of the group, as well as the individual, need to be given consideration by the therapist; (c) relationships involve the understanding that mutual rights and responsibilities are both given and received; (d) all living things, including humans, possess intrinsic worth; (e) people possess a drive toward the achievement of self-realization; (f) individuals and society as a whole can be understood; and (g) each individual possesses the capacity for change. (p. 197)

The values and beliefs, such as those listed by Austin (2013), constitute the philosophy of practice of any RT unit. The conceptual model (e.g., Health Protection/ Health Promotion Model, Leisure Ability Model) embraced by the RT unit provides the philosophical basis for the day-to-day RT practices carried out by recreational therapists within the unit.

Effective Organizational Development

Effective organizing reflects the mission, vision, and philosophy of the overall organization and the units within the organization, such as the RT unit. The development of organizational structures is how the sought ends are achieved and philosophies expressed.

Organizing is the function of management in which the manager brings together available human, physical, and financial resources to get results. Put another way, organizing is the process managers use to promote the most efficient and effective use of resources. Organizing establishes means by which staff work together to achieve the aims of the overall organization and particular units (e.g., RT units). The purpose of the organizing function of management is to establish a clear structure so every staff member knows who is responsible for what has to be done and the means are in place for them to accomplish what needs to be achieved. Successful organizing includes establishing formal relationships between people in specific positions and organizing resources in a way that allows staff to achieve desired results.

A sense of invigorating energy will likely be in the air when walking into an RT unit that rests on a foundation of sound organization, as staff function harmoniously for the common good. Without sound organization, the unit will only be a collection of recreational therapists carrying out their individual interests, instead of a group or team with a sense of unity and pride in what they are achieving together.

First-Line Managers and Organizing

Key Actions

What are the essential actions first-line managers must take during the organizing process? Astute first-line managers must first identify what is necessary to achieve the outcomes that have been identified for their unit. Their second action is to determine who is responsible for what and to allocate responsibilities and authority.

Steps

To accomplish these actions, the first-line manager of an RT unit needs to execute the following steps:

- Determine the tasks that need to be accomplished.
- Group or organize the tasks into related activities.
- Assign specific activities to individuals.
- Provide necessary resources.
- Designate the organizational relationships needed. (ISPAT GUEU, 2015; Waldron, Vsanthakumar, & Arulraj, 1997)

Determine tasks. Here the first-line manager determines what programs need to be conducted (e.g., classes, special interest groups, clubs, leisure counseling groups, adventure therapy groups).

Organize related activities. The first-line manager then categorizes identified activities to cluster together similar activities. For example, aquatic programs would represent one cluster. Another could be activities for geriatric patients. Children's activities could constitute another. Supportive areas of activity might involve providing clinical supervision for recreational therapists and supervising physical resources, such as outdoor recreation areas.

Assign specific activities to individuals. An important step is assigning responsibilities so individual staff members know their specific responsibilities. It is critical that therapists have the backgrounds and credentials to conduct the specific activities to which they are assigned. Closely related is granting individuals the necessary authority to discharge their assigned responsibilities.

Provide necessary resources. The first-line manager, working with staff, allocates necessary resources to each area of activity. Resources include human resources (e.g., determining staffing patterns for specific program areas), physical resources (e.g., allocating areas, such as pools, gyms, and classrooms, to specific activities), and fiscal resources (e.g., budgets assigned for equipment and supplies to conduct specific programs).

Designate organizational relationships. Organizing also involves developing an organizational structure and chain of command. Organizational structures typically take the form of an organizational chart or diagram depicting reporting relationships and formal arrangements of positions within the unit. Establishing a structure ensures that clear relationships exist among those in the unit. The identification of relationships within the structure facilitates communication channels. When relationships are designated, each staff member knows to whom to report and with whom they will work.

A related activity not to be forgotten is coordinating activities with other departments. Thus, in addition to internal communication channels within the department or unit, the first-line manager communicates with managers from other departments or units within the organization to ensure resources are available. For example, the first-line RT manager will likely need to coordinate with the volunteer director to secure volunteers and with the maintenance director to ensure the maintenance of program areas, such as gyms or pools.

Organizational Structures

Organizational structures are typically represented within organizational charts showing the lines of authority and communication channels that employees need to follow. An example would be the tall, bureaucratic, highly centralized chart commonly found in large hospitals that contains a hierarchy consisting of any number of layers, at the top of which is the chief executive officer (CEO), who only reports to the hospital board. In contrast to the centralized model often found in large hospitals, the organizational framework follows a matrix design. The matrix design uses a decentralized approach in which managers regularly interact without going through a bureaucratic maze of administrators (Kelly, 2010).

Large RT departments may employ a more traditional central organizational framework. There may be an RT director to whom several supervisors report. In turn, staff may be assigned to report to a specific supervisor. Smaller RT units typically do not subscribe to organizational structures with several layers. Instead, a flat organizational structure is followed without layers in the chain of command, which functionally may follow a matrix approach in which supervisors freely interact among themselves and with the first-line manager. In small RT units, there may be only a designated first-line manager to whom all staff and volunteers report.

Span of Control

Span of control is a management term used to designate the number of staff reporting to one person. If the span of control is too narrow, the organization is thought to be inefficient and "top heavy," with unneeded communications going up and down the chain of command. If it is too broad, it is difficult for the people being reported to simply because they cannot give an adequate amount of attention to every individual they are supervising (Kelly, 2010).

Unity of Command

Traditionally, the term *unity of command* referred to each employee reporting only to one supervisor. Today, however, not all organizational structures are set up to strictly adhere to a reporting system in which each staff member reports to only one supervisor. McConnell (2014) explained use of the term *unity of command* has changed because of "matrix management arrangements, split-reporting relationships, and other complex organizational patterns. . . ." (p. 41). So unity of command now means that for each task that is carried out, the staff member doing the task is accountable to a designated individual (McConnell, 2014).

Authority

Authority is the right to direct others given to an individual for being in an authorized position, such as a manager. First-line managers require authority to fulfill their responsibilities because they must direct others from their place in the *chain of command*. Thus, the organizational chart for an RT unit would place the RT manager at the apex of the hierarchy or on the top of the unit's organizational chart.

An example of an organizational chart for an entire organization is shown in Figure 6.1. Advantages and disadvantages of using organizational charts are shown in Table 6.1.

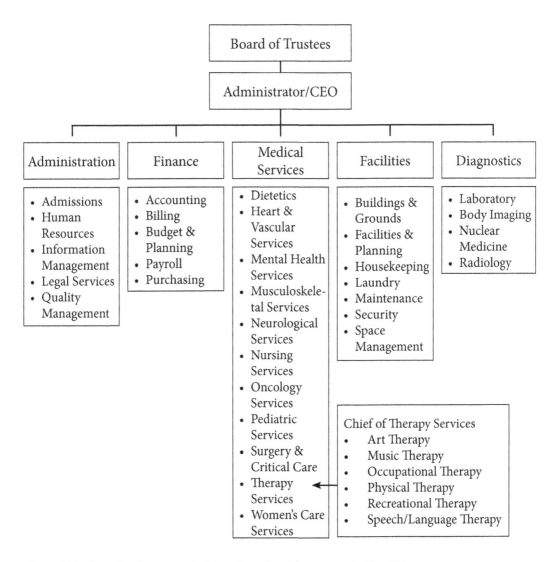

Figure 6.1. Example of an organizational chart showing an organizational hierarchy.

McConnell (2014) wrote: "Authority possessed by an individual in the organizational hierarchy is formal power that is delegated: that is, passed on down the hierarchy to the point at which it is to be applied" (p. 40). Therefore, for example, first-line managers possessing authority by virtue of their position can pass on their authority to subordinates. This is an important concept because giving responsibility to subordinates without the accompanying authority to carry out their responsibilities is a poor management style. Staff need the authority to do their jobs.

McConnell (2014) warned, however, that the granting of authority can be relatively weak in application:

To be effectively applied, authority must be supplemented by other conditions or characteristics as follows:

- Expertise, for example, licensure, certification, knowledge, skill, or experience
- Credibility, as in being trusted and respected
- Leadership skill, whether natural or acquired
- Persuasiveness or charisma
- Influence, sometimes as determined by whom one knows or is connected with (p. 40)

Hopefully, first-line managers possess many of the conditions and characteristics listed by McConnell. This is highly likely, otherwise the individual would not have been promoted into a management position. Similarly, staff who are granted authority are likely to possess characteristics that enhance their authority. For instance, aquatic therapy supervisors are apt to possess specialized certifications and training that provide them with enhanced credibility.

Table 6.1
Advantages and Disadvantages of an Organizational Chart

Advantages

- It provides a quick visual illustration of the organizational structure.
- It clearly delineates formal lines of authority and accountability.
- It shows who supervises whom and to whom each employee is responsible.
- It indicates channels of communication.

Disadvantages

- Charts may become quickly outdated.
- Charts do not show informal relationships.
- Charts do not show duties and responsibilities.
- Poorly prepared charts may be misleading.

Note. Adapted from *Organizational Structure,* by M. A. Adlong, 2013 (http://www.slideshare.net/xenna_85/organizational-structure-26872255).

Time Management as a Leadership Skill

One leadership skill particularly related to organizing is exemplifying good organization in time management. The use of refined time management skills by the first-line manager can help get work done efficiently and effectively, and the manager's behavior offers a positive model for staff to follow.

> "Time management is an oxymoron. Time is beyond our control, and the clock keeps ticking regardless of how we lead our lives. Priority management is the answer to maximizing the time we have."
>
> John C. Maxwell

Two Areas of Time Management

First-line managers typically interact with staff in their office or during staff meetings. Therefore, key areas for time management are organizing the office environment and planning and conducting meetings.

An Office Environment to Enhance Time Management

One step in organizing an office environment is simply to keep it neat and orderly. Yoder-Wise (2011) suggested that "file management" is a better system than "pile management." Her hints for good file management include the following:

- Plan where things should go; your desk or your computer files.
- Keep a clean workspace.
- Create a to-do folder.
- Create a to-be-filed folder for any papers.
- Schedule time to work your way through the folders. (p. 566)

To-do list. Ponte and Conlin (2014) indicated the importance of managers creating a *to-do list;* it has the benefit of keeping them concentrating on defined tasks. The to-do list should reflect the manager's priorities and goals, and the manager should revise it each day to ensure the most functional use of time. A review of the to-do list at the end of the day provides a helpful assessment of the manager's productivity in meeting set goals and determines what still needs to be done.

Avoiding the stacked-desk syndrome. In regard to keeping an orderly workplace, Ponte and Conlin (2014) proposed that managers need to avoid *the stacked-desk syndrome.* By this they mean not allowing the desk to become cluttered with papers, books, or anything else that may find its way to the top of a desk. To ward off the stacked-desk syndrome, they suggested that managers clear their work area and their minds. They proposed managers do the following:

- Remove everything from the work surface that does not directly relate to the project at hand; only things you need every day should be on the desk
- Place the telephone out of sight, but within reach
- Remove all personal items, such as calendars, clocks, or photographs, if they are distractors
- Close the door to the work area when possible, but communicate to colleagues that you may be interrupted in the case of an emergency (p. 453)

The art of "wastebasketry." Employing *the art of "wastebasketry"* is another technique suggested by Ponte and Conlin (2014) to enhance the office environment for greater time management. They wrote:

Perfecting the art of "wastebasketry" is mandatory for better use of time. The art of physical wastebasketry involves "circular filing" (in the trash can or with the delete key on the computer) or any documents, including e-mails or other paperwork that has limited use or needs no response. The goal is to handle a paper (or e-mail) only once, then either act on it (do it), or throw it away (dump it). Some also refer to this as the TRASH approach: T: Throw it away, R: Refer it to someone else, A: Act on it, S: Save it, or H: Halt it (e.g., stop junk mail from coming to you). (p. 453)

Minimizing e-mail mania. Another item that could be added to Yoder-Wise's (2011) list of file management, rather than pile management, is dealing with e-mail so messages do not pile up but are dealt with efficiently. Like many things, the expression "easier said than done" can certainly be applied to dealing with e-mails, as they have become perhaps the primary way of communication among those in healthcare, so the manager will likely have many e-mails to which to attend.

Ponte and Conlin (2014) indicated that managers need to keep their e-mails brief and to the point, while following correct form and proper etiquette and being accurate. They suggested that managers keep in mind the e-mail is a professional form of communication that should meet the following criteria: (a) messages should contain a greeting; (b) a clear body of text should follow; (c) specific and clear requests for information need to be made; (d) an acceptable closing to the message needs to conclude the message; and (e) the message should be free of grammatical or typographical errors.

They also suggested that managers set aside periods during the day to review and respond to e-mail. One of these periods is 10 minutes at the beginning of the workday for managers to review e-mail to prioritize time-sensitive items. Managers should additionally check e-mail a couple of times during the day and again at the conclusion of the day to wrap up any unfinished business.

> "If you had to identify, in one word, the reasons why the human race has not achieved and never will achieve its full potential, that would be meetings."
>
> Dave Barry

Planning and Conducting Meetings

RT departments or units often hold weekly or monthly staff meetings. Staff often complain about how their time is wasted by participating in staff meetings. Typical complaints are the length of meetings (i.e., too long) and information items taking up time when the information could have been distributed to staff by e-mail.

Astute first-line managers employ basic strategies to minimize staff complaints and model for staff how to best conduct meetings by following a few tips. Yoder-Wise (2011) offers a number of tips that may be helpful to first-line managers.

Scheduling and arranging meetings. First, before scheduling a meeting, first-line managers should ask themselves if the meeting is necessary. For example, can an e-mail message get across the information that would be covered in the meeting? Or can a brief "huddle" (5-minute opportunity to touch base) suffice to serve the needs to be met? Or, if key staff will be absent, can the meeting be rescheduled? In short, meetings should not be held for the sake of meeting.

Regular meetings should be scheduled just prior to lunch or at the end of the workday. Anticipating lunch or going home will serve as an incentive for all to stick with the agenda. The first-line manager should schedule meetings to be held in appropriate settings where interruptions will not be apt to occur and always start and end meetings on time. If the same members meet regularly, they should be involved in setting rules for conduct and behavior. Recreational therapists are typically action oriented, so few will wish to sit in meetings for long periods (e.g., 1.5–2 hours) and will probably be pleased to actively participate in establishing rules by which to conduct meetings.

Inform staff and prepare agendas. The wise manager makes known what the meeting is about (i.e., the goal for the meeting) and distributes a written agenda in advance. If group members have to prepare for the meeting, the agenda should go out well before the scheduled meeting to allow staff sufficient time to ready themselves to participate.

According to the purposes they serve, different types of agendas can be used. *Timed agendas* specifying the specific amount of time to be given to each item help move the meeting along if realistic time frames are established. *Action agendas* indicating needed actions can be used to take formal action on items, such as approving minutes or accepting proposals. *Structured agendas* can be employed when especially controversial topics are being considered. This type of agenda requires that a negative comment be preceded by a positive comment.

Yoder-Wise (2011) indicated that following formal structures makes for better meetings. She commented that even though Robert's Rules of Order appear too structured, it is a good idea to employ them so the group is kept on task. The leader chairing the meeting, typically the first-line manager, can use Robert's Rules of Order to conduct an orderly meeting and to set limits on discussion. Additionally, Yoder-Wise suggested that minutes of meetings be kept and distributed to participants and those unable to attend.

Informal Organizational Structures

Thus far only formal organizational structures have been discussed, but anyone who has worked for an organization realizes that in addition to formal organizational structures, there exist *informal organizational structures*, also referred to as *informal social networks*. McConnell (2014) noted:

> Every organization has beneath its visible surface a network that constitutes another arrangement of interrelationships not represented on any organizational chart. This is the informal organization, which at times is perhaps even more powerful simply because of its lack of visibility. This informal organization even has its own communication system; we refer to it as "the grapevine." (p. 44)

Huning, Bryant, and Holt (2015) portrayed informal social networks as follows:

> Informal networks are those channels that carry information and connect organizational members through routes not prescribed by the organization. Networks provide their members with many opportunities such as tracing task information, work standards and expectations, rumors, and social norms. (p. 20)

Informal organizations or informal social networks are well-developed social structures within an organization that exist without written rules or procedures but have group norms that are followed by its members and maintained by its leaders. Informal networks are unofficial and not typically deliberately developed. They emerge out of a variety of mechanisms, including interpersonal attraction, family ties, common tasks or interests, common schedules, common geography origins, and common backgrounds, according to Huning et al. (2015). But Huning et al. went on to explain that self-interests also play a role: "There are also self-interests that members of a shared informal network pursue. Individuals seek out their own personal benefit by belonging to informal networks of other people. . . ." (p. 21). Among possible personal benefits derived from social interactions in social networks are the giving and receiving of material and intangible resources. Those in the informal networks certainly benefit personally by gaining psychological and emotional satisfaction from their participation in the social network. Employees within the network maintain their own communication system, sometimes referred to as the group's grapevine (McConnell, 2014; Saritha Pujari Organization, n.d.).

At one time, the grapevine consisted of networking through face-to-face interactions, e-mails, and telephone conversations. Today, the grapevine is supported by the speed of the Internet and broadband technology. Thus, managers need to monitor social media to keep track of concerns circulating within the grapevine network of their unit or organization as well as keep staff informed of the proper protocols for social media use (Dunn, 2016).

Effects of Informal Organizations

Huning et al. (2015) conducted an extensive analysis of informal social networks in organizations. Following their examination of how informal social networks influence areas including knowledge transfer, informal learning, communications, and leadership and power, they concluded: "Informal social relationships drive organizational practice and everyday operations" (Huning et al., 2015, p. 28).

Cross, Nohria, and Parker (2015) further explained the effects of informal social networks. They expressed that formal structures often have less influence than informal social networks: "Informal networks of employees are increasingly at the forefront, and the general health and connectivity of these groups can have a significant impact on strategy execution and organizational effectiveness" (Cross et al., 2015, p. 11). Thus, the conversations around the coffee machine or in hallways may have a greater effect on the organization than do the formal organizational charts that appear in employee orientation manuals.

The First-Line Manager and Informal Organizations

Informal organizational structures or informal social networks can be either good or bad. Social networks can serve to enhance the goals and objectives of the organization or to derail them. Therefore, first-line managers of RT units need to become aware of informal social networks and work with the leaders of the networks so they, as managers, can gain and maintain support for the formal goals and objectives sought by their units.

For example, McConnell (2014) provided the illustration that astute managers speed communications by tapping into the grapevines of informal social networks to hasten the flow of information throughout the unit or to squelch rumors. Furthermore, McConnell suggested that managers identify the leaders of informal networks and make sincere attempts to cooperate with them. In time, these informal leaders should be considered for promotion to supervisory positions or be delegated formal authority for achieving particular tasks.

Clarke (2010) indicated that those in management positions need to ask themselves a series of questions to work with informal social networks effectively: (a) What internal social networks exist within my unit? (b) Why do I want the informal network to do? What is my priority? (c) How can I change my habits, rituals, and regular modes of operation to better integrate what I am doing on the informal organizational side?

To Sum Up

Formal organizational structures clearly spell out responsibilities, authority, and relationships to achieve the goals and objectives of the organization. In contrast, informal social networks develop out of common ties and have as a major purpose gaining psychological or emotional satisfaction. Informal social networks can enhance or deter the work of the organization. The wise manager joins with informal groups to reach the goals and objectives of the organization, thus using formal and informal organizational structures to accomplish the work needed to maintain a successful program.

Summary

Organizing is the second management function. It is establishing the structure to get work done at the levels of the overall organization and of the individual departments or units, such as an RT department or unit. Guided by the mission, vision, and philosophy of the organization and individual department or unit, organizing involves identifying the management structure needed to accomplish identified goals and expressed philosophical values and beliefs.

The essential actions first-line managers take during the organizing process include identifying what is necessary to achieve the outcomes established for the unit and then determining who is responsible for what and to allocate responsibilities and authority. Organizational structures provide means for the manager to organize tasks, make decisions, and identify individual authority and responsibilities. Organizational charts are typically used to illustrate organizational structures by showing the hierarchy of formal authority and communication channels.

By virtue of being put in charge, the first-line manager is granted authority by the organization. It is desirable that such granted authority be supplemented by exhibiting characteristics such as having expertise; being trusted and respected; displaying leadership skills; and possessing persuasiveness, charisma, or influence. One leadership skill particularly related to organizing is exemplifying good organization in time management. The use of time management skills by the manager provides staff with an example of personal organizing that gets work done efficiently and effectively.

Informal organizations exist in all organizations. Informal social networks emerge out of common ties and develop into social structures within an organization that exist without written rules or procedures but have group norms that are followed by its members and maintained by its leaders. Astute first-line managers recognize the existence of informal social networks and learn to work with them to further the goals of their unit.

References

Adlong, M. A. (2013). *Organizational structure* [Slide show]. Retrieved from http://www.slideshare.net/xenna_85/organizational-structure-26872255

Austin, D. R. (2013). *Therapeutic recreation processes and techniques: Evidence-based recreational therapy* (7th ed.). Urbana, IL: Sagamore.

Brill, N. L., & Levine, J. (2002). *Working with people: The helping process* (7th ed.). Boston, MA: Allyn and Bacon.

Cherry, B. (2014). Nursing leadership and management. In B. Cherry & S. R. Jacob (Eds.), *Contemporary nursing: Issues, trends, & management* (6th ed., pp. 285–308). St. Louis, MO: Mosby Elsevier.

Clarke, K. (2010). Inside the informal organization. *Associations Now.* Retrieved from https://www.asaecenter.org/resources/articles/an_magazine/2010/nov/inside-the-informal-organization

Cross, R., Nohria, N., & Parker, A. (2015). Six myths about informal networks – and how to overcome them. *MIT Sloan Management Review.* Retrieved from http://sloanreview.mit.edu/six-myths-about-informal-networks-and-how-to-overcome-them/

Dunn, R. (2016). *Dunn & Haimann's healthcare management* (10th ed.). Chicago, IL: Health Administration Press.

Huning, T. M., Bryant, P. C., & Holt, M. D. (2015). Informal social networks in organizations: Propositions regarding their role in organizational behavior outcomes. *Academy of Strategic Management Journal, 14*(1), 20–29.

ISPAT GUEU. (2015). Organizing – A management function. Retrieved from http://ispatguru.com/organizing-a-managment-function/

Kelly, P. (2010). *Essentials of nursing leadership & management* (2nd ed.). Clifton Park, NY: Delmar.

McConnell, C. R. (2014). *Umiker's management skills for the new health care supervisor* (6th ed.). Burlington, MA: Jones & Bartlett Learning.

Ponte, P. R., & Colin, G.J. (2014). Managing time: The path to high self-performance. In B. Cherry & S. R. Jacob, (Eds.), *Contemporary nursing: Issues, trends, and management* (6th ed., pp. 444–460). St. Louis, MO: Elsevier.

Saritha Pujari Organization. (n.d.). 7 main characteristics of informal organisation. Retrieved from http://www.yourarticlelibrary.com/organization/7-main-characteristics-of-informal-organisation/956/

Waldron, M. W., Vsanthakumar, J., & Arulraj, S. (1997). Improving the organization and management of extensions. In B. E. Swanson, R. P. Bentz, & A. J. Sofranko (Eds.), *Improving agricultural extension: A reference manual.* Retrieved from http://www.fao.org/docrep/W5830E/w5830e0f.htm

Yoder-Wise, P. S. (2011). *Leading and managing in nursing* (5th ed.). St. Louis, MO: Elsevier Mosby.

Chapter 7
Staffing

Objectives
- Define the terms *staffing, position description, scheduling, orientation program,* and *in-service training.*
- Identify steps in the recruiting process.
- Indicate basic principles of interviewing.
- Describe the importance of interviews in the selection process.
- Name pitfalls to avoid when selecting new employees.
- Describe important components of a position description.
- Describe what is included in an orientation program.
- Describe ways to increase staff retention.

Key Terms
- **Staffing:** A management function that provides the appropriate and adequate provision of staff to meet the organization's objectives and involves recruiting, interviewing, hiring, orientation, in-service training, scheduling, and retention.
- **Position description:** A position or job description summarizes the duties of the person doing the job.
- **Scheduling:** Developing a plan for where and when personnel are to work within the parameters dictated by the organization (Carter & O'Morrow, 2006, p. 291).
- **Orientation programs:** Introduce new employees to the agency and the RT unit.
- **In-service training:** Helps staff to keep current by updating their skills and knowledge to perform on the job.

In the management of recreational therapy (RT) services, understanding the many steps and facets of staffing is important to developing a well-functioning team. Staffing takes attention to detail and often a substantial amount of time, but it is essential for the manager to invest time in this process, which will ultimately affect the services provided by the RT staff. Dunn (2002) presented the following definition of staffing:

Staffing represents the manager's responsibility to recruit and select employees to ensure qualified employees to fill the various positions needed based on the organization of duties to achieve the plan, while at the same time remaining within the budgeted labor amount for the department. (p. 18)

As defined by Grohar-Murray and Langan (2011), "**staffing** is the management activity that provides for appropriate and adequate personnel to fulfill the organization's objectives" (p. 154). They explained that the term *staffing* is used to describe a process and an outcome. It describes the number of staff required to meet client demands in a particular setting and the process involved in hiring staff.

As indicated earlier in Chapter 4, the five steps in staffing, modeled from Marquis and Huston (2009), have been described by Cherry (2011):

1. Determine the number and type of staff needed based on goals and budget requirements.
2. Recruit, interview, select, and assign personnel based on job description requirements and performance standards.
3. Get new employees off to a good start by offering excellent orientation, training, and socialization programs.
4. Implement an ongoing staff-development program to ensure employees at all levels have opportunities to develop personally and professionally and to enhance knowledge and skill levels.
5. Implement creative and flexible scheduling based on patient care needs, employee needs, and organizational productivity requirements. (p. 346–347)

These steps are discussed in this chapter. First-line managers may have a say in establishing staffing levels for their unit, but such decisions are typically made by middle managers and higher level administrators. First-line managers are regularly involved in identifying, recruiting, and retaining well-qualified recreational therapists. They often assist with establishing criteria for selecting new personnel and interview candidates for positions. As such, first-line managers need to know legal requirements for hiring. Additionally, first-line managers need to plan and carry out orientation and training programs for new employees and to build a workplace environment conducive to staff development and retention.

It is critical that staffing be given a tremendous level of importance because of the effects it will have on the organization. Ashurst (2010) indicated that the time and resources used in getting the recruitment and hiring process right will be repaid many times over. The benefits include (a) staff having the right skills to deliver the services needed by clients; (b) improved teamwork as those hired achieve the right fit for developing an effective team; and (c) having the right people, which allows for unit growth and development to meet new challenges that must be addressed in the future.

> "In most cases being a good boss means hiring talented people and getting out of their way."
>
> Tina Fey

Not getting the recruitment and hiring process right can prove costly. Costs include (a) time and money spent on marketing positions, interviewing, orientation, training, managing, resignations or terminations, and rehiring; (b) negative staff morale as it relates to a new employee's lack of skills, poor attitudes, or unprofessional behaviors; and (c) reduced performance caused by efforts needed to manage inappropriate hires, resulting in an overall detrimental effect on the organization (Ashurst, 2010, p. 61).

Position Descriptions

The purpose of the position description, or job description, is to summarize the duties of the individual performing the job, but it does not provide a detailed listing of duties. Ellis and Hartley (2009) indicated: "A formal job description never gives a complete description of everything individuals do as part of their jobs, but it should provide the broad general guidelines under which the individual will function" (p. 60).

The title of the position should reflect the responsibilities of the job, and the position description should specify the general requirements of the job, major duties and responsibilities, and organizational relationships for the position. Equal employment opportunity laws require that job descriptions not discriminate against any class of individual (e.g., based on their age, disability, or national origin). Important elements in position or job descriptions are the qualifications needed for being appointed to the position. Qualifications usually include the minimum acceptable education; experience; knowledge, skills, and abilities; and special requirements, such as certification or licensure (Marriner Tomey, 2009). Recreational therapists who provide direct care should be required to not only hold a bachelor's degree but also be certified as Certified Therapeutic Recreation Specialists (CTRSs). In states with licensure programs, a license to practice will also be required. Should the individual be required to perform in a certain area (e.g., aquatic therapy), additional credentials specifically related to the area of expertise may be required. First-line managers and middle managers are likely to be called upon to have a number of years of experience in RT (e.g., 5 years) and may be required to hold a master's degree. See Table 7.1 for other important information to be covered in a job description.

Authors of nursing management texts have cautioned that position descriptions cannot ever cover every aspect of an employee's full scope of practice or keep up with the rapid changes in the work environment that continually affect staff and programs (Fry, 2010; Porter-O'Grady & Malloch, 2013). Porter-O'Grady and Malloch (2013) wrote:

> Organizations have historically placed a great deal of stock in these job descriptions as a justifiable and legitimate framework for defining functional performance expectations. The problem with this approach is that the dynamic nature of professional work, the significant dependence on individual relationships and critical judgments, and the highly variable nature of the user professional service seriously belie the validity and value of work defined as a fixed, finite, functional, and incremental set of activities. (pp. 502–503)

These authors also described that job descriptions do not fully capture all of the components of jobs with changing or variable demands, such as those in healthcare.

Thus, although position descriptions are helpful in the staffing process, the caution portrayed in the literature of nursing management to not rely on position descriptions as rigid, inflexible documents seems warranted. Fry (2010) wrote: "Because of the complexities of the practice environment and patient acuity, staff members must be flexible and do whatever it takes within their scopes of practice to properly care for patients and clients" (p. 30).

Table 7.1
Important Job Description Information

Title of the position (descriptive enough to be clear)
 Position description, including primary functions
  *Often includes statement "and other duties as appropriate."

Major duties and responsibilities, including
 Mental/cognitive demands
 Physical demands
 Working conditions

Organizational relationships for the position being described, including
 Those who the employee in this position will report to
 What positions will report to this employee

Qualifications, including
 Certification (CTRS)
 Education
 Experience
 Knowledge
 Skills and abilities
 Special requirements, such as certification in specific skills or licensure

---

Recruiting

Once position descriptions are in place, what follows is typically the recruitment of personnel. Before beginning recruitment, however, managers should ask whether anyone on the existing staff might fill the position (Ashurst, 2010). For instance, in the case of an opening for a recreational therapist to do direct care, an intern completing an internship might be a good fit for the opening. This is considered internal recruiting, or recruiting from inside the agency

Should it be determined that an external recruiting effort is necessary (going outside the agency to find a qualified candidate), an overall strategy for recruitment needs to be determined because it is critical that the best candidates for the position be attracted. At this point, the first-line manager having responsibility for hiring should seek the advice and counsel of the human resources department (sometimes referred to as the personnel department). It is the responsibility of the first-line manager to do the hiring, but the manager needs to work closely with human resources staff to ensure policies, procedures, and regulations are followed. The human resources department can also conduct screening interviews to determine if applicants meet basic qualifications (e.g., education, certification) for the job and do reference checks with former employers (Dunn, 2002). Another point of collaboration for the first-line manager is the agency's marketing department. Marketing staff are useful in determining how their connections and information systems can help with recruitment.

Clark (2009) suggested the following steps in the recruitment process:

- *Define the job description* so all necessary skills are clear as well as how candidates will fit into the grow from the organization's structure.
- *Determine an appropriate strategy,* first deciding whether to hire internally or from outside the agency. When recruiting from outside, those recruiting should use contacts with universities and colleagues at other agencies, as well as national professional societies (e.g., ATRA), RT conferences and publications, websites, and any listserv dealing with RT. Marriner Tomey (2009) indicated that marketing content is more important than the form it takes. She suggests that recruiters should identify the needs of potential applicants and then show how the organization will be able to address those needs. For example, applicants may be interested in: being a part of a team that delivers the highest quality of care; the possibility for advancement within the organization; opportunities for personal and professional growth; adequate income and fringe benefits; and fellowship with colleagues. Those who are newly graduated may be apt to be particularly interested in opportunities for orientation, in-service training, and clinical supervision.
- *Set interviewing and selection processes* to be able to move quickly as candidates may be offered other positions. At this point, the first-line manager may wish to conduct one-on-one interviews with candidates already screened by the human resource department or may want to call upon staff to help interview and make recommendations for selection.
- *Offer tailored incentives to attract top staff* in order to recruit only quality people into the organization. It is a good idea to listen for the things that may make the RT unit attractive to applicants. Clark (2009) has suggested being upfront with candidates by asking them during interviews: "What is most important to you – salary, autonomy, location, or something else?" (p. 342)

Interviewing

After the initial screening, applicants who appear to be the most qualified should be invited to interview for the position. The overall purpose of the interview is to predict whether the applicant is a good fit for the job. During the interview, the interviewee should become acquainted with the position, receive information about the agency's policies and procedures, and have any questions answered.

Because of the high level of importance of the interview, the interviewer needs to be thoroughly prepared by being acquainted with the background information available on the applicant, including the individual's résumé. If questions arise while the interviewer is studying the applicant's information, the interviewer should note these so they are clarified during the interview. The interviewer also must have in mind the specific qualities the ideal candidate will possess. A list of essential and desirable qualities should be constructed to assess the applicant's qualifications. Being well prepared for the interview, the interviewer can concentrate on listening to and observing the candidate (Dunn, 2002).

Marriner Tomey (2009) suggested that during the interview the interviewer needs to judge the applicant on the following:

- Dependability
- Willingness to assume responsibility for the job
- Willingness and ability to work with others
- Interest in the job and adaptability
- Consistency of the applicant's goals with available opportunities
- Conformity of the applicant's manners and appearance to job requirements (p. 340)

Furthermore, Marriner Tomey (2009) indicated: "Job interest, poise, manners, appearance, and aspirations are other areas to investigate" (p. 341). Suggested areas for the interviewer to probe include whether the applicant is (a) cooperative, (b) able to work well as a team member or prefers to work alone, (c) successful in working with managers and peers, (d) open to criticism or reacts excessively to criticism, (e) involved in the community, and (f) open and candid during the interview.

It is important during the interview that questions posed to the applicant be based on the job description, the qualities needed for the job and the skills and abilities the candidate possesses, and the background information the applicant has provided. The interviewer must avoid questions that could be considered discriminatory or illegal (e.g., about the person's age being over 40 or general questions about disability). The human resources department typically provides guidelines on avoiding discriminatory or illegal questions. Examples of appropriate and inappropriate questions are listed in Table 7.2.

To begin the interview, the interviewer should greet the applicant and introduce himself or herself to the applicant and make a brief comment about the agency and position available. The interviewer should then explain the plan for the interview (Marriner Tomey, 2009).

The interview should be conducted in a manner that puts the applicant at ease because the interviewee will likely be under a great deal of strain. A positive atmosphere may be set by the interviewer offering the interviewee a cup of coffee or taking them on a walk through the workplace to put the applicant at ease and build rapport. To relax the applicant, the interviewer might begin with a brief warm-up period making small talk about the weather or some other topic of general interest before moving into the formal interview. To begin the interview, the interviewer should discuss details of the job (e.g., working conditions, wages, hours, vacations, how the job relates to other jobs in the unit). The interviewer should then ask what else the applicant would like to know about the job. Following this, the interviewer should ask questions to determine how well qualified the applicant is for the job (Dunn, 2002).

Table 7.2

Examples of Appropriate and Inappropriate Questions

Appropriate Questions:

- What did you like best about your present (most recent) job? Why? What did you like least?
- What special assignments have you taken on in the past (or your current job) that will make you successful here?
- Have you ever been convicted of any crime or misdemeanor other than parking violations?
- Is there anything that would preclude you from traveling out of town overnight or working overtime?

Inappropriate Questions:

- Were you born in Cuba or the United States?
- Will your husband (wife) have any problems with your working hours?
- Have you ever been arrested for any crime?
- Do you have babysitters arranged for your children?
- Do you dislike your current job because you are reporting to a woman?

Note. From *Haimann's Healthcare Management* (7th ed., p. 335), by R. Dunn, 2002, Chicago, IL: Health Administration Press.

Nondirective, open-ended questions tend to reveal applicants' feelings and attitudes. Examples of open-ended questions include the following: What aspects of your last job appealed to you? How did you enjoy your relations with your coworkers? The interviewer can use a funnel technique by starting with nonthreatening open-ended questions (e.g., What subjects did you like most in school?) and closed-ended questions (that can be answered briefly), such as who their last employer was and how long they worked there. Following these, questions should be funneled down to self-appraisal questions to elicit subjective information, such as why the applicant liked those courses in particular (Marriner Tomey, 2009).

Once the interviewer has obtained the information to help determine if the individual is qualified for the job and will fit into the unit's culture, the interviewer should close the interview. At this point, the interviewer should ask if the applicant has further questions. This question, in itself, may reveal the level of interest the person has in the job and whether the applicant prepared for the interview by having developed questions to ask. The closing should also include telling the applicant the next steps in the hiring process, such as when and how the applicant will be informed about the outcome of the search (Dunn, 2002).

Selection

It has been stated that "hiring an employee is truly making an investment in your organization. When you hire someone to work for you, you will invest time, money, training, and trust. If you do it right, your organization can move forward much faster than ever before" (Quicken, 2000, as cited in Dunn, 2002, p. 327). On the other hand, if you do not do it right, you pay all costs involved, including replacing the person and reinvesting your time, money, training, and trust. So it certainly pays to select wisely when hiring.

The final decision of whom to hire rests with the person who will supervise the new staff member, the first-line manager in the case of an RT unit. Others, however, can assist the first-line manager in making the selection. These include the first-line manager's supervisor, recreational therapists who will be colleagues of the new hire, and the human resources department.

Typically, interviews are used as selection devices. First-line managers interview applicants and, based largely on the interview, select who will fill the vacant position. The interview is a necessary and critical aspect of the recruitment process because the interviewer must put together a good match between the abilities and personality of the applicant and the culture of the unit and the demands of the position (Dunn, 2002). An alternative to simply having the first-line manager conduct an interview is having RT staff interview applicants as well and, based on their interviews, make recommendations on who should be invited to join the staff. The first-line manager's supervisor and human resources staff may also conduct interviews and share their evaluations of applicants with the first-line manager.

Marriner Tomey (2009) stated that the essential qualities and desirable qualities for those who would occupy the open position should be identified. Then the first-line manager and others can assess the essential and desirable qualities of the applicants, and these observations can serve as means to evaluation. Furthermore, Marriner Tomey suggested the development of an evaluation instrument listing essential and desirable qualities on which candidates may be appraised with columns labeled yes, ?, and no, along with a column for comments.

To conclude this segment on selecting the right person for the job, consideration should be given to items to avoid when making a selection. Ashurst (2010) listed pitfalls first-line managers should avoid:

- Feeling extremely busy, managers may not devote the time they need for recruiting.
- Managers may recruit in their own likenesses thinking that because the applicant has a similar approach to life that they will be a good candidate for the position.
- Taking the best of a bad bunch is a common mistake made in desperation to get the position filled.
- Basing a hiring decision on subjective feelings, such as whether you like the person, and not exploring whether the individual can do the job.
- Interviewing too many people and not taking enough time to do a thorough job so you lack the information needed to make good decisions. (p. 62)

Scheduling

As defined by Carter and O'Morrow (2006), "scheduling is developing a plan for where and when personnel are to work within the parameters dictated by the organization" (p. 291). Scheduling may be centralized (done by the central administration) or decentralized (done at the unit level), or a hybrid model of both approaches may be used (Porter-O'Grady & Malloch, 2013). No matter the approach, the major objective in scheduling is to have adequate coverage of staff to meet client needs. An ideal scheduling pattern does not understaff or overstaff and accommodates the needs of clients and staff (Grohar-Murray & Langan, 2011).

RT units tend to follow the decentralized approach in which the manager is responsible for the staffing schedule. RT managers typically involve their staff in determining the staffing plan, thus ensuring the staff's commitment to the plan (Carter & O'Morrow, 2006). Staff generally feel that decentralized scheduling, done at the unit level, is a more personalized approach. Managers responsible for scheduling for their units need to be careful not to give some staff individualized treatment at the expense of others or to use scheduling as a punishment–reward system (Marriner Tomey, 2009).

Staffing plans are complex because of the large number of variables to consider when constructing a plan. Factors that may affect scheduling include the types and numbers of clients; complexity of care required; education and experience of staff; intervention skills of staff; time needed for charting, in-service training, staff meetings, and attending conferences; time for program planning and the organization of supplies and equipment; and personnel policies for weekends off, trading shifts or days off, tardiness, funerals, vacations, holidays, educational leave, and sick leave (Carter & O'Morrow, 2006; Grohar-Murray & Langan, 2011; Marriner Tomey, 2009).

Porter-O'Grady and Malloch (2013) adapted considerations for staffing published by the American Nurses Association (ANA). These served as the basis for the list of principles for RT scheduling that appear in Table 7.3.

Table 7.3
Principles for Recreational Therapy Scheduling

- The needs of clients drive scheduling patterns.
- In addition to client needs, the skills of the recreational therapist and the influences of the environment also must be considered.
- The needs of recreational therapists should be considered.
- Input from recreational therapists into scheduling is always necessary.
- Evaluation of the staffing effectiveness should completed and should involve the multiple variables impacting staffing.

Note. Adapted from *Leadership in Nursing Practice* (p. 178), by T. Porter-O'Grady and K. Malloch, 2013, Burlington, MA: Jones & Bartlett Learning.

Orientation and Training

Providing ongoing professional development opportunities for staff is a central function of RT units. The first-line manager must ensure a well-conceived orientation program is in place to introduce new staff to the organization and the RT unit and that in-service training sessions are offered regularly for all staff. Both are long-term investments into staff, the most important asset available to any organization (Ashurst, 2010).

Orientation Programs

Orientation programs are necessary to introduce new employees to the agency and the RT unit. Given the increased complexity of healthcare environments and the support needed to ensure a smooth transition from school to practice, it is especially critical that newly graduated recreational therapists receive well-designed orientation programs that launch them on a positive trajectory that will propel them toward a long and enjoyable career at the agency. Having stated that proper orientation is critical for the job satisfaction and retention of new graduates does not diminish the importance of orientation for all new staff, no matter their age or experience. The way all new staff are treated during the first days and weeks of employment tends to play a large part in their future job satisfaction and performance.

The first two or three days of orientation may be carried out by the human resources department for all new hires. Information typically included in orientation is the history of the organization, along with its vision, purpose, and structure. Information is usually then provided about work hours, holidays, vacation time, sick time, paydays, performance standards and evaluation, grievance procedures, parking facilities, eating facilities, health services, and educational opportunities offered. Manuals containing the information reviewed are normally given to those taking the orientation program because of the vast amount of information covered (Marriner Tomey, 2009).

The RT manager then introduces the new staff member to his or her new job; co-workers; unit policies; areas, facilities, equipment, and supplies; protocols; standards of practice; performance expectations; and the availability of clinical supervision, in-service training, and mentoring programs. Marriner Tomey (2009) emphasized: "Orientation is important, and the manager who does not take the time to assist a new employee is making a serious mistake" (p. 364).

Marriner Tomey (2009) suggested that orientation alone does not, however, socialize new employees into the organization:

Socialization is the sharing of attitudes and values through role modeling, myths, and legends. It is less structured than orientation. All employees need socialization. Instilling a clear understanding of the value system throughout the organization is the socialization process for creating team spirit that is found in excellent organizations. It is correlated with lower levels of dissatisfaction, absenteeism, and attrition. (p. 365)

In-Service Training

In-service training helps staff to keep current by updating their skills and knowledge to perform on the job. Topics may be far ranging, but often involve new client care procedures, learning how to use new equipment, reviewing charting methods, or learning how to use an intervention technique. The RT manager's responsibility is to "provide responsive training programs that address staff needs quickly, cost-effectively, and accurately" (Carter & O'Morrow, 2006, p. 235).

A logical beginning place for the RT manager in planning in-service training is to assess the needs of staff members while keeping in mind the organization's goals. Carter and O'Morrow (2006) indicated: ". . . Systematic determination of staff operational needs based on organizational and department goals is the basis for determining specific content (of in-service training programs)" (p. 237).

There are several means to determine in-service training needs. One of the best is to discuss the topic during a staff meeting. Staff often have areas in mind they wish to pursue. Another source of ideas is to have an outside consultant conduct a needs appraisal for RT. Still another way in which needs are surfaced is through accreditation visits during which visitors report areas that need strengthened. Some ideas for in-service training will likely come from higher up in the organization. These are typically passed on to the first-line RT manager from the manager's superior.

Once needs have been identified, the manager, often assisted by staff, identifies ways to meet the needs. Of course, the resources available to the manager will influence the type of training that will be possible. Larger organizations, and units within them, tend to have greater resources (e.g., financial support, internal staff) available to assist with organizing and conducting staff training. Wise managers network with peers within other units of the organization and with colleagues in the community to become familiar with possible internal and external resources for conducting in-service training sessions. University faculty offer an additional resource available to RT units, as professors are often willing to assist with the training of staff at a reasonable fee or for no cost.

When a topic has been selected for an in-service training session, the RT manager needs to first work with the individual who will be leading the session to determine the content and to establish the learning objectives for the session. The time allotment should be made clear to the person doing the session, and if a question-and-answer period is to occur, the person needs to know this so time may be factored in to include it. Arrangements should be made for a place in which to hold the session and the audiovisual equipment required by the session leader needs to be identified and reserved. Once the arrangements have been put in place and the session has been scheduled, the RT manager should begin to interpret to staff the benefits of receiving the training so they will be motivated to attend and to learn.

As a follow-up to the training session, it is worthwhile to discuss with staff what they found useful from the presentation and how they plan to use it in their practices. RT managers can do this by interviewing individual staff members or by discussing this in a staff meeting. Another typical means of evaluation is to have staff complete evaluation forms immediately following the training session. Central to this evaluation is the degree to which the learning objectives were achieved, assessment of the delivery of the person leading the session, and determining whether the setting and audiovisual aids were helpful. RT managers should analyze all types of evaluation data and use them as a basis for making needed adjustments in the unit's in-service training program.

Clinical Supervision

In addition to regular in-service training sessions, RT managers should ensure that RT clinicians are provided clinical supervision as a part of their ongoing staff development. Clinical supervision is a means of helping recreational therapists develop and deliver the highest quality of clinical services to clients. It is discussed in detail from a management perspective in Chapter 11.

Retention

All organizations, including RT units, strive for staff retention. Research on retention in RT is lacking, but nursing researchers have found that reducing turnover results in a higher quality of care, as reflected in improved treatment outcomes (Aiken, Clarke, Sloane, Lake, & Cheney, 2008; Hinson & Spatz, 2011). Ensuring the retention of competent staff requires providing a positive workplace that leads to staff being happy in their positions in contrast to staff feeling a lack of satisfaction, recognition, and reward as a result of working in a negative workplace (Hinson & Spatz, 2011; Porter-O'Grady & Malloch, 2013).

Clark (2009) indicated four critical factors involved in staff retention: (a) job satisfaction, (b) supervision, (c) the work environment, and (d) personal factors. Job satisfaction is heavily influenced by factors such as heavy client loads, continuing mental and physical demands of the job, little autonomy, and excessive paperwork. Problems in supervision result from a lack of support and encouragement by supervisors. The work environment is a negative factor when it contains a lack of civility and mutual respect among staff. Unpleasant and uncooperative coworkers are impairments to happiness at work, as is having to work in crowded conditions with little personal space or privacy. Personal factors, such as not having opportunities for personal development or not being able to have autonomy, may lead to dissatisfaction and leaving the employment of the organization.

An intriguing and creative approach to retention was reported by Hinson and Spatz (2011) in a study on improving the retention of nurses working in a large tertiary acute-care hospital. Resulting from the five innovative retention concepts they employed was a significant effect on increasing staff satisfaction and reducing turnover. The five retention concepts were termed on-boarding, employee rounding, social networking, employee recognition, and developmental "stretch" assignments.

On-boarding involved retaining newly hired staff through a program led by the orientation coordinator. Among the on-boarding approaches were mailing a personalized welcome letter to new staff members along with a T-shirt to congratulate them on their new position and to welcome them to the nursing team. New hires also received an e-mail during the second week explaining the orientation process. A "New Hire Leadership Welcome Breakfast" was organized so the new staff could meet nursing leaders and preceptors. A picture board was constructed on which the pictures, names, and interests of new nurses were posted. Finally, support groups were organized run by seasoned nurses for the new nurses to learn about procedures followed at the hospital. These support groups were enjoyed by the experienced nurses, who welcomed the opportunity to share their knowledge with the new nurses. *Employee rounding* involved enhancing two-way communication between staff nurses and senior leadership staff. Staff nurse team leaders met weekly with nurses to gain understandings of their most critical needs. Another dimension had to do with leadership staff (the division chief, nursing director, and nurse manager) meeting with staff nurses for a number of sessions. Initially, sessions were focused on staff engagement around what were thought to be complex patient cases, and later, sessions were focused on nurse–physician partnerships. The concept of *social networking* involved units holding social networking events to connect employees to one another and to the organization. Several events were held for all units (e.g., a big league baseball game, a wine and cheese event, and a mom and baby pool party). Other team events included wedding and baby showers, holiday dinners, and cultural outings. *Employee recognition* was a critical component of the retention program because nurses had revealed in prior surveys that they were not feeling recognized. An online employee recognition program called "BRAVO" was established by management to recognize staff. This included the monthly recognition of the "Star of the Month" for each unit. Another recognition effort awarded staff with "Priceless" T-shirts for their parts in the hospital receiving a national award. The *developmental "stretch" assignments* had the purpose of improving staff satisfaction and increasing feelings of attachment to the hospital by engaging them through autonomy and leadership roles. This program fostered the creation and implementation of staff-initiated projects that served as means for staff to increase their involvement in decision making, providing a sense of autonomy and bringing recognition to staff.

Although the five concepts presented by Hinson and Spatz (2011) were employed within a retention program for nurses, they certainly provide models for retention programs in RT. Skillful RT managers may borrow from the five concepts to replicate them successfully when attempting to retain competent recreational therapists.

Summary

Staffing is a key management function that if done right ensures the RT unit will hire and retain competent staff who will meet client needs and fulfill unit objectives. Areas for the first-line manager to become well versed include position descriptions, recruiting, interviewing, staff selection, scheduling, organizing orientation and in-service training programs, and retaining staff.

References

Aiken, L. H., Clarke, S. P., Sloane, D. M., Lake, E. T., & Cheney, T. (2008). Effects of hospital care environment on patient mortality and nurse outcomes. *Journal of Nursing Administration, 38,* 223–229.

Ashurst, A. (2010). *Developing management potential.* London, England: Quay Books.

Carter, M. J., & O'Morrow, G. S. (2006). *Effective management in therapeutic recreation service* (2nd ed.). State College, PA: Venture.

Cherry, B. (2011). Nursing leadership and management. In B. Cherry & S. R. Jacob (Eds.), *Contemporary nursing: Issues, trends, & management* (pp. 333–363). St. Louis: Elsevier Mosby.

Clark, C. C. (2009). *Creative nursing leadership & management.* Boston, MA: Jones & Bartlett.

Dunn, R. (2002). *Haimann's healthcare management* (7th ed.). Chicago, IL: Health Administration Press.

Ellis, J. R., & Hartley, C. L. (2009). *Managing and coordinating nursing care* (5th ed.). Philadelphia, PA: Wolters Kluwer/Lippincott Williams & Wilkins.

Fry, B. J. (2010). *Fast facts for the clinical nurse manager: Managing a changing workplace in a nutshell.* New York, NY: Springer.

Grohar-Murray, M. E., & Langan, J. (2011). *Leadership and management in nursing* (4th ed.). Upper Saddle River, NJ: Pearson.

Hinson, T. D., & Spatz, D. L. (2011). Improving nurse retention in a large tertiary acute-care hospital. *The Journal of Nursing Administration, 41*(3), 103–108.

Marquis, B. L., & Huston, C. J. (2009). *Leadership roles and management functions in nursing: Theory and application* (6th ed.). Philadelphia, PA: Wolters Kluwer/ Lippincott Williams & Wilkins.

Marriner Tomey, A. (2009). *Guide to nursing management and leadership* (8th ed.). St. Louis: Mosby Elsevier.

Porter-O'Grady, T., & Malloch, K. (2013). *Leadership in nursing practice.* Burlington, MA: Jones & Bartlett Learning.

Chapter 8
Influencing

Objectives
- Define the terms *influencing, coaching, autocratic technique, consultative technique, motivation, communication, delegating,* and *conflict.*
- Provide approaches to giving directives.
- Describe the role of the first-line manager in effecting change.
- Describe ways for the first-line manager to create a climate to keep staff motivated.
- Explain how the job environment affects staff morale.
- Describe ways to assess staff morale.
- Describe leadership styles.
- Name common ways RT managers communicate with staff.
- List competencies useful to managers in interpersonal communications.
- Describe points for giving positive feedback.
- Describe points for delivering criticism.
- Provide questions the manager should ponder before delegating.
- Outline guidelines for a manager to follow when delegating.
- Provide strategies for dealing with conflict.
- Provide tips for thriving in a changing workplace.

Key Terms
- **Influencing:** A major management function involving the supervisor eliciting action from staff to reach an organization's objectives.
- **Coaching:** Provides staff with a feeling of being heard, valued, and encouraged by the person they work for as they develop professional skills and learn to take on increasing levels of responsibility.
- **Autocratic technique:** The autocratic technique to supervision calls for close supervision.
- **Consultative technique:** Characterized by general supervision or what may be termed loose supervision and allows opportunities for staff to employ individual ingenuity.
- **Motivation:** Involves inspiring staff to put forth sustained effort in their jobs while they perform caringly and competently.

- **Communication:** A two-way sharing of meaning involving a message being sent and received.
- **Delegating:** The process that facilitates the accomplishment of work by entrusting a staff member with the responsibility and authority to reach desired objectives.
- **Conflict:** "A metaphor for difference. It is more normal than it is exceptional" (Porter-O'Grady & Malloch, 2013, p. 562).

The recreational therapy (RT) manager must engage in the fourth management function of influencing. The influencing function connects the preparatory functions of planning, organizing, and staffing with the fifth and final function of controlling. The function of influencing is sometimes referred to in the literature as coordinating, leading, directing, or motivating (Dunn, 2002; McConnell, 2014).

Dunn (2002) defined influencing as "the managerial function by which the supervisor evokes action from others to accomplish organizational objectives" (p. 383). Dunn stated: "Influencing is the process around which all performance revolves, it is the essence of all operations" (p. 18).

Influencing has to do with giving staff their assignments so they know what is expected of them and supervising them to achieve the objectives of the organization (Cherry, 2011). Cherry's description is correct, but perhaps does not go far enough. Influencing has to do with giving assignments and seeing they are carried out correctly, but it involves more than simply handing out staff assignments and overseeing staff performance. Dunn (2002) interpreted this role as follows:

> It is the role of every supervisor to influence in order to get the work done through and with the help of employees. Influencing is the managerial function that *initiates* action. In most work settings, very little may be accomplished without influencing by the manager. Influencing includes issuing directives, instructions, assignments, and orders, as well as guiding and overseeing employees. It also addresses the problems of how to motivate one's employees. (p. 384)

Furthermore, Dunn explained:

> Moreover, the manager should consider the influencing function as a means not only for getting the work done and motivating the employees, but also for *developing* them. The most effective way to develop employees is diligent coaching and teaching by their immediate superior. Thus, influencing is more than just giving orders or supervising the employees to make certain that they follow directives. Influencing means building an effective workforce and inspiring its members to perform their best, in effect getting the employees to work in a large enterprise as effectively as possible and with the same enthusiasm that they would display if they were working for themselves, either in their own enterprise or as a hobby. (p. 384)

Coaching

RT managers use coaching in the influencing function to help staff develop their potential. The goal of coaching is to help RT staff develop and enhance their clinical or managerial skills and to prepare them for increased responsibility. In the relationship of managers as coach to recreational therapists, managers share their knowledge to help staff members grow and achieve goals. In turn, staff tend to develop loyalty toward managers who devote time out of their responsibilities to help them to grow (Clark, 2009).

Coaching and mentoring support the development and growth of another person, but coaching differs from mentoring. Perhaps the most significant difference is that the coach is the employee's manager and the mentor is typically outside the mentee's chain of command. Coaching provides staff with a feeling of being heard, valued, and encouraged by the person they work for as they develop professional skills and learn to take on increasing levels of responsibility. Mentoring is an exclusive one-on-one long-term relationship in which the mentor (an experienced senior staff member) helps the mentee (an inexperienced staff member) settle into the organization and then supports the mentee's advancement within the organization (Clark, 2009). Detailed information on mentoring is provided in Chapter 13.

Clark (2009) provided the following process for coaching:

- *Observing.* By observing the manager gains information about how coaching may prove to be helpful to the staff member. The manager should observe the staff member in both formal and informal situations, asking himself or herself: "What is the person doing or not doing effectively?" "What's the impact of the individual on others (e.g., members of the treatment team)?" "What's the person's impact on the achievement of organizational goals? Individual goals?"

- *Examining coach motives.* When an employee is not performing effectively, the manager should ask himself or herself: "Am I realistic? Am I expecting too much?" "Do I harbor anger or frustration toward the person that is interfering with my observations and analysis?" "Have I provided enough positive feedback to the person so I am not contributing to a problem behavior or attitude?" "Am I modeling excellent listening skills?" In this stage of the process it may be good for the manager to do a "reality check" with a trusted colleague in order to become aware of his or her own development needs.

- *Creating a discussion plan for the coaching session.* The manager should think about what he or she will discuss, pondering the following questions: "What's the purpose of this session?" "What is the outcome sought?" "What are potential difficulties that could come up and how will I handle them?" It is a good tact to share the plan for the discussion with the individual being coached for their input.

- *Initiating.* Remain positive and focused on the personal development of the staff member. Emphasize with the individual that you wish to be helpful to them. Discuss your observations with the individual (e.g., "This is what I observed. If I were in that team member's shoes, I might think…"). Remaining supportive, always describe the behavior and its impact in a calm, truthful, and straightforward way. Emphasize positive communication skills such as maintaining good eye contact, seeking clarification, providing reflective feedback, and using open-ended questions.

- *Providing and eliciting feedback.* Being clear and balanced, present your ideas and advice to the individual. Express specific desired behaviors (e.g., improving charting, working as a member of a team). Employ initiating comments such as "You sounded interested in that." Give explicit feedback to support your suggestions, such as "I observed you interrupting Charles three times during the last staff meeting" or "The support you gave Mrs. Chancellor was very effective." Encourage feedback from the staff member ("Were my suggestions helpful to you?" or ""Can you give me an example?").
- *Follow-up meetings.* Meet at regular checkpoints to evaluate progress. Ask the staff member what is going well and what needs more assistance. Give your observations with an emphasis on progress toward goals. Identify any needed changes in the plan. Gain feedback on what was helpful to the individual in coaching sessions. (p. 400)

Giving Directives: Communicating Performance Expectations

Two techniques may be used in giving directives or communicating performance expectations. One is the *autocratic technique* that calls for close supervision. The second is the *consultative technique* characterized by general supervision or what may be termed loose supervision. At times the autocratic technique (e.g., following exact safety procedures) may be called for, but on most occasions the consultative technique is preferable. It is more efficient and leads to higher motivation and morale among supervisees, as employees do not want to feel that the supervisor is "breathing down their neck" (Dunn, 2002).

In routine directives given in the daily performance of staff, the consultative general supervision approach should be employed. In this approach, once staff have been provided the standards and goals to be achieved by the supervisor, they are open to make their own decisions on how to get the job done. This more democratic, participatory approach provides staff with the opportunity to employ their individual ingenuity to getting the job done, which leads to enhanced feelings of satisfaction for staff members. The supervisor's focus is on getting results and not the way the desired results are achieved. The employees feel they are their own boss. Dunn (2002) stated: "All indications are that general supervision produces better results than close supervision" (p. 412).

Role Modeling

Positive role modeling is an effective means by which to bring about quality performance outcomes. Positive role modeling involves demonstrating a high level of performance staff can use as an example for their own job performance. Managers, for example, who show dignity and respect toward staff influence staff to similarly treat clients with dignity and respect. Likewise, managers who model caring and respectful attitudes toward staff promote camaraderie among staff. Additionally, managers who display effective communication skills, conflict management skills, and team-building skills create a climate that motivates staff to achieve their goals (Cherry, 2011).

Implementing Change

Anyone who has worked in the healthcare field for any time can attest that healthcare is always in a dynamic state of affairs with resulting substantial changes (Dunn, 2002). Being in the middle of healthcare systems, RT managers must learn how to deal with and implement change whether from internal or external forces (see Table 8.1).

Table 8.1
Forces That Influence Change

Internal Forces:

- Shift in priorities
- Need for increased productivity
- Need for cost containment
- Staffing pattern changes
- Shifts in philosophy
- Work processes changes
- Need for quality of work life

External Forces:

- Healthcare economics
- Technology
- Restructuring
- Diversity
- Changing demographics

Note. From *Nursing Management and Leadership* (8th ed., p. 315), by A. Marriner Tomey, 2009, St. Louis, MO: Mosby/Elsevier.

No matter the change, some employees will likely resist it. Because of this typical resistance to change from staff, or even the manager, change is frustrating. Nevertheless, the first-line manager's responsibility is to help staff deal with change and to bring it about. Dunn (2002) indicated: "The supervisor is the front line, and it is his or her responsibility to accommodate change and make it into a reality" (p. 413).

Reasons for resistance to change are wide ranging. Causes to resistance to change provided by Clark (2009), Dunn (2002), and Marriner Tomey (2009) include the following:

- Uncertainty about the effects of change
- Disrupts the equilibrium of the current state of affairs
- Threatened self-interest
- Misunderstanding
- Embarrassment
- Insecurity
- Habits
- Complacency
- Cynicism
- Inaccurate perceptions
- Perceived loss of status, power, rewards, or relationships

- Objective disagreement based on different perceptions of the situation
- Psychological reactions
- Low tolerance for change
- Opposition of the change to current trends
- Previous system stability for a long time

Can resistance to change be overcome? Happily, the answer is yes, but the task will not always be easy for the RT manager. Dunn (2002) suggested:

> The supervisor should assume that a considerable amount of time is necessary to implement a change; a rigid timetable for change is unrealistic. The change must be planned far in advance, and its impact on each position and job should be anticipated. Even if the change is well thought out and carefully planned, some ramifications will probably be overlooked. With the proper attitudes and the right techniques, the supervisor can facilitate the introduction of change. Involving subordinates in change discussions and decisions will help to overcome the various types of resistance. (p. 409)

Furthermore, Dunn (2002) indicated that the critical aspect in influencing change is the supervisor's responsibility to explain the change to staff in advance of implementation. The explanation should include what is to be accomplished by effecting the change and how the change relates to the overall goals of the organization. In the process of explaining the change, supervisors should put themselves in the place of the subordinates to understand the pluses and minuses of the change from the view of the staff. In doing so, supervisors conduct a *force field analysis* from the subordinates' views with the aim of trying to gain acceptance for the change by showing more pluses than minuses in bringing about the change (Dunn, 2002).

Dunn (2002) indicated that a key in implementing change is to allow enough time for the process to occur. Before changes are made, time has to be provided for staff to become familiar with the change, allowing them to think about the change and have questions answered so they understand the reasons for the change. Another key to reducing resistance to change is allowing for staff participation in planning for and implementing the change. This involvement allows staff to invest in the planning and implementation of the change and should decrease their anxiety over the change as they work with it and begin to accept it. Dunn (2002) stated: "If the plan for change is *their* plan, acceptance by the employees is greater" (p. 411).

Following a similar approach to that of Dunn (2002), Clark (2009) specified ways to reduce resistance to change. These appear in Table 8.2.

Table 8.2

Approaches to Dealing With Resistance

- *Communicate.* One of the best ways to reduce resistance is to provide accurate information about a change. By presenting information before the change, staff can see the logic of the change effort. This can reduce the number of unfounded rumors, and it's polite and respectful. Never just spring a change on staff.
- *Involve.* The more staff are involved in changes, the less likely they are to resist those changes.
- *Support.* By helping staff deal with their fears and anxieties during the transition period, you can provide a valuable service and reduce resistance to change.
- *Negotiate.* You can offer incentives to staff so they will not resist change or can allow team members who are resisting the chance to veto certain threatening elements of the change.
- *Co-opt.* Co-opt with staff who resist change by bringing them into a change planning group and giving them a role that does not threaten the change effort.
- *Coerce.* Use coercion only when speed is essential and only as a last resort. You can force staff into accepting change by making it clear that resistance to change can lead to job losses, dismissals, transfers, and/or fewer promotions.

Note. From *Creative Nursing Leadership & Management* (p. 303), by C. C. Clark, 2009, Sudbury, MA: Jones & Bartlett.

Creating a Motivating Climate

One difference between a mediocre organization and a highly successful one is having a motivated staff willing to put forth sustained effort in doing their jobs while performing their responsibilities caringly and competently (Baron & Byrne, 1994). Grohar-Murray and Langan (2011) stated: "Motivation is sparked by internal and external interacting forces that modify one's perception of, and commitment to goals" (p. 198). Helping staff become motivated to work hard and perform at a high level to achieve the organization's goals is part of the role of the first-line manager during the influencing function of management.

It is hoped that recreational therapists would naturally be highly motivated to assist their clients to achieve health-related outcomes by reaching the goals and objectives jointly agreed upon by staff and clients. Recreational therapists, however, typically have minimal control over the environment, or climate in which they work, an element that can positively or negatively affect therapists' motivational levels. Grohar-Murray and Langan (2011) indicated:

Climate influences the quality of performance that can take place in a given situation. High-quality performance is more likely to take place in settings where the climate is predominantly positive relative to both the organization and its goals and to individual workers and their needs. (p. 203)

The effectiveness of first-line managers of RT units greatly influences the climate in which recreational therapists function. The best managers help create a work environment in which recreational therapists can realize their full potential. Typically, this means allowing autonomous decision making by staff, minimizing rigid bureaucratic policies and procedures, and providing staff with supportive comments.

Cherry (2011) suggested that it is necessary for the supervisor to provide positive encouragement and support for staff, to create a good work climate. She stated: "Positive reinforcement in the form of a sincere 'thank you, you did a good job' is one of the most powerful yet most often underused motivational resources available to the manager" (p. 348).

> "Lead by inspiration, not intimidation."
>
> Rebecca Aguilar

Clark (2009) followed *Herzberg's Motivation–Hygiene Theory* as a basis for improving the environment so healthcare workers could achieve satisfaction from their jobs. Per Herzberg's theory, improvements in the work environment are brought about by providing motivators or *satisfiers* (e.g., achievement, recognition, gratifying work, responsibility, and advancement/growth) and ensuring "hygiene factors"—that may serve as *dissatisfiers*—do not produce negative reactions from staff. Hygiene factors, such as negative policies, strained relationships with the boss and colleagues, and inadequate salaries, create dissatisfaction among employees and work against staff motivation. To bring about employee satisfaction, Clark stated that supervisors must do the following:
- Be concerned with hygiene factors to avoid employee dissatisfaction and provide motivators intrinsic to the work itself.
- Provide sufficient challenge to workers.
- Provide increasing levels of responsibility once ability has been demonstrated or replace the employee with one who has a lower level of skill to ward off motivation problems. (p. 231)

Additionally, Clark (2009) provided a number of ways to increase the motivation of staff members. RT managers may use these tips to motivate their staff to perform their best. Drawn from the work of Clark, the following are steps RT managers should consider to increase motivation:
- Rewarding therapists who give the best care
- Giving therapists more power by helping them achieve leadership positions
- Helping meet therapists' needs for achievement by challenging them to succeed and by providing training and orientation
- Helping meet staff needs for affiliation by providing opportunities to enjoy social relationships, empathize with others in trouble, and work side by side with colleagues to decide on client care
- Improving physical working conditions to satisfy basic needs for safety
- Increasing the level of training and skills to raise self-esteem
- Placing staff in positions that help fulfill their self-actualization needs
- Providing assignments that satisfy and give value to employees, encouraging them to perform well

- Enhancing positive motivation by using a democratic leadership model, rewarding good work, and encouraging positive peer group interaction
- Providing annual awards for best client care or other actions by therapists
- Avoiding scolding in front of others or humiliating staff
- Stating what was not completed adequately and demonstrating a better performance
- Observing (not hovering over) staff carefully to make sure that they are taking responsibility
- Providing warmth and support and respecting individual capabilities (p. 235)

In addition to the aforementioned ways to enhance a positive climate, RT managers should also consider celebrating RT month each February. During this month, managers can develop or provide tokens of appreciation for each recreational therapist employed at the facility, such as RT paraphernalia (e.g., water bottles with the agency name and RT on it, or a nice work shirt embroidered with recreational therapist). By celebrating RT month, managers not only enhance the climate for the RT staff, but also provide internal marketing about the benefits and roles of RT within the facility.

In sum, wise first-line managers of RT units remain conscious of the importance of maintaining a positive climate for their staff and take steps to ensure that staff are satisfied with their work environment. Such an approach is the essence of management assisting staff to be motivated to perform their best.

Maintaining Morale

Closely related to a positive climate in the workplace is staff morale. Morale "is a state of mind and emotion affecting the attitudes, feelings, and sentiments of groups of employees and individuals toward their work environment" (Dunn, 2002, p. 474). Marriner Tomey (2009) presented the following description of morale:

> Morale is a state of mind related to cheerfulness, confidence, and discipline. A person who works confidently, courageously, and with discipline demonstrates high morale. A person who is apathetic, cowardly, disorderly, devious, fearful, complaintive, or rebellious demonstrates low morale. Morale is related to productivity, quality, job satisfaction, and motivation. (p. 111)

Morale in the workplace is contagious and spreads quickly. Positive attitudes spread rapidly, but negative attitudes seem to spread at warp speed. Whatever the level of morale, high or low, it affects not only the staff but also clients. Therefore, maintaining a high level of morale needs to be a concern for managers (Dunn, 2002).

Many factors affect morale, and they either arise outside the work environment or originate within the workplace. Supervisors have little or no control on outside factors that have repercussions on staff morale, but they can influence factors that affect morale within the workplace. Factors that managers can influence result from their leadership style (e.g., participatory or bureaucratic), interpersonal skills (e.g., whether people are treated as winners, whether supportive comments are made to staff), communication skills (e.g., keeping staff informed), and working conditions that affect the quality of life of employees (e.g., whether flexible work schedules are provided, if troublemakers who destroy morale are terminated). Positive influences on morale brought about by managers are likely to result in increased productivity by the staff.

Although managers can gauge the level of morale by observing staff, gaining a clear reading of the state of staff morale is always difficult. A technique to assist in gauging staff morale is the use of surveys to draw out workers' perceptions about job factors and their levels of satisfaction. Surveys are used to find out how employees view a number of aspects including their jobs, colleagues, salaries, benefits, working conditions, and the supervision they receive. Sometimes, the surveys are conducted by outside consultants or the organization's human resources department (Dunn, 2002; Marriner Tomey, 2009).

Suggestions for managers to employ to improve morale on a daily basis and serve as a positive role model have been presented by Clark (2009), who drew on the work of Baldrige (1994). She pointed out that it is important to do the following:

- *Greet everyone.* Saying "good morning" or "good afternoon" sets a tone of openness, warmth, and caring.
- *Avoid misusing beepers and cell phones.* Turn off beepers and/or cell phones during meetings. On the rare occasions when you must stay in touch, set your beeper or cell phone to vibrate.
- *Take invitations seriously.* Accepting an invitation and then not showing up or showing up late is rude and gives the impression that you're disinterested or disorganized. Invitations must be replied to within a week. If you accept, you should attend. Unless the invitation specified bringing a guest, it is not wise to bring one.
- *Return phone calls and e-mails.* Set aside a certain time during the day to return phone calls and e-mails. Not doing so may convey an air of self-importance. And even a seemingly unimportant message could be a vital one.
- *Apologize after a mistake.* After making a verbal or nonverbal gaffe, it is important to apologize in person and then follow it up with a phone call apology. For serious mistakes, a small thoughtful gift accompanied by a note of apology is in order.
- *Listen carefully.* Avoid getting caught up in personal agendas. When someone needs to talk with you, listen. Do not forget that important information may be transmitted during even a short communication. If there is an emergency, set a time to talk with the person later, and then follow through and be available as agreed.
- *Say no.* Learn to say no to unreasonable demands or invitations that do not support your priorities. (pp. 153–154)

Relating to Peers

Another factor to consider in influencing is the relationship managers maintain with peers. To be truly effective in accomplishing the work of their unit smoothly, managers must relate positively to not only their subordinates but also to their peers. Thus, building positive relationships with other managers and leaders within the organization is also vital to the influencing function (McConnell, 2014).

Employing Leadership Styles

A number of leadership styles are available to managers. Leadership styles were briefly introduced in Chapter 1. They are described in greater detail in the following sections. As explained elsewhere in this text, even though the term *leadership styles* is employed in the management literature, the approaches could be called management styles because they are adopted by managers and some approaches rely on directing employees rather than on leading them.

Although the popularity of leadership styles tends to come and go, managers in today's healthcare environment tend to place value on collaboration and teamwork. Astute managers recognize that contemporary healthcare systems are complex and require cooperative, coordinated efforts so those in managerial and clinical roles join together to produce positive results for the organization (Sullivan, 2012). Thus, the controlling nature of the first leadership style discussed, authoritarian leadership, generally does not fit well with the needs of today's healthcare organizations.

Authoritarian Leadership (Theory X)

McConnell (2014) described authoritarian leadership as follows:

Leaders who use this style are often described as task-oriented, paternalistic, or autocratic. They "run a tight ship," and they order or direct their employees. This style is also referred to as top-down or "I" (the leader comes first) management (also referred to as Theory X). (p. 211)

One form of authoritarian leadership is using a paternalistic approach in which the leader assumes the role of a critical and oppressive parent or benevolent dictator. This approach is perhaps only appropriately employed in emergency situations (e.g., fire or disaster), with employees who are inexperienced or insecure, or with hostile individuals who challenge authority.

Micromanagement is a second form of authoritarian leadership. Although it is condemned by most staff and managers, many cling to the notion of micromanaging because they believe staff are not capable of functioning without them. Micromanagers do not want their employees to make decisions, because they do not deem them capable of decision making. Thus, they operate with minimal regard for or trust in staff. Employees working under micromanagers tend to consider them as meddlers.

Participative Leadership (Theory Y)

McConnell (2014) portrayed participative leaders as follows: "Leaders who behave according to this style are often referred to as people-oriented. They run a 'happy ship.' This style is also described as bottom-up or 'we' (all of us together) management (Theory Y)" (p. 212). McConnell further described participative leadership:

Participative leaders believe that people want to work and are willing to assume responsibility. They believe that, if treated properly, people can be trusted and will put forth their best efforts. Participative leaders motivate by means of internal factors (for example, task satisfaction, self-esteem, recognition, and praise). They explain why things must be done, listen to what employees have to say, and respect their opinions. They delegate wisely and effectively. (p. 212)

Thus, managers who use a participative leadership style (sometimes referred to as participative management) encourage employees to participate in decision making by providing input and giving feedback. Such a style offers opportunities for staff to be involved in making suggestions, setting goals, and solving problems; such two-way communication brings about feelings of shared governance and empowerment for employees and has been found to improve employee job satisfaction (Kim, 2002). The scientific method of assessment, planning, implementation, and evaluation is used throughout the process of participative leadership (Muller, 1995). Recreational therapists are already familiar with this process, which is termed the recreational therapy process or APIE process by those in RT and is employed in working with clients (Austin, 2013).

The approach of *Management by Objectives* (MBO) was introduced by famed management author Peter Drucker in 1954. Because of Drucker's notoriety, his MBO method became well known and widely used. In the MBO approach, the supervisor and employee sit down together to jointly set specific objectives for the employee to accomplish within a time frame. The central concept of MBO is that the employee having been involved in setting the objectives and deciding how they will be achieved will be more likely to take responsibility for them (Thomson, 1998). Like many management approaches, MBO is not as widespread as it once was, but many managers still use it to influence staff performance.

Theory Z Leadership

Ironically, the third leadership style, termed Theory Z, is not related to authoritarian leadership (also referred to as Theory X) or participative leadership (referred to as Theory Y). McConnell (2014) explained Theory Z leadership as follows:

> Unrelated to Theory X and Theory Y, Theory Z was labeled as such primarily to distinguish it from authoritarian leadership. Originated by the Japanese, Theory Z is characterized by employee participation and egalitarianism. It features guaranteed employment, maximum employee input, and strong reliance on team mechanisms such as quality circles. (p. 213)

Theory Z reflects Japanese cultural traditions and values that seem to be compatible with the paternalistic approach of authoritarian leadership. Theory Z focuses on management establishing a caring, benevolent relationship with employees in which interest in the well-being of employees is a principal component. This concern for employees even extends outside the workplace in concepts such as ensuring job security and lifetime employment. Theory Z assumes that having been treated well, employees reciprocate by developing a strong dedication and loyalty to the organization. Thus, social relations and strong bonds play a large role in this management approach (Reference for Business, 2014). Marquis and Huston (2009) indicated that Theory Z has lost favor with American management theorists because of their inability to apply it within American organizations.

Bureaucratic Leadership

McConnell (2014) described bureaucratic leadership (perhaps better termed bureaucratic management, as the manager directs rather than influences) as follows:

> Terms descriptive of this style include rules-oriented, by-the-book management, and "they" management (essentially impersonal). Bureaucratic managers act as monitors or police. They enforce policies, rules, procedures, and orders from upper management. They tend to be buck-passers who take little or no responsibility for directives and who often experience near-paralysis of thought and action when encountering a situation for which not rule exists. (p. 213)

Only for the most mundane tasks (e.g., sorting mail) that must always be completed in the same way would a bureaucratic approach be satisfactory. Certainly it is difficult to envision situations in RT for which bureaucratic leadership would be appropriate.

Situational Leadership

McConnell (2014) coined the phrase "different strokes for different folks leadership" to describe situational leadership because this leadership style is flexible and adaptive as it is based on the contingencies at hand. McConnell described situational leadership this way:

> As the name suggests, flexible leaders adapt their approach to the specific situations and to the particular needs of different members of the team. As employees gain experience and confidence, the leadership style changes from highly directive to supportive (from task-related to people-related). For example, two new employees may start work on the same date. If one has had previous experience and the other has had none, different directive styles are needed. A show-and-tell approach is required for the novice, but the same may not be appropriate for the experienced person. (pp. 213–214)

Because of its flexible nature, situational leadership is well suited to instances in which a collaborative, collegial approach is called for with seasoned therapists as well as when a more directive approach is needed with emerging therapists. Thus, it seems situational leadership has application in RT.

Laissez-Faire Leadership

McConnell (2014) used terms such as *hands-off*, *fence-straddling*, and *absentee* to describe laissez-faire leadership. He wrote: "Laissez-faire managers avoid giving orders, solving problems, or making decisions. They are physically evasive and are sometimes nowhere to be found when needed. Verbally, they are often masters of double-talk" (p. 214).

This description of laissez-faire managers is hardly flattering. Yet McConnell stated that this hands-off style of leadership can be positive in situations in which a strong team exists that consists of members who are well trained, motivated, and highly productive. Given such a team has been clearly charged with a task and appropriately oriented, a laissez-faire approach can work. On the other hand, McConnell warned that the laissez-faire approach can be devastating when the manager is incompetent or lazy and therefore does not have the support of the members of the strong, self-directed team.

Which Leadership Style?

Which leadership style is best? The answer provided by Dunn (2002) is that no single leadership style has all the answers. Of the leadership styles presented in this section, the situational style may have the most application in RT. RT managers must know the leadership options available and determine which may be best applied when considering the people, place, and time. In short, managers should adapt leadership style to each situation, although it seems that the participative leadership style might most commonly be employed by RT managers, as they are primarily working with skilled and educated staff who would be thought to respond positively to a participatory approach.

Communicating

Communication has been defined as "a two-way sharing of meaning in which a message is both sent and received" (Austin, 2013, p. 253). The ability to communicate effectively is a basic skill for recreational therapists, so it may be assumed that RT managers have some level of competency in communicating. RT managers can communicate with staff in a number of ways, including everyday face-to-face communications, communicating by e-mail, staff meetings, and monthly one-on-one meetings with staff members.

It is a good practice for managers to maintain daily face-to-face communications with staff because this allows regular exchanges of information and permits the manager and staff member to react to verbal and nonverbal cues. E-mail can be an effective mechanism for communication, but miscommunication may occur because of the lack of nonverbal cues. Therefore, it is best to ensure that all e-mail messages are clear and to the point.

Weekly or monthly staff meetings are typically held by managers to bring about the opportunity for all staff to communicate. In conducting regular staff meetings, the manager should use an agenda and ensure that minutes are taken and distributed to staff in a timely fashion following the meeting. During staff meetings, the manager's responsibility is to not only share information, but also to facilitate the exchange of ideas by staff. The manager should be conscious of the tendency of some managers to dominate staff meetings by devoting too much of the time to providing staff with information, which reduces the amount of time for staff discussion.

It is a good practice for managers to schedule monthly one-on-one meetings with each employee. These meetings can be particularly useful in coaching staff members to advance their professional and personal development. Staff members also tend to appreciate having the opportunity to be heard and to share their ideas for improving the functioning of the unit.

Of course, wise managers communicate regularly with their supervisors and colleagues throughout the organization. Supervisors need to be apprised of occurrences within the RT program, and it is sound practice to build relationships with others within the system, as they are often helpful in meeting the needs of the RT unit.

Clark (2009) drew on information provided by the Nursing Leadership Institute to provide useful competencies for managers to follow in their interpersonal communications:

- Listens attentively to others' ideas and concerns
- Invites contact and is approachable
- Treats employees with respect
- Develops collaborative relationships within the organization
- Builds and sustains positive relations in the organization
- Shares information readily with staff
- Recognizes and uses the staff's ideas
- Articulates ideas effectively both verbally and in writing
- Succinctly communicates viewpoints
- Involves staff in building consensus on issues
- Models healthy communication and promotes cooperative behaviors (p. 137)

RT managers may find the extensive chapter titled "Communication Skills" in Austin's (2013) book *Therapeutic Recreation Processes and Techniques* to be a useful resource in refining communications skills. Managers or clinical supervisors may also refer the chapter to staff who need to review a particular area of communication (e.g., listening skills or interviewing skills).

Giving Feedback

The best means for the supervisor to know if a staff member is performing a job correctly is to observe the employee in action and then provide the employee with feedback on observed strengths and weaknesses through an honest two-way discussion in which the staff member's perspectives and feelings are allowed to surface. Following this, the supervisor and employee need to jointly develop a plan to overcome issues that may be preventing the employee's highest level of performance (Cherry, 2011).

Clark (2009) provided useful suggestions for managers to employ when giving positive feedback and delivering criticism. In terms of giving positive feedback, Clark's first suggestion is that praise needs to be linked to results. Second, if verbal praise might disrupt work, managers need to find another means to provide positive feedback. Third, managers need to learn what type of praise the employee most values (e.g., written memos, certificates, approving special requests, receiving occasional perks) and use that approach with the employee. Finally, she suggests that praise be used to build up other performance areas requiring improvement. She provides this example: "That was well done. Excellent work. What about complimenting your clients once in a while to show them you respect their work, too?" (p. 150).

To deliver criticism in a respectful manner, Clark (2009) suggested the following:

- *Begin with two positive statements.* "You really have presented some very good ideas, and I like working with you."
- *State the criticism.* "I'd like us to stay on topic and not stray off it."

- *Add another positive statement and a ray of hope.* "You've shown the ability to work on complex goals, and I believe we'll get this accomplished by tomorrow." (p. 150)

Delegating

Delegating facilitates the accomplishment of work by entrusting a staff member with the responsibility and authority to reach desired objectives. Delegation is the tool that allows managers to manage, as it permits work to be accomplished through others. Delegation involves assigning work to the right person for the job and then giving that person clear directives in terms of the work to be accomplished. Managers' success largely depends on their ability to delegate skillfully by assigning staff to tasks that they are competent to perform and able to accomplish. Staff who are delegated work that fits their skill sets typically feel they are playing a vital role within the organization by taking on responsibilities, being their own bosses by exercising control over their work, and successfully accomplishing the task. This builds staff morale (Grohar-Murray & Langan, 2011).

> "The first rule of management is delegation. Don't try and do everything yourself because you can't."
>
> Anthea Turner

By delegating, managers do not relinquish their responsibility but retain overall authority and responsibility for the assignment being carried out. Grohar-Murray and Langan (2011) explained that delegation does not reduce the responsibilities of the manager because "the manager remains accountable to superiors for those below the manager" (p. 171).

It is, of course, imperative that managers consider the level of experience and training of staff members prior to delegating direct care responsibilities. The following questions, adapted from a list presented by Clark (2009), need to be answered before delegating a task:

- Will the client receive quality RT care if the task is delegated?
- Should the task be delegated?
- How much supervision will the person doing the task require?
- Is the person to whom the task is being delegated competent to do the task?
- Is the person functionally able to perform the task based on other assignments?
- Can the person perform the task without an adverse client occurrence?

Are there additional guidelines for the beginning manager to follow to be effective in delegating? The answer is yes. Grohar-Murray and Langan (2011) offered the following guidelines:

- Give a clear description of what it is you want the employee to do. Describe the overall scope and background of the current task. Give the reason for the assignment, and tell the employee if other departments or people are involved to achieve the desired outcome. If there are special problems, share this information with the employee.

- Share with the employee the outcome you expect and by when.
- Discuss the degree of responsibilities and authority the employee will have.
- Ask the employee to summarize the main points of the delegated task.
- Know what cannot be delegated. This includes confidential matters, contractual responsibilities, discipline of the workforce, and ultimate responsibility for the work output. (p. 175)

From the discussion of delegating, it should be clear that effective managers must learn to delegate. Managers must concentrate their efforts on performing the duties expected within their management position and learn to delegate tasks the staff is competent to perform.

Managing Conflict

Conflict occurs when clashes transpire between individuals or groups who have have different values, beliefs, or needs. Because we as human beings exist together in a diverse society, differences will lead us into conflict. Conflict, in fact, is a naturally occurring phenomenon when human beings interact. Porter-O'Grady and Malloch (2013) wrote: "Indeed conflict is more normal than it is exceptional" (p. 122). Similarly, Clark (2009) portrayed conflict as "part of the ebb and flow of any human relationship" (p. 160) and something that is typically seen as being detrimental but can have beneficial outcomes. Conflict, for example, is beneficial when the manager uses conflict to further communications among members of a healthcare team with the result that it becomes a learning experience producing insights into others' values and beliefs. It has even been suggested that the complete resolution of conflict might lead to stagnation with a stifling effect on creativity and growth (Clark, 2009).

Yet we tend to fear conflict. Some polarized broad-based conflict can be frightening, as extremists can become provoked into dangerous ways of expressing positions about which they are passionate. Although such broad-based conflict exists, most conflict does not reach intense large-scale levels. Interpersonal conflict tends to exist between individuals and between small groups. In fact, Porter-O'Grady and Malloch (2013) reported: "Well over 90 percent of the conflict that occurs between human beings is local and is completely resolvable" (p. 122).

The view that conflict is relatively normal and should be expected when humans interact is probably a good perspective for RT managers because they will almost certainly encounter conflict. Conflict will be easier to deal with if RT managers do not live in fear of clashes between individuals and groups but accept such conflicts will occur and prepare to deal with them as inevitable eventualities.

Conflict Among Healthcare Professions: The Manager's Responsibility

Being a healthcare professional is not always easy. Clinical work can be stressful. Feelings of stress can then accentuate feelings of conflict among healthcare employees whose jobs produce aggravation or exasperation and put them on edge. When stress occurs, managers need to remain alert to potential conflict. Porter-O'Grady and Malloch (2013) suggested: "The most important and best first step in the management of all conflict is early recognition of signs and early addressing of the issues" (p. 123). Early recognition of conflict means that steps can be taken to keep it from escalating into a major conflict.

Conflict tends to grow from personality differences, individuals with differing personal needs and values, issues that remain continually unresolved, and issues related to excessively demanding or not equitable workloads. If the manager can identify conflicts spawned by such triggers early in their development, interventions can be established to keep the conflict in check and head off further development. Porter-O'Grady and Malloch (2013) outlined a number of strategies for RT managers to adopt to address conflicts before they get out of hand:

- Develop an awareness of the norms of conflict in all the professional peers so they can be coagents in the early identification of the potential for emerging conflict.
- Work with colleagues to organize a unit strategy for normalizing and addressing conflict that includes professional colleagues, interdisciplinary colleagues, associates, and managers.
- Develop specific protocols and processes that automatically begin when a particular conflict is identified and noted by any member of the staff.
- Make sure that there is a portion of the regular staff meeting that addresses a particular challenging issue, circumstance, or event for which there is a potential for conflict or for which signs of conflict already exist.
- Make sure that there are sufficient social and relational outlets that are regularly scheduled for socialization, friendly dialogue, celebration of key events, acknowledgment of successes or accomplishments, or recognition of important life occurrences.
- Regularly undertake feedback, evaluation, problem identification, complaints, or assessment of potential concerns with staff in an emotionally neutral, safe environment that makes such activities a regular part of the way of doing business in the unit or department.
- Establish communication, interaction, and communication norms that represent nonjudgmental, balanced, self-directed communication styles and patterns that eliminate judgment, threats, reactions, or aggression. Make these norms a part of the structure of meetings and of staff and leadership communication styles. (pp. 124–125)

Confronting Continuing Conflicts

Continuing conflict should not be ignored. It needs to be dealt with so it does not produce constant discord that may lead to severe psychological or physiological harm for those directly involved and may be disrupting to the entire unit. In ongoing cases of conflict, the manager or an outside individual (e.g., perhaps someone from the human resources department) needs to mediate the situation. Whoever serves as mediator, the first step is to decipher the core issues underlying the conflict. The individuals experiencing the conflict have to be given opportunities to express their concerns and feelings. During this process, the mediator's role should not be to solve the issues for the combatants, but instead to help those in conflict to resolve it (Porter-O'Grady & Malloch, 2013).

Types of Conflicts

Five types of conflicts have been identified: relationship conflicts, information conflicts, interest-based conflicts, organizational conflicts, and values-based conflicts. Each category of conflict is unique and requires different approaches.

Relationship conflicts. Relationship conflicts are typically emotionally charged. Therefore, the mediator needs to create a safe space for the parties involved to express their feelings on the issue. According to Porter-O'Grady and Malloch (2013), in this space the mediator does the following actions:

- Moves the parties away from each other and the place of conflict
- Supports each person in his or her feelings and emotions
- Accepts each individual's own perceptions of how he or she feels
- Makes sure each person has an opportunity to verbalize feelings
- Doesn't attempt to resolve the issue before individuals express feelings
- Is caring and supportive of each person experiencing the conflict
- Accepts whatever emotions are expressed in an appropriate place for it (p. 138)

Furthermore, Porter-O'Grady and Malloch (2013) suggested four elements to be included in the mediation process. First, the mediator needs to remind the participants of the respect they want to be shown and should attempt to ensure they offer as much respect for one another as possible under the circumstances. Anger should be directed to the issues and not at each other. Second, the mediator needs to help the parties to understand what they need versus what they want so they may have their true needs recognized and met. Third, the mediator should help each party to hear the other's position. Finally, because in relationship conflicts there is a tendency to blame the other person, the mediator needs to remind the parties to not use "you" statements, but instead to begin statements with "I" (e.g., "I think," "I feel," "I see").

Information conflicts. Information conflicts arise largely because of the filtering of information through the perceptions and values held by each individual. Thus, the parties involved in the conflict need to analyze how their personal perceptions and values affect their understandings of information. Porter-O'Grady and Malloch (2013) stated that the parties involved need to consider the following questions:

- Are judgments being made before all of the information is available to support them?
- Is the meaning of the information clear to all parties before conclusions can be drawn from them about what action needs to be taken?
- Are all parties' perceptions appropriately clarified so there is a mutual level of understanding and insight about what action needs to be taken?

Interest-based conflicts. When interest-based issues exist, conflict may occur over the expressed interests by the parties, rather than the legitimate interests they hold.

Thus, the mediator needs to help the individuals clarify the real underlying interests generating the conflict. Sometimes, parties discover that they share the same real interests.

Organizational conflicts. Organizational conflicts occur when some within the organization have their own agenda and are not committed to the overall organization. Managers affect how their unit functions within the total organization. They affect how well the unit relates to and aligns with the goals, mission, and purpose of the overall organization. The more the organization's goals, mission, and purpose are reflected by the actions of those in the unit, the less opportunity for conflict. The role of effective managers becomes seeing that a good fit exists between the unit and the overall organization.

Values-based conflicts. Porter-O'Grady and Malloch (2013) said: "Perhaps the most difficult conflicts to address in the workplace are those that relate to personal values" (p. 145). Any number of sources may bring about values conflicts. These include values related to religious beliefs, political ideologies, socioeconomic status, and culture. Within RT, values conflicts may relate to the philosophical positions held by staff. Those who hold a therapy orientation may find conflict with those with a leisure facilitation orientation.

Often, staff respond to values conflicts by proselytizing and taking positions rather than by listening to others. Values conflicts are often difficult to resolve, and Porter-O'Grady and Malloch (2013) presented practices to minimize the potential for values conflicts:

- Make a true and abiding commitment to finding common ground and developing win–win compromises in values adjustments between individuals and groups.
- Expand the vocabulary and language of the workplace to include broader terms, expressions, and definitions that are inclusive and respectful.
- Find the common themes and elements between and among values that can anchor relationships and demonstrate the foundation for the expression of value.
- Articulate and define as a system your unit that includes the fundamental elements of dignity and respect, which informs all behavioral expressions among members and colleagues.
- Enumerate the legitimacy of the individual differences, the right to have them, and the appropriate forum within which they can be legitimately expressed. At the same time, define and acknowledge environment, context, and situations where the expression of such differences is not legitimate or appropriate.
- Make sure a specific and well-designed ethics process or committee is in place to deal with significant values challenges or intractable values issues in an effort to establish a common frame for behavioral expectations and expression.
- As with other differences, make values conflict a normative expectation of the dynamics of a diverse membership group, creating a safe space for exploration, an effective process for dialogue and clarification, and a mechanism for conflict resolution. (pp. 147–148)

Summing Up the Management of Conflict

In the end, no matter the type, conflict in the workplace is a reality that managers must face and address. If not addressed, conflict tends to escalate and produces harmful consequences. Thus, managers have to understand conflict and develop techniques to deal with it. Although there are no easy answers to addressing conflict, Clark (2009) listed ways to deal with conflict:

- Acknowledge conflict so it can be resolved before it escalates.
- Develop conflict prevention and management guidelines so staff can refer to them.
- Focus on behavior that contributes to the conflict, not the person.
- Identify conflicting values and beliefs that may be fueling conflict.
- Avoid postponing dealing with conflict.
- Use open body language, and display a respectful attitude.
- Develop efficient reporting systems to help manage conflict before it escalates.
- Allow concerns to be raised at team meetings.
- If you're a manager, adopt an open-door policy, and take action to make a fair workplace environment.
- When you're at fault, give the other persons what they want or request.
- Strive to understand the problem from all viewpoints.
- Work with other parties to create a solution that meets everyone's needs.
- Always use tactful messages—for example, "I have a problem, can you help me?" "I need your help with . . ." "I feel this way about . . ." (p. 175)

Influencing in a Nutshell

In her book with the subtitle of *Managing a Changing Workplace in a Nutshell*, Fry (2010) synthesized many of the complex elements involved in the management function of influencing. She titled these the "Top Twelve Management Tips for Thriving in a Changing Workplace," although (for some unknown reason) she lists only 11:

1. *Always tell the truth.* Staff members know when you are not being upfront and will "fill in the blanks" with what *they think* is missing. Before you know it, the grist for the organizational rumor mill is churned out at warp speed.
2. *Authentic leaders have nothing to hide.* They inspire trust.
3. *Expect respect for all.* Require respectful behavior from and toward all staff members, physicians, patients, families, and visitors.
4. *In crisis, look for opportunities; in opportunities, expect snags!* Most change can create reactions ranging from the good to the bad to the ugly. Snags may be blessings in disguise. Look for the possibilities.
5. *Create a place where staff wants to work!* Creating a practice environment grounded in excellence begins with you. You set the tone, you hire the right staff, you communicate expectations, you inspire staff through regular feedback and you challenge them to soar both personally and professionally.
6. *Create opportunities for fascinating group conversations, inspired dialogue, and possibilities!* Staff meetings are one of the most powerful tools for a manager. Craft agendas that excite, energize, and invite conversations and laughter. Then, staff will attend! If you supply refreshments, staff will beat down the door!

7. *Breathe life into Standards of Practice.* When staff performance deviates from the Standards of Practice and members are not held accountable, they start on a slippery professional slope that can negatively affect the quality of care and work life. You cannot monitor adherence to the Standards if you are not present in the practice setting to draw attention to them! If you are present, you can assess staff's competence, identify their learning needs, and determine where they fit on the professional practice autonomy scale.

8. *Build your workplace mission, vision, and values to guide professional practice and quality of work life.* Staff members do well when they are confident that there is a good organizational fit between their skills and the required work. They also need to know how their workplace fits into the context of the organization, as well as the guidelines and actions that govern behaviors to accomplish what needs to be done. A practice setting mission, vision, and values statement is a compass that gives direction to the workplace and all who work there.

9. *Deal with unacceptable behavior by reinforcing professionalism at all times and practicing performance management.* Although one of the most uncomfortable processes that managers must face, dealing with untoward behavior is never optional. The longer the behavior goes unchecked, the greater the potential for destroying workplace relationships essential to professional practice, staff well-being, and quality of care.

10. *You cannot be a friend to staff and manage them at the same time.* Being a friend to staff is a boundary issue about meeting your needs and not about meeting staff needs.

11. *Facilitate self-directed learning, listen to what is not being said, and encourage solution-focused conversations.* (pp. 191–193)

Tips from Happywork

Similar to Fry (2010), in his book titled *Happywork*, Reimer (2015) integrated many of the complex elements involved in the management function of influencing. He termed these The Happywork Agreement. In one portion, he listed a manager's commitments to employees. Table 8.3 draws upon Reimer's list of commitments.

Table 8.3
Manager's Commitments to Staff

1. First and foremost, I will not ask my staff to do anything I would not be willing to do myself. And I will not create rules that I cannot follow myself. I realize that acting in such a manner destroys morale.

2. I will not publicly take credit for my staff's great ideas and hard work.

3. I will give my staff direction. I want people with initiative (self-starters, as it were), but I do not want members of my staff to have to wonder what is most important to me.

4. I will provide my staff the tools and training they need to have a chance to succeed. I will mentor them and give them opportunities to advance when I can.

5. I will give my staff constructive feedback, considering both their career advancement and their feelings.

Table 8.3 (cont.)

6. I will try to provide some variety to my staff's workdays.

7. I will listen to the ideas of members of my staff.

8. I will not be afraid to hire individuals who are smarter than me. It is the sign of a great manager.

9. I will not keep dead weight around. I promise to build a workforce in which staff members can excel, even if that means pulling the trigger on tough decisions. Other staff members should not have to pick up the slack for underperforming staff.

10. I promise to take arguments between upper management behind closed doors. Staff do not need to see or hear such things. Often, such strife can hurt staff morale and can even make staff fear for the future.

11. I will remember that I may possess certain skill sets that my staff do not. Therefore, it may not be reasonable to expect from others sterling performance in areas where I excel. I will be patient.

Note. Adapted from *Happywork* (pp. 160–162), by C. Reimer, 2015, Shippensburg, PA: Sound Wisdom.

Conclusion and Summary

Grohar-Murray and Langan (2011) nicely summed up the role of the manager performing the function of influencing: "It is the manager's job to motivate, stimulate, and foster excellence and ambition in the staff" (p. 10). McConnell (2014) offered a number of points for managers to facilitate the influencing function. McConnell's points provide a good means of concluding this chapter as they summarize many of the key dimensions involved in influencing. These are listed in Table 8.4.

Table 8.4
Means to Improve the Influencing Process

- Make all service requests clear and direct. Whenever possible, make the request directly to the person or persons who provide the service.

- Anticipate negative responses to requests and problems, and be ready to respond positively.

- When a request is initially made, secure agreement on the date or time by which the necessary action will be taken.

- Always follow up a verbal request with the same in written form; a verbal request can be forgotten or ignored, but any request is less likely to fall by the wayside if documented.

- Listen to the problems of employees and do your best to empathize.

- Seek collaborative (win–win) solutions whenever possible, but be prepared to compromise when necessary.

- Treat others as partners or collaborators; let them know this is "ours" rather than "mine."

- Always place teamwork above competition.

- Be patient and reasonable; never demanding or critical.

- Avoid becoming upset and avoid upsetting the other person; anger only hinders the cooperative process.

Table 8.4 (cont.)

• Eliminate all kidding and sarcasm from your repertoire. You never know when innocent kidding could be taken to heart. Also, sarcasm is never found among the legitimate tools of communication.

• Always strive to know your staff and your colleagues better and to improve your understanding of their work.

• Always express sincere appreciation for the efforts of others. Honest appreciation of work well done is one of the surest ways of ensuring that future work is well done.

Note. From *Umiker's Management Skills for the New Health Care Supervisor* (6th ed., pp. 46–47), by C. R. McConnell, 2014, Burlington, MA: Jones & Bartlett Learning.

References

Austin, D. R. (2013). *Therapeutic recreation processes and techniques: Evidence-based recreational therapy* (7th ed.). Urbana, IL: Sagamore.

Baldrige, L. (1994, March 1). 10 mistakes in manners that executives make over and over again. *Bottom Line Personal, 1994,* 10–11.

Baron, R. A., & Byrne, D. (1994). *Social psychology: Understanding human interaction.* (11th ed.). Boston, MA: Allyn and Bacon.

Cherry, B. (2011). Nursing leadership and management. In B. Cherry & S. R. Jacob (Eds.), *Contemporary nursing: Issues, trends, & management* (pp. 333–363). St. Louis, MO: Elsevier Mosby.

Clark, C. C. (2009). *Creative nursing leadership & management.* Sudbury, MA: Jones & Bartlett.

Dunn, R. (2002). *Haimann's healthcare management* (7th ed.). Chicago, IL: Health Administration Press.

Fry, B. J. (2010). *Fast facts for the clinical nurse manager: Managing a changing workplace in a nutshell.* New York, NY: Springer.

Grohar-Murray, M. E., & Langan, J. (2011). *Leadership and management in nursing* (4th ed.). Upper Saddle River, NJ: Pearson.

Kim, S. (2002). Participative management and job satisfaction: Lessons for management leadership. *Public Administration Review, 62,* 231–241.

Marquis, B. L., & Huston, C. J. (2009). *Leadership roles and management functions in nursing: Theory and application* (6th ed.). Philadelphia, PA: Wolters Kluwer/ Lippincott Williams & Wilkins.

McConnell, C. R. (2014). *Umiker's management skills for the new health care supervisor* (6th ed.). Burlington, MA: Jones & Bartlett Learning.

Muller, M. (1995). Participative management in health care services. *Curationis, 18*(1), 15–21.

Porter-O'Grady, T., & Malloch, K. (2013). *Leadership in nursing practice.* Burlington, MA: Jones & Bartlett Learning.

Reference for Business. (2014). Theory Z. In *Encyclopedia of management.* Retrieved from http://www.referenceforbusiness.com/management/Str-Ti/Theory-Z.html

Reimer, C. (2015). *Happywork.* Shippensburg, PA: Sound Wisdom.

Sullivan, E. J. (2012). *Effective leadership and management in nursing* (8th ed.). Boston, MA: Pearson.

Thomson, T. M. (1998). *Management by objectives* (2nd ed.). San Francisco, CA: Jossey-Bass/Pfeiffer.

Marriner Tomey, A. (2009). *Nursing management and leadership* (8th ed.). St. Louis, MO: Mosby/Elsevier.

Chapter 9
Controlling

Objectives
- Define what is meant by controlling.
- Describe the relationship between the management functions of planning and controlling.
- Describe considerations important to the controlling function.
- Describe operations that first-line RT managers are responsible for controlling.
- Describe what is meant by performance appraisal.
- Outline disciplinary steps managers may take.
- Describe the role of the RT manager in managing risk.
- Describe the four steps involved in identifying, evaluating, and managing risk.
- Describe the elements of structure, process, and outcomes in quality health and human services.
- Create measurable indicators of service quality.
- Describe standards RT units typically have to meet.
- Describe the role of the RT manager in budgeting.

Key Terms
- **Controlling:** Involves follow-up and correction to ensure plans are carried out and goals and objectives are being achieved.
- **Performance appraisal:** The formal evaluation system in which periodic evaluations are completed to indicate how well an individual has performed.
- **Risk management:** A process through which managers seek to maximize the safety of their services to all stakeholders and minimize the risk of negative outcomes.
- **Quality management:** A process of control and evaluation to provide safe, effective, client-centered, timely, efficient, and equitable services.
- **Rules and regulations:** Rules and regulations (i.e., policies and procedures) are standards set to meet goals and objectives.
- **Operating budget:** Involves planning and accounting of income and expenses.

The final management function is known as controlling. Controlling is the means to transforming planned goals and objectives into the provision of high-quality services. Controlling has to do with monitoring the performance of the organization or unit to determine if the goals and objectives stated in the organization's or unit's plan are being carried out. In essence, controlling is an evaluative function that guides managerial decision making. If deviations occur, controlling involves making corrections that need to be made in performance or, alternatively, modifying the goals and objectives of the original plan.

Planning and Controlling Functions

A close relationship exists between the planning and controlling functions. The plan sets the goals and objectives and the methods for achieving them. Controlling involves measuring performance against the planned goals and objectives of the unit or organization. Therefore, planning and controlling seem to be inseparable functions of management. Controlling is meaningless without planning, and without controlling, planning is a fruitless enterprise.

> "Plans are only good intentions unless they immediately degenerate into hard work."
>
> Peter F. Drucker

Definitions of Controlling

McConnell (2014) briefly defined controlling: "The simplest and perhaps most appropriate definition of controlling is follow-up and correction" (p. 47). Dunn (2007) offered a more extensive definition:

> Controlling is the function that ensures that plans are followed, that actual performance matches the plan, and that objectives are achieved. A more comprehensive definition of controlling includes determining whether the plans are carried out, if progress is being made toward objectives, and whether other actions must be taken to correct deviations and shortcomings. Again, this relates to the importance of planning as the primary function of the manager. A supervisor could not check on whether work was proceeding properly if there were no plans to check against. Controlling also includes taking corrective action if objectives are not being met, and revising the plans and objectives if circumstances require it. (p. 19)

Similarly, Carter, Smith, and O'Morrow (2014) explained:

> Controlling is the evaluative function of management. It is the process of measuring performance against planned outcomes. *Controlling* is the process of establishing and implementing mechanisms, or processes, for ongoing evaluation to compare results with plans and goals. Managers establish performance standards as benchmarks, or targets, and evaluate and measure progress toward achievement. Controlling also includes identifying and implementing corrective actions that are needed to improve performance in the work unit. (p. 12)

Thus, in short, the controlling function involves the following:

1. Establishing standards to measure performance
2. Measuring actual performance
3. Comparing performance with the adopted standards
4. Taking needed corrective action

Considerations in Controlling

Controlling Deals With More Than Budgeting

Controlling is certainly a budgeting function to ensure that finances are in line with the planned budget. Controlling involves managers meeting financial criteria but also includes controlling processes, procedures, and policies related to providing safe and high-quality recreational therapy (RT) services. Thus, in addition to budget matters, controlling functions are also important in managerial activities such as evaluating staff, monitoring quality and effectiveness of services, managing risk, and applying performance standards based on written policies and procedures or rules and regulations adopted by the unit.

Communication Is Key

Successful managers first clearly communicate to staff the plans for the unit in terms of the sought goals and objectives and the standards (i.e., rules and regulations) that will be used to achieve them. Good communication of plans by the manager and the staff's understanding of the goals and objectives and the standards are basic considerations in carrying out the controlling function.

Establishing a Positive Tone and Sense of Trust

There can be what Roussel (2009) termed "unintended consequences of control" (p. 501). Inexperienced managers, in particular, must guard against assuming paranoid interpretations of the behavior of staff members (e.g., managers thinking staff resent them for exercising control and therefore are uncooperative). Also lacking experience, managers new to their roles sometimes feel uncomfortable with exercising control. Roussel explained: "Because control can be perceived as a threat from unwanted power or authority, it can trigger defense mechanisms such as aggression and repression" (p. 501). For instance, to protect their egos, when unsure of themselves new managers may become unnecessarily aggressive toward an employee they feel is not respecting their authority. On the other hand, managers may repress exercising control because it is difficult for them to do. Therefore, it is important for managers to build trust with their staff by assuming an "I'm okay, you're okay" relationship with those they supervise.

To carry out controlling functions successfully, managers need to strive to establish a high degree of mutual trust with individuals on their staff. As their supervisors, managers need staff to see them as people who will not fail to adhere to standards, as well as people they can trust to treat them fairly and who wish for them to develop to their fullest potential.

Roussel (2009) indicated a series of approaches important in carrying out the controlling function: "a high degree of mutual trust, a high degree of mutual support, open and authentic communications, clear understandings of objectives, respect for differences, use of member resources, and a supportive environment" (p. 504). Roussel concluded that employing these approaches will "lead to conflict resolution, changed beliefs and attitudes, genuine innovation, genuine commitment, strengthened management, and prevention of unintended consequences of control" (p. 504).

Recruit and Retain Talented, Self-Controlling Staff

To minimize the discrepancies between the desired goals and objectives and the actual outcomes, an obvious strategy is to recruit excellent staff who possess self-control, the highest form of control. Staff who exercise self-control are reflective practitioners who examine what they do and why they do it. They assess themselves and make self-corrections (Roussel, 2009). Once top staff members are in place, they need to be retained by reinforcing high-quality performance with the provision of positive feedback from the first-line manager and competitive salaries. High-quality staff will also want to grow and develop, so the first-line manager's job is to ensure that many opportunities are available for staff training and development. Additionally, wise first-line managers who have the advantage of having a superior staff allow staff to have autonomy to do their jobs so they gain job satisfaction and experience a sense of achievement from work well done.

> "Choose a job you love, and you will never have to work a day in your life."
>
> Anonymous

A Perfect Correspondence Between the Desired Goals and Objectives and the Actual Outcomes Is Uncommon

It would be ideal if planning was impeccable and managers could rely on their exemplary staff to achieve sought outcomes. It is rare, however, that a perfect correspondence exists between the desired goals and objectives and the actual outcomes. Thus, first-line managers typically need to monitor and analyze what is occurring within their unit to take corrective actions to meet the goals and objectives or adjust the goals and objectives so they are more realistic (Porter-O'Grady & Malloch, 2013).

When corrective actions need to be taken to improve staff performance, the manager needs to take steps to make changes. The manager can engage in disciplinary actions against employees. Or the manager can provide staff with training and development opportunities to improve performance (Roussel, 2009).

Controlling Activities of the
First-Line Recreational Therapy Manager

The first-line manager in RT has primary responsibility for the daily operating activities of the RT unit. Thus, RT managers serve as operational managers most concerned with exercising operational control dealing with day-to-day processes. RT managers should have a master plan for control that incorporates all standards related to the operations of the unit. Elements involved will likely include evaluating the performance of individuals (performance appraisal), controlling and managing risk, evaluating the quality of care, overseeing the rules and regulations in force within the service, and planning and monitoring the budget.

Performance Appraisal

Marriner Tomey (2009) stipulated that managers must "adjust closeness of supervision to the needs of the employee, take disciplinary action as soon as it is justified, and fire personnel who are not meeting minimum standards" (p. 60). These words indicate the seriousness of performance appraisal.

Performance appraisals, sometimes termed employee evaluations, are the formal evaluations to indicate how well staff members have performed as compared with job standards. Performance appraisals are conducted with the intent of informing staff members of how well they are meeting performance expectations.

Performance appraisals may also reveal staff training and development needs. If a number of staff share the same need, the first-line manager can establish staff training and development opportunities. Having properly trained staff is a means to problem prevention.

First-line managers generally are expected to conduct performance appraisals for the RT staff. First-line managers may employ informal and formal means when developing assessments of therapists. Informal assessment involves incidental observation of programs while they are being provided. Individual therapists may be observed to determine the quality of the provision of RT care and how they interact with clients and co-therapists. Formal methods of assessing therapists delivering clinical programs may involve checklists with one column listing behaviors in the expected performance of the therapist and another column for the manager to mark if the therapist displayed each desired behavior. A rating scale could also be used to assess therapists on items representing the different tasks in their job descriptions, with the manager rating the extent to which they achieved each task while conducting a program. Another method is the use of anecdotal recordings by the manager, who describes technical and interpersonal skills exhibited by a therapist on a particular occasion. In addition to assessing staff for performance appraisals, managers can also apply information from informal and formal methods to assess if programs are being conducted as planned.

Once the staff member's assessment has been completed, the first-line manager meets the staff member to discuss the individual's performance. Hopefully, the meeting will be constructive and result in improved performance of the employee being evaluated. The purpose of conducting performance appraisals is to assess and improve the performance of the staff being evaluated. The performance appraisal also provides evaluation information that can be used as a basis for pay raises, promotions, demotions, or terminations.

New employees are typically provided a performance appraisal following a probationary period (e.g., after 6 months). Typically, formal employee performance appraisals are conducted annually. However, feedback should be provided to each individual on a continuing basis. Of course, the manager needs to maintain ongoing documentation regarding employee job performance.

Most recreational therapists who have participated in performance appraisals will attest that the interview is typically stressful for the first-line manager conducting the interview and the employee being evaluated. Thus, first-line managers need to do their best to conduct the evaluation in a professional manner, yet set as relaxed a tone as possible to lessen the stress of participants. To neutralize the position of the power of the manager, the interview may be conducted in a private conference room, rather than in the manager's office, with seating arrangements that help create a collegial environment. The manager should promote an atmosphere throughout the interview that reinforces that the purpose of the meeting is to have two-way communication that will result in the manager and employee working together to improve the staff member's performance. Carter et al. (2014) offered suggestions for ensuring a productive assessment appraisal interview:

- Realize most employees believe they are meeting expectations and are surprised to hear otherwise.
- Focus on two or three specific areas needing improvement.
- Specify a follow-up plan to assess progress in the specific areas needing improvement and set review dates.
- Close the interview with positive comments that include praise and gratitude for work well done and express confidence in the employee's ability to improve and meet expected levels of performance. (p. 149)

Organizations typically provide a performance appraisal form for the first-line manager to complete prior to the formal interview. At the end of the interview session, the usual protocol is for the employee to sign the completed evaluation form, and then it is filed in the individual's personnel file. The manager and employee may then work together to prepare a performance improvement action plan that prioritizes areas needed to improve the employee's performance. Of course, individuals who consistently display high levels of performance and growth should be provided with positive feedback to reinforce their behaviors and motivate them toward further achievement.

Individual Performance Improvement

Many organizations have a form for use by the manager and employee in preparing a performance improvement action plan. The aim is to assist the staff member by developing concrete steps to take to improve performance. For instance, the first-line manager may stipulate that certain readings be completed by the employee and that the employee meet with the manager to discuss the readings to ensure the employee comprehends them. Next, the action plan may call for the manager to observe the performance of the employee to determine if the concepts obtained from the readings are displayed in the employee's work and provide feedback to the employee.

"Hard work never killed anybody, but why take a chance?"

Edgar Bergen

Disciplinary Steps

Should an employee be performing poorly, Carter et al. (2014) suggested a series of steps for the first-line manager to adopt in disciplining the employee:

1. *Verbal reprimand*: In this initial step, the manager meets with the employee to discuss the performance deficiency and means for improvement. The manager may document this meeting in the employee's personnel file.

2. *Written warning*: A formal written reprimand is the next step. The manager meets with the employee and presents the written warning that states the violations and the consequences of any further violations, as well as the expectations for actions to take to make corrections in order to avoid further violations. Both the manager and employee should have copies of the reprimand document. Most organizational procedures permit the employee to respond in writing to the reprimand. The reprimand contains a specific time period after which the employee and manager will again meet to discuss whether the employee has complied with the expectations set forth.

3. *Final written warning*: If the employee fails to perform at an appropriate level, a final written warning is issued and the employee is suspended without pay for a period of time.

4. *Terminate*: Dismissal is the final step in disciplining an employee. Some employees will agree to resign, rather than be fired. (p. 150)

During the steps in any disciplinary procedures, first-line managers should always work closely with the human resources department to be sure they are correctly following the organization's procedures and are documenting on the proper forms. First-line managers also need to obtain from the human resources department the grievance procedures followed within the organization by employees who may have formal complaints.

Controlling and Managing Risk

Welcoming Risk

Risk taking is an inherent aspect of healthcare work. Mistakes can be made, and this is not a reason to never try something new or to keep doing things the same old way, neglecting procedures that need to be improved. Porter-O'Grady and Malloch (2013) emphasized the need for rational risk taking:

Risk taking has not been perceived as a positive leadership behavior, nor is it traditionally welcomed and encouraged. Instead, risk taking is viewed negatively and as something that increases the organization's exposure to unforeseen hazards and to loss of new income and reputation. Playing it safe and being a hardworking employee is the more preferred behavior, but the reality is that playing it safe will lead the organization nowhere because the intent is to live in the past and continue the practices that have been deemed to work yesterday. (p. 55)

Thus, some risk taking should be seen as appropriate so recreational therapists or other healthcare professionals do not get locked into old patterns because they are frightened to take risks. New ways of offering optimal client care should be brought into practice, especially when old ways do not work well. Choices made in providing client care that are rational and carefully considered should be put in place even though staff may have to learn new skills. In short, some level of risk taking should be embraced to move the organization forward in providing quality care (Porter-O'Grady & Malloch, 2013).

Porter-O'Grady and Malloch (2013) presented strategies to minimize risk when making innovations. Their first strategy to minimize risk is to speak up when change is needed. Of course, the suggested changes need to be evidence based. The second strategy is not to rush change but to ensure the timing is right for its adoption. Staff need to communicate with one another and look carefully at current dogma and raise issues so new approaches may be considered to improve services. The third strategy is for the organization to encourage upward communication so staff ideas reach decision makers. Staff need to realize leaders do know everything and to share information respectfully with those in decision-making positions. The fourth strategy is for staff to develop their personal competence so they are knowledgeable about current evidence-based practices and can bring forth new concepts to those who are risk avoidant. The final strategy is to admit mistakes, to apologize quickly, and then to discuss ways to avoid repeating them.

Risk Management Programs to Minimize Risks

All healthcare institutions today have a risk manager (Kavaler & Alexander, 2014; Roussel, 2009), but risk management should also be a concern of RT first-line managers because they are in a position to have firsthand knowledge of the specific policies and procedures being followed by RT staff. Of course, the RT first-line manager can turn to the risk manager for advice and consultation.

All healthcare staff, including those in RT, should receive risk management education during their orientations and again annually. Kavaler and Alexander (2014) suggested that during in-service training the following be covered:

- Organization and goals of the risk management program
- "Patients' Bill of Rights"
- Patient relations and complaint program
- Incident-reporting program
- Reporting responsibilities for alleged professional misconduct
- Safety program and department-specific safety practices (p. 22)

As is true for other therapies, within RT, risks are unavoidable. It is human to make mistakes, so risks cannot be eliminated completely. Risks can, however, be minimized. Minimizing risks is the concern of risk management.

Risk Management Defined

Because outcomes are not always as expected, uncertainty needs to be reduced as much as possible. This is why organizations have risk management programs. As defined by Kelly (2010), "risk-management programs in health care organizations are designed to identify and correct system problems that contribute to errors in patient care or to employee injury" (p. 335).

Kavaler and Alexander (2014) specifically defined risk management for healthcare entities: "Risk management for healthcare entities can be defined as an organized effort to identify, assess, and reduce, when appropriate, risks to patients, visitors, staff, and organizational assets" (p. 5). Kavaler and Alexander also provided a second definition: "Risk management is a program designed to reduce the incidence of preventable accidents and injuries to minimize the financial loss to the institution should an injury or accident occur" (p. 5).

Solely from a financial perspective, risk management has the following goals:

- Reducing the organization's risk of a malpractice suit by maintaining or improving quality of care
- Reducing the probability of a claim being filed after a potentially compensable event (PCE) has occurred
- Preserving the institution's assets once a claim has been filed (Kavaler & Alexander, 2014, p. 10)

Thus, risk management is about having strategies that minimize the possibility of an adverse outcome that would harm a patient or client. Risk management is also typically concerned with staff and visitor safety. The goal of risk management is to improve the quality of care provided to clients; to ensure client, staff, and visitor safety; and to ultimately reduce malpractice costs to the healthcare organization. Marriner Tomey (2009) listed specific goals of risk management programs: (a) to provide patients, staff, and visitors safety and prevent injury or harm to all concerned; (b) to avoid liability exposure by evaluating new and existing services, practices, and procedures, including consultation with a professional liability carrier; (c) to maintain an incident-reporting system to identify trends and patterns of practice and occurrences with the potential of causing an adverse occurrence and to improve measures to prevent such events; and (d) to maintain a quality improvement program to identify areas of risk in specific clinical applications and reduce their untoward effect on client care (p. 482).

Risk Events

Whitehead, Weiss, and Tappen (2007) listed several risk events: (a) service occurrences that do not result in a clinically significant interruption of services and that are without apparent client or employee injury (e.g., minor equipment damage); (b) serious incidents in which there is a significant interruption of therapy, minor injury to a client or employee, or significant damage of equipment or property; and (c) sentinel events involving serious adverse outcomes, such as an unexpected death or serious physical or psychological injury (or "risk thereof"). These events are termed sentinel events because they require an immediate investigation and response.

Steps in Risk Management Programs

Steps in risk management programs include (a) risk identification, (b) risk evaluation, (c) risk management strategies, and (d) risk management implementation and reporting. The four steps in risk management programs are illustrated in Figure 9.1.

Figure 9.1. Steps in the risk management process.

Thus, during the first step of risk identification, RT managers need to identify potential and actual risks and safety concerns. One means to identify risk is to describe events that may occur during the RT process (e.g., failure to identify a client need during assessment, not following protocols or standards, and errors in documentation). Another way to ascertain risks is to identify potential hazards that may cause safety concerns (e.g., slippery surfaces by pools or in shower areas, uneven surfaces or protruding objects, improper safety rule enforcement). Concerns may arise through means such as incident reports, quality reviews or audits, and state inspections. "Red flags" that should alert healthcare providers to take actions to correct risk management concerns are summarized in Table 9.1.

Table 9.1

"Red Flags" for Risk Management Actions

- Treatment Conditions: poor treatment results, repetition of a problem, lack of follow-up care, and equipment malfunction
- Patient Relations: dissatisfied patients, antagonistic patient or family members, complaining relatives, patient discharged against medical advice, intimidated patient, poor physician–patient relationship, and poor staff–patient relationship
- Practice Management: poorly maintained medical records, lack of critical policies and procedures, and excessive volume of patients
- Conduct of Staff: acting outside the scope of training, lack of qualified supervision, performance of a procedure for the first time without supervision, outspoken or rude behavior, personality conflict, and poor physician–staff relationship

Note. From *Risk Management in Healthcare Institutions* (3rd ed., p. 11), by F. Kavaler and R. S. Alexander, 2014, Burlington, MA: Jones & Bartlett Learning.

During risk evaluation, a review of errors and threats is conducted. The severity of occurrences or the frequency of problems is analyzed to categorize them as representing high, medium, or low risks. Risk management strategies involve ways to control the consequences of risk issues. Perhaps the easiest strategy (termed avoidance) is to simply do away with the service or activity because it is too risky. Another strategy (termed reduction) minimizes the frequency or severity of potential incidents using planning procedures, staff training, information management, and improved procedures. A third strategy is retention, in which the organization accepts there always will be risk and therefore makes fee adjustments or self-insures to cover potential losses. The final strategy of transference involves financial risks being assumed by means such as hold-harmless clauses or commercial insurance. Once strategies have been selected and are in place, policies and practices in line with them are prepared for staff to follow. The final step is risk management implementation and reporting. This step involves (a) ensuring each unit's policies and procedures documents incorporate all aspects of the plan; (b) following all practices while providing staff with continuing education and training; and (c) evaluating and reporting goals. The RT manager, while monitoring the plan's goals, may need to recommend possible preventive or corrective actions. Typically, based on their continual evaluations, RT managers make reports to the risk manager. Wise RT managers involve personnel (i.e., staff, volunteers, interns) from their unit when recommending policies and procedures (Carter et al., 2014).

To conclude this segment on risk management, a number of critical items that RT managers may wish to consider to minimize risks and enhance the quality of the clinical program provided by their unit are provided in Table 9.2.

Table 9.2
Means to Minimize Risks and Enhance the Quality of Care

- Care needs to be driven by the needs of clients.
- Staff need to communicate with clients regularly and keep them informed.
- Staff need to treat clients with kindness and respect.
- Recreational therapists need to be reflective practitioners who strive for continuous care improvements.
- Recreational therapists need to have access to professional standards of practice through professional organizations and evidence-based practices through continuing education (e.g., professional literature, conferences, and workshops).
- Documentation procedures need to be followed closely and should include reporting on client outcomes. Good charting practices can decrease liability risks.
- New recreational therapy graduates must not be assigned to duties beyond their competencies.
- Managers need to ensure staff have the competencies and skills and the documented education to provide the levels of care demanded of them.
- Managers need to see for themselves what is occurring within their programs to grasp situations thoroughly.
- Managers need to make sure to have sufficient numbers of qualified recreational therapists to conduct the programs offered by the unit.
- Managers need to build a culture of fixing problems to get quality right.
- Managers need to establish clear policies and procedures for all programs and strive to improve them when warranted.
- Policies and procedures need to be clear for all areas, including delegation, supervision, and the chain of command to be followed.
- Staff need to have the skills and competencies to care for the clients they serve (e.g., being prepared to serve older clients with chronic conditions).
- Staff need to be aware of the latest techniques and best practices.
- Staff need to ensure, to the greatest extent possible, that clients have a good experience in recreational therapy.
- Staff need to acknowledge unfortunate incidents and show concern for these events without taking the blame, blaming others, or reacting defensively.

Controlling Service Quality

Tracing the evolution of quality in healthcare services gives some indication of the controlling function. For example, the Joint Commission on Accreditation of Healthcare Organizations (JCAHO) first developed standards to accredit hospitals in 1953, but not until 1975 did the first standards specifically addressing the quality of care appear (McCormick, 2003). Prior to 1975, the basic assumption appeared to be that healthcare providers would implicitly provide quality care (Scalenghe, 1991). By 1996, the Joint Commission was no longer including standards specific to service quality, but had instead evolved to standards related to *performance improvement*

(McCormick, 2003). This evolution in the Joint Commission's standards reflected the evolution in healthcare quality from a system known as quality assurance, to continuous quality improvement and performance improvement.

The critical issue of quality services in healthcare was brought to public attention first in the Institute of Medicine's (IOM, 2000) report *To Err Is Human: Building a Safer Health Care System*. This report identified that as many as 98,000 deaths annually were due to medical errors. This was soon followed by another IOM (2001) report, *Crossing the Quality Chasm: A New Health System for the 21ˢᵗ Century*, which sought to identify ways that the healthcare system in the United States could be designed to improve care. This report advocated that the highest quality healthcare has the aims of safe, effective, patient-centered, timely, efficient, and equitable services (Table 9.3). Thus, the IOM's initial report focused on the safety of services and the goal of eliminating medical errors, and the subsequent report asserted that eliminating errors was only one dimension of high-quality services.

Table 9.3
Institute of Medicine's Six Aims for High-Quality Healthcare

- *Safe.* avoiding injuries to patient from the care that is intended to help them.
- *Effective.* providing services based on scientific knowledge to all who could benefit and refraining from provided services to those not likely to benefit (avoiding underuse and overuse, respectively).
- *Patient-centered.* providing care that is respectful of and responsive to individual patient preferences, needs, and values and ensuring that patient values guide all clinical decisions.
- *Timely.* reducing waits and sometimes harmful delays for both those who receive and those who give care.
- *Efficient.* avoiding waste, including waste of equipment, supplies, ideas, and energy.
- *Equitable.* providing care that does not vary in quality because of personal characteristics such as gender, ethnicity, geographic location, and socioeconomic status.

Note. From *Crossing the Quality Chasm: A New Health System for the 21ˢᵗ Century* (pp. 5-6). by Institute of Medicine, 2001, Washington, DC: National Academies Press. Copyright 2001 by National Academy of Sciences. Reprinted with permission.

Identifying High-Quality Services

Most discussions of quality of services begin with Donabedian's (1986) model of the elements of quality. In this model, the quality of a service is dependent upon (a) the structures in place, (b) the processes that occur, and (c) the outcomes that result. This framework is pervasive in health services, and the American Therapeutic Recreation Association (ATRA, 2013) Standards of Practice (SOP) follow this framework. At its most basic description, structural elements of care are likely to lead to high-quality services. These often include written plans of operation, policies defining staff–client ratios, and the credentialing of staff, as a few examples. One problem with evaluating the quality of care on structural elements alone is that although the presence of these structures is assumed to lead to high-quality care, this is not always the result. The healthcare provider being credentialed may meet a structural standard; however, across all credentialed providers there is great variability in expertise, knowledge, and skill. Process elements of high-quality service focus on the things that are done and how they are done. For example, when and how the assessment process is conducted provides a way to examine this process element of services. Part of the challenge in examining the quality related to services is that it may be hard to observe. This is where completeness and accuracy of the record of care become important (Donabedian 1985). In health services, a frequent saying is, "If it wasn't documented, it didn't happen." Finally, outcome elements of quality identify the results of activities. Examples of outcome elements include achieving treatment goals, client satisfaction with services, and engaging in the discharge plan. Although there is a current emphasis on outcomes as a clear indicator of the quality of care, structures and processes produce outcomes. Without knowing the elements of service producing outcomes, it is difficult to institute practices to control them.

Care Monitoring and Evaluation

With an understanding of the ways to examine the quality of services, managers now have to translate that into actions that allow them to monitor and determine if the care the unit is providing meets quality expectations. The place to begin this process is through establishing standards that identify structural, process, and outcome expectations for practice. Within RT, the ATRA (2013) SOP are the best starting place. At the same time, RT managers need to consider if agency-wide standards related to organizational accrediting bodies, such as the Joint Commission (formerly JCAHO) or the Commission on Accreditation of Rehabilitation Facilities (CARF International), apply to elements of RT services. Finally, managers need to identify if state or federal regulations apply to the provision of RT services in their agency.

Identification of standards is only the first step. For example, although more than 100 structure, process, and outcome criteria are related to the 12 standards in the ATRA SOP, many of them require specification to the nature of service. For example, ATRA process criteria 1.2.1 related to assessment identifies that the recreational therapist responds to orders and requests for RT assessment in a timely manner. The challenge is that what constitutes timely in an inpatient psychiatric facility (IPF) with an average length of stay of 3–5 days is considerably different from what constitutes timely in a long-term care facility (LTC) in which the average length of stay may be in months or years. Another challenge is that although it is important to examine an RT service's compliance with all applicable standards and criteria, keeping track of this volume of information becomes difficult to manage because it requires significant staff resources (e.g., time) to gather, which takes these resources away from the provision of care.

One approach to managing this large volume of quality criteria is the use of care *indicators* that highlight critical aspects of care (Mainz, 2003a). Through the identification of and tracking performance against indicators, managers can determine if high-quality services are being provided as well as have some indication of where to begin to investigate if services are falling short. One place to begin to identify useful indicators is by considering aspects of care that may be considered high volume, high acuity, or high cost (Mainz, 2003b). For example, within RT services assessment is likely to be high volume and high acuity, as all other service is influenced by the quality of the assessment process and outcomes. Poor assessment processes may be linked to poor assessment outcomes, which have a lower probability of producing effective intervention services. Examples of clinical indicators that might be developed relevant to RT services in a specific setting are provided in Table 9.4.

Once indicators are developed, two other useful elements of care monitoring and evaluation should be developed. First, it is useful to define the *data source* to identify where the indicator should appear in the record of services. As noted, without documentation, making determinations about the nature of care is difficult. Second, it is useful to define a threshold or target compliance rate. Carter et al. (2014) indicated that these are frequently identified as a percentage of cases in which the service complies with the indicator, but setting this at 100% is unrealistic. The idea behind these targets is that when service performance drops below the threshold or compliance rate, the manager has to investigate to determine the causes behind performance that are not meeting the target. At the same time, in a continuous quality improvement or performance improvement model, the philosophical goal is 100% success on the indicators. Finally, the example thresholds in Table 9.4 are based on the assumption that the assessment processes and treatment plan structures are within the control of recreational therapists, but the discharge outcomes are dependent upon a number of factors beyond the control of recreational therapists.

Table 9.4

Examples of Clinical Indicators

Assessment	*Indicator:* Assessment is completed within 72 hours of referral and identifies client's strengths and limitations in the areas of physical, cognitive, social, and behavioral/emotional functional independence in life activities.
	Data Source: Assessment summary in client record of care
	Threshold: 95%
Planning	*Indicator:* When referred, recreational therapy services are included within the individualized plan of care with measurable functional goals described in behavioral terms with a time frame for achievement.
	Data Source: Individualized plan of services
	Threshold: 95%
Discharge Plan	*Indicator:* Client benefits from RT services as documented by achievement of treatment goals.
	Data Source: Discharge Plan
	Threshold: 90%

The final component of the care monitoring and evaluation plan is to develop the monitoring period. In this aspect of the management of the quality of RT services, the manager has to identify the review cycle. Review cycles are best determined based on knowledge of client length of stay and volume of services provided. Again, the manager must balance the staff resources required to monitor care and resources required to provide care. For services with a high volume of clients, with shorter lengths of stay, a shorter review cycle, such as monthly, may be warranted. The logic here is that if there are quality concerns, they are caught earlier, and thus, fewer clients may be affected. In services with longer lengths of stay and a lower volume of clients, a longer review cycle, such as quarterly, may be appropriate.

The RT Manager and Overseeing Rules and Regulations

Every first-line RT manager needs to display a strong commitment to the rules and regulations of the unit. It is important that the manager completely understand and subscribe to the rules and regulations of the unit. This sets a good example for staff and establishes a positive tone for following established rules and regulations. The job of the first-line manager is to instill in employees a feeling of responsibility to deliver quality performances by following written rules and regulations.

As should be evident from the previous segment on controlling service quality, rules and regulations are put in place by RT units to meet SOP, such as those established by ATRA (2013). The self-assessment guide provided in the ATRA SOP affords means to assess written plans of operation, audit documentation, assess treatment outcomes, evaluate staff competency, and evaluate clinical performance. The rules and regulations of governmental agencies (i.e., state and federal) and accreditation bodies (e.g., Joint Commission, CARF International) related to the delivery of RT services are equally important.

Budget Planning and Monitoring

As indicated in Chapter 5, RT managers are apt to be directly involved in developing and maintaining operating budgets that contain statements of revenues and expenses. Operating budgets account for the income and expenses associated with the day-to-day activities of an RT unit.

The planning of operating budgets includes the determination of costs by cost accounting to provide data on the amount of resources required to provide a service. Another part of determining operating budgets is determining charges that will bring in revenue (Kelly, 2010; Nowicki, 2008). Detailed explanations of these procedures are presented in Chapter 5. In maintaining operating budgets, first-line RT managers monitor the allocations for supplies and equipment, as well as other operating expenses, to ensure that they do not exceed budgeted funds. Because budget preparation and monitoring can be complicated, it is suggested that when preparing budgets RT managers work closely with financial officers within their organization.

Summary

It should be clear that the controlling function is the means to accomplishing the ends established during planning. Through controlling, the goals and objectives of the unit are realized. As in client planning, in the controlling function when it is discovered that the goals and objectives are not realistic, they are modified. Controlling is a budgeting function to ensure that finances are in line with the operating budget.

Controlling involves managers meeting financial criteria but also includes controlling processes, procedures, and policies related to service delivery.

Managers must consider a number of aspects to carrying out controlling responsibilities. These include maintaining clear communications with staff so they understand the goals and objectives being sought through their performances and the standards being employed to reach them, establishing a positive tone and a mutual trust between the manager and staff, and recruiting and retaining talented staff capable of self-controlling. At the same time, managers must realize it is rare that a perfect correspondence exists between the deemed goals and objectives and the actual outcomes.

First-line RT managers have the primary responsibility for the daily operating activities of their unit. Thus, they should have a master plan for control that incorporates standards related to the operations for which they are responsible. Elements involved will likely include evaluating the performance of individuals (performance appraisal), controlling and managing risk, evaluating the quality of care, overseeing the rules and regulations that are in force within the service, and planning and monitoring the budget.

References

American Therapeutic Recreation Association. (2013). *Standards for the practice of recreational therapy and self-assessment guide.* Hattiesburg, MS: Author.

Carter, M. J., Smith, C. G., & O'Morrow G. S. (2014). *Effective management in therapeutic recreation service* (3rd ed.). State College, PA: Venture.

Donabedian, A. (1985). Twenty years of research on the quality of medical care. *Evaluation and the Health Professions, 8,* 243–265.

Donabedian, A. (1986). Criteria and standards for quality assessment and monitoring. *Quality Review Bulletin, 12*(3), 99–108.

Dunn, R. T. (2007). *Haimann's supervisory management for healthcare organizations* (8th ed.). Chicago, IL: Health Administration Press.

Institute of Medicine. (2000). *To err is human: Building a safer health system.* Washington, DC: National Academies Press.

Institute of Medicine. (2001). *Crossing the quality chasm: A new health system for the 21st century.* Washington, DC: National Academies Press.

Kavaler, F., & Alexander, R. S. (2014). *Risk management in healthcare institutions* (3rd ed.). Burlington, MA: Jones & Bartlett Learning.

Kelly, P. (2010). *Essentials of nursing leadership & management* (2nd ed.). Clifton Park, NY: Delmar Cengage Learning.

Mainz, J. (2003a). Defining and classifying clinical indicators for quality improvement. *International Journal for Quality in Health Care, 15,* 523–530.

Mainz, J. (2003b). Developing evidence-based clinical indicators: A state of the art methods primer. *International Journal for Quality in Health Care, 15*(Suppl. 1), i5–i11.

Marriner Tomey, A. (2009). *Guide to nursing management and leadership* (8th ed.). St. Louis, MO: Mosby Elsevier.

McConnell, C. R. (2014). *Umiker's management skills for the new health care supervisor* (6th ed.). Burlington, MA: Jones & Bartlett Learning.

McCormick, B. P. (2003). Outcomes measurement as a tool for performance improvement. In N. Stumbo (Ed.), *Client outcomes in therapeutic recreation services* (pp. 221–231). State College, PA: Venture.

Nowicki, M. (2008). *The financial management of hospitals and healthcare organizations.* (4th ed.). Chicago, IL: Health Administration Press.

Porter-O'Grady, T., & Malloch, K. (2013). *Leadership in nursing practice.* Burlington, MA: Jones & Bartlett Learning.

Roussel, L. (2009). *Management and leadership for nurse administrators* (5th ed.). Boston, MA: Jones & Bartlett.

Scalenghe, R. (1991). The Joint Commission's "Agenda for Change" as related to the provision of therapeutic recreation services. In B. Riley (Ed.), *Quality management: Applications for therapeutic recreation* (pp. 29–42). State College, PA: Venture.

Whitehead, D., Weiss, S. A., Tappen, R. (2007). *Essentials of nursing leadership and management* (4th ed.). Philadelphia, PA: FA Davis.

Chapter 10

Internship Supervision

Objectives

- Define the term *internship.*
- Define the term *fieldwork.*
- Describe what is meant by the term *site supervisor.*
- Describe what is meant by the term *academic supervisor.*
- List two or more benefits of conducting internship programs.
- Describe the minimum requirements for someone to serve as a site supervisor.
- Identify major student concerns when selecting an internship site.
- Describe the importance of having the endorsement of the internship program by staff, the first-line manager, and the agency administration.
- Analyze the list of items to consider when planning the internship program and then determine which three to five you believe are most important.
- Explain why gaining knowledge of college and university internship manuals is important for affiliated agencies.
- List what you believe are the top five functions of site supervisors and be prepared to defend your determination.
- List at least three qualities involved in good supervision.
- Explain which role the site supervisor will most likely assume in clinical supervision.
- Explain possible tasks of the first-line manager, site supervisor, and internship coordinator prior to the arrival of student interns at the agency.
- Identify three to five activities that typically occur during the first week of orientation.
- Identify three to five activities that typically occur during the second week of orientation.
- Explain how the theme of continually increasing the responsibilities of interns is reflected in the schedule developed for them.

Key Terms

- **Internship:** An extensive full-time capstone field placement accomplished under a credentialed recreational therapist who provides supervision for an intern.

- **Fieldwork or practicum:** The term *fieldwork* is typically used to describe hands-on practical field experiences completed by students prior to the internship. The term *practicum* is sometimes used to describe field experiences that occur prior to the internship.
- **Site supervisor:** The recreational therapist at the agency who provides direct supervision for the intern for the duration of the internship.
- **Academic supervisor:** The university representative who advises the student intern throughout the internship.

The internship is the final phase of academic preparation and, as such, the pinnacle experience in professional preparation. It is a full-time capstone field placement accomplished under a credentialed recreational therapist. Completing an internship is a necessity for recreational therapy (RT) students who wish to become credentialed professionals. Because the internship is a vital element in the professional preparation of RT students, it needs to be well structured, and high-quality supervision should be provided throughout the experience. Ideally, the internship should provide supportive supervision, structured learning experiences, and on-the-job training. Agencies that offer internships have to recognize the crucial nature of the internship and look upon carrying out an internship program as a weighty responsibility. This chapter focuses on the roles and responsibilities of the first-line manager, the site supervisor, and the agency in providing the RT internship.

> "Tell me and I forget,
> Teach me and I may remember,
> Involve me and I learn."
>
> Benjamin Franklin

Defining the Term Internship in Recreational Therapy

Beck, in a presentation at the 2013 Illinois Recreation Therapy Association Conference, defined the RT internship as a "means by which a student translates knowledge into clinical skills and abilities in a structured, supervised setting." She went on to define the internship being completed at one agency for at least 14 consecutive weeks, with a minimum of 560 hours being completed under a credentialed supervisor. The parameters indicated by Beck match those required by the National Council for Therapeutic Recreation Certification (NCTRC), which are the standards typically followed in the completion of RT internships, although the NCTRC (2014a) offers an alternative of interns completing 20 hours/week for 28 weeks to meet the required minimum of 560 hours.

The NCTRC (2014a) defined the internship in the following manner:

Highly structured, field-centered and professionally supervised: An acceptable field placement must have one (1) identified primary agency supervisor. The primary supervisor works on a consistent basis with the student, coordinates all other secondary supervision and completes all evaluation materials and weekly reports pertaining to the field placement experience. An acceptable internship must be based on the therapeutic recreation process as defined by the knowledge and tasks in the current NCTRC Job Analysis. This means the student must have exposure to all areas of the current NCTRC National Job Analysis. Additionally, the internship program should be well established at the agency. If an internship program and agency manual is not available, the student should question how the field placement experience will be structured to insure the student completes the necessary knowledge and tasks for professional eligibility. The student may investigate how professional supervision will be conducted in practice. The primary supervisor is the one who works on a consistent basis with the student. The professional should not merely sign their CTRS on student evaluations. (p. 13)

From the definitions provided by Beck and the NCTRC, RT internships clearly allow students to integrate academic knowledge with clinical practice through a structured experiential learning process under the guidance of a supervisor. Through the internship, the intern should acquire clinical skills and understandings of what is involved in being a professional. This experience needs to cover all areas identified by the 2007 NCTRC "Job Tasks and Knowledge Areas for the Certified Therapeutic Recreation Specialists" as they appear in the NCTRC (2014a) *Certification Standards Part II*.

Other Terms Related to the Internship

In addition to the term *internship*, several other terms are used within the context of the RT internship. These include *fieldwork, intern, site supervisor,* and *academic supervisor*. The term *fieldwork* or *practicum* is typically used to describe the practical experiences gained by students as prerequisites to the internship. Fieldwork assignments provide students with hands-on experiences with clients, to help them begin to assess themselves as helping professionals. *Intern* is the term applied to the university student engaged in an internship. Students have to complete the majority of their RT coursework to be eligible to become an intern. The term *site supervisor* is used to describe the recreational therapist at the agency who provides clinical supervision for the intern during the duration of the internship. This individual has to have a strong clinical practice background and must be certified by the NCTRC for the intern to meet NCTRC standards. The *academic supervisor* is the university representative who advises the student intern throughout the internship. Like the site supervisor, this individual needs to be certified by the NCTRC. The academic supervisor's responsibility is to assign the student intern a grade for the internship following a formal evaluation of the intern by the site supervisor. It is common practice for the academic supervisor and intern to have regular communications throughout the internship and for the academic supervisor to visit the student intern at the agency during the internship. Typically, while on site, the academic supervisor speaks with the intern and the site supervisor and observes the intern conducting a program.

Benefits of Conducting Internship Programs

There are a number of benefits to having an internship program. Boeve presented the following benefits of having an intern at the 2013 Michigan Therapeutic Recreation Association Conference:

- Keep abreast of new information or trends at the university level by learning from your student.
- Hone your skills by instructing others.
- Lessen your workload or increase productivity, as the intern is able to take on more responsibilities.
- Increase your creativity by brainstorming with others (the intern) for programming.
- It is rewarding and satisfying to be a mentor for your dedicated profession and to contribute to the skill set in qualified, educated, and excellent CTRS practitioners.

Another advantage experienced by the authors of this text when working as site supervisors with student interns was having to respond to the inquisitive nature of interns who asked many "why" questions. At times, the authors found that they were challenged to think, as they did not have ready answers as to why they did some things a certain way. This helped them to stop and ponder exactly why they did things. It caused them to be thoughtful, rather than habitual, in their clinical practices.

Finally, internship supervisors can obtain continuing education (CE) credit for providing internship supervision. Since July 1, 2014, NCTRC standards allow for up to 2 CE credits per recertification cycle for those overseeing interns. Further information on the NCTRC CE program can be found in the *NCTRC Internship Supervision Guidelines for Continuing Education Credit* (NCTRC, 2014b).

The Internship From the Student's Perspective: Students Selecting an Internship Site

Agencies should keep in mind that student interns need to give a great deal of consideration to the selection of the internship site. Key factors in the student internship selection process include (a) the student's own needs and (b) the learning opportunities afforded them by the agency.

Students should have in mind what type of client they wish to work with (e.g., older adults, adults, adolescents, children), the area of practice (e.g., physical medicine and rehabilitation, mental health, substance abuse), and what type of setting they prefer (e.g., inpatient or outpatient, or fast-paced or slow-paced, or short-term or long-term facility).

Students also need to think about the educational opportunities at potential sites. For example, students should inquire about how much direct client contact they will have. Will they be treated as a true member of the treatment team, or will they be discredited because they are a student? Will they get the support and supervision required during an internship? Will they be exposed to evidence-based practice? Will standardized instruments be used in outcome measurement? Therefore, agencies should prepare to help students think about themselves and their personal needs as well as to interpret what the agency has to offer.

Prospective student interns and agencies should know that universities typically maintain written evaluations of the experiences that prior interns have had at each agency where the university places students, and students have access to these evaluations when selecting an internship placement site. Therefore, agencies naturally wish to perform well to achieve positive evaluations from student interns.

Establishing the Internship

The first factor in establishing an internship is for the agency and staff to determine that providing training for students is a part of the agency mission. Without a strong commitment to student training by the agency and its staff, any internship program is destined to fail.

So first-line RT managers must meet with their staff to discuss the initial establishment of an internship program. If the staff are enthusiastic about establishing an internship program, first-line managers need to approach senior administrators (working in concert with their immediate supervisor) to gain their support for the internship program verbally and in writing.

Once staff members have indicated their support for hosting an internship program and it is set in place, the first-line manager should annually discuss the prospect of having interns for the approaching year so staff can discuss whether they have a continuing commitment and available resources to maintain the internship program.

Of course, a necessary element central to inaugurating or continuing an internship program is having a person on staff with the credentials and clinical expertise to assume the role of the site supervisor who provides the direct clinical supervision of the intern. At a minimum, the site supervisor must be a Certified Therapeutic Recreation Specialist (CTRS) credentialed by the NCTRC, and when applicable, the individual should also hold state certification, licensure, or registration. Additionally, the site supervisor needs to be a full-time employee of the agency. Furthermore, it is recommended that at a minimum the site supervisor have 2 years of clinical experience and have been on the agency's staff for at least 1 year (Grote & Hasl, 2003).

Initiating Planning for Internships

Agreement by the administration and staff to establish an internship program must be followed by planning the internship program. The first-line manager may play a direct role in developing an internship program or may delegate the responsibility to a group of therapists on the staff. The decision for the first-line manager rests, at least in part, on the size of the staff within the RT unit. The first-line manager will most likely take direct responsibility for planning the internship program when the staff is small in size. With a larger sized staff, the first-line manager may delegate the responsibility for planning the program.

Occasionally, when the RT department is under a larger unit (e.g., rehabilitation services), an internship coordinator oversees all internship programs (e.g., for RT, occupational therapy, and music therapy). This individual handles administrative issues, and the site supervisor is responsible for the direct day-to-day clinical supervision provided to the intern. In such cases, the internship coordinator and site supervisor should work together to plan, coordinate, and market the RT internship program (Grote & Hasl, 2003).

When an overall internship coordinator exists, that individual is normally responsible for setting up and maintaining formal agreements or contracts between colleges and universities and the agency. When no agency internship coordinator exists, the first-line manager would likely handle getting approval for formal agreements or contracts between the agency and colleges and universities. In either case, agreements or contracts normally have to be approved and signed by senior managers before they are put into place.

Components to Consider in Internship Planning

Grote and Hasl (2003) outlined the following components of comprehensive internship planning:

- Goals and objectives of the internship.
- Agency expectations of the intern.
- Description of the agency and the particular program or service unit where the intern will work.
- A statement about a required affiliation agreement between the academic curriculum and the agency, and any required agreement between the agency and student.
- What assistance the agency offers the intern in terms of locating housing, stipends, meals, parking, immunizations, access to medical libraries, work space, keys, identification badges, books and other resources.
- The hours of operation of the RT program and the intern's work schedule.
- Intern selection criteria.
- Policies and procedures governing issues such as: illness on the part of the intern or site supervisor; requesting a letter of recommendation; the intern's role in the professional environment; the agency's requirement for clinical supervision; the need to co-sign the intern's clinical documentation; the agency's return policy; what happens if the site supervisor is unable to complete supervision of the internship; and internship termination procedures.
- A performance schedule that outlines the intern's progression of daily and weekly tasks and responsibilities, so that the intern is taking on more complex activities throughout the internship.
- A position description of the duties and responsibilities of the intern.
- Prerequisites for the intern, including required coursework and/or readings, proof of liability insurance and required immunizations, fees that may be assessed to the student, confidentiality statements, and any required certifications such as CPR or first aid training.
- Application procedures, including an application form.
- Secure approval of the internship plan from the agency's administration.
- Develop a strategy for marketing internship opportunities.
- Review and evaluate applications for internships.

- When the selection is made, complete the affiliation agreement with the academic institution. This is often initiated by the agency, but may also be initiated by the college or university. Remember to allow sufficient time if legal decisions are necessary to develop an agreement between the agency and the college or university.
- Send a formal letter of acceptance to the student. (pp. 13–15)

Additionally, because of NCTRC requirements, in internship planning the agency should consider the site supervisor's obligations to be the direct supervisor of the internship student and to ensure that the student is exposed to the "Job Analysis Task Areas" outlined by the NCTRC. Furthermore, the primary site supervisor, who also serves as the liaison to the university, must sign official documentation, including midterm and final evaluations as well as the NCTRC field placement verification form. Additionally, the site supervisor needs to keep logs to provide evidence to verify the intern has completed the minimum number of hours and weeks (NCTRC, 2014a).

Once all of the components to be included in comprehensive internship planning have been addressed, they should be documented in an internship manual for the agency. Such documentation provides everyone involved with a written account of the policies and procedures to be followed. Copies of the agency's internship manual should be shared with the administration of the agency; RT staff; the internship coordinator (if one exists within the organization); universities or colleges with which the agency has agreements; and, of course, the intern.

Internship Manuals of Colleges and Universities

Like agencies, colleges and universities develop RT internship manuals to outline goals for the university internship program; their policies and procedures; and expectations for interns, university supervisors, and site supervisors. Wise agencies obtain internship manuals from colleges and universities with which they are affiliated to gain insights into the goals, policies, procedures, and expectations related to the responsibilities of not only interns but also academic and site supervisors (from the perspective of the colleges and universities).

The *Internship Manual* of the University of North Carolina at Wilmington (UNCW, 2014) is an example of a college or university internship manual. The UNCW manual strongly encourages agencies to provide student interns with weekly clinical supervision meetings in which interns discuss clinical issues, such as the client–therapist relationship or the progress of a client. The UNCW manual also lists the expectation that the site supervisor will meet with the student intern during the first week of the internship and use a format provided by the university for the student to establish learning objectives for the internship. Another university requirement is that the site supervisor meet with the intern to conduct midterm and final evaluations using an evaluation instrument provided by the university. In a fashion similar to most college and university internship manuals, the UNCW manual delineates "Student Responsibilities During Internship." This heading contains requirements that UNCW students must achieve to complete their internships successfully (e.g., biweekly reports to the academic supervisor).

Having knowledge of the requirements in college and university internship manuals is helpful to agencies. For instance, if several college and university internship manuals contain similar expectations or procedures, the agency may wish to incorporate these into its own internship manual. Also, knowing what is expected by colleges or universities ensures that the agency is willing and able to perform the tasks delineated in their manuals.

Site Supervisor's Responsibilities

Most college and university internship manuals list the responsibilities expected of site supervisors. Colleges and universities usually require that site supervisors become familiar with their internship manuals. Other responsibilities of the site supervisor that routinely appear in college and university internship manuals include assisting the intern to establish personal objectives for the internship; orienting the intern to the agency and its policies and procedures; acquainting the intern with the organizational hierarchy of the agency; holding a meeting each week with the intern; establishing weekly schedules for the intern; gradually increasing the responsibilities of the intern as the internship progresses; consulting with the academic supervisor regarding the intern's performance; preparing midterm and final evaluations of the intern and meeting with the intern to discuss these evaluations; and at the end of the internship, completing a form to verify the internship. Common functions of site supervisors appear in Table 10.1.

Almost all colleges and universities expect the site supervisor to have daily contact with the student intern. In addition, most colleges and universities call for the site supervisor to hold a weekly formal meeting with the intern. Some institutions expect that the weekly meeting will be largely organizational, focusing on issues such as scheduling or required student projects or reports. Colleges and universities with more sophisticated curricula, however, may wish to have their interns receive clinical supervision during the weekly meeting between the intern and site supervisor so their interns can examine their clinical skills and how they may be developed and enhanced. Clinical supervision offers the opportunity for interns to discuss clinical skills and their own performances with an experienced and accomplished clinician. The authors of this text believe the weekly meetings should involve the site supervisor providing clinical supervision for the intern. Skills in applying the RT process of assessment, planning, implementation, and evaluation are particularly important. The development of skills in clinical reasoning should be a focal point while helping student interns apply the RT process.

Table 10.1

Common Functions of Site Supervisors

1. Teaching student interns to follow the recreational therapy process (sometimes referred to as the APIE Process).
2. Providing emotional support for student interns.
3. Being available in times of crisis.
4. Helping students to develop strong collaborative relationships with clients.
5. Training students to complete client assessments.
6. Teaching students how to engage in clinical reasoning.
7. Training students to use intervention skills.
8. Developing students' skills in evaluation.
9. Developing students' skills in evidence-based practice by integrating research findings into practice.
10. Encouraging students to be realistic about their own limitations and strengths.
11. Helping students to understand the importance of developing good professional and personal support networks.
12. Developing students' awareness and skills for dealing with diverse clients.
13. Developing students' ethical awareness and decision-making skills.
14. Developing students' skills in using supervision time wisely.
15. Providing students with knowledge about opportunities for continuing professional and personal development.
16. Dealing with the formal administrative and evaluative aspects of supervision.

Note. Adapted from *Essential Counseling and Therapy Skills* (p. 341), by R. Nelson-Jones, 2002, Thousand Oaks, CA: Sage.

The Good Site Supervisor

Thomlison and Corcoran (2008) suggested three qualities involved in providing good supervision. These are (1) a supportive supervisory relationship, (2) opportunities for critical reflection and thinking, and (3) strategies for learning competency-based practices.

The *supervisory relationship* is perhaps the key to a successful internship. Good supervisors are supportive of interns, and interns see good supervisors as respected and accomplished clinicians who will recognize and promote the interns' personal strengths and abilities. Good supervisors also have the ability to empathize with interns in their struggles and take pride in their interns' accomplishments. Finally, good supervisors take time for interns and are approachable, are flexible, and model the qualities of being genuine and congruent.

In regard to *critical reflection and thinking,* Thomlison and Corcoran (2008) wrote:

Supervisors who use critical reflection and thinking processes turn novice learners into informed learners. Through the supportive supervisory relationship and open communication, these supervisors encourage students to actively explore alternative ways of thinking about practice and practice situations. (p. 103)

Thus, good supervisors use open communications to require student interns to critically examine themselves (i.e., beliefs and values) and their interpersonal and technical skills employed in practice.

The third component in good supervision, the provision of *strategies for evidence-based practice (EBP),* involves several elements. Supervisors need to demonstrate the mastery of EBP and to assist student interns to develop understandings and skills in applying EBP. This involves not only developing interns' clinical reasoning and skills, but also increasing their self-awareness of their professional competence.

Furthermore, Thomlison and Corcoran (2008) analyzed the research on internship supervision in social work. Their findings would likely be replicated if similar research was done on internship supervision in RT. Their results appear in Table 10.2.

Table 10.2

Research on Quality Internship Supervision

1. Student interns' perceptions of the quality of the supervision is the most important factor in satisfaction with the placement.
2. A good site supervisor is a respected individual who is accomplished and competent as a clinician.
3. A good site supervisor clearly separates supervision from psychotherapy or personal counseling.
4. Personal abilities such as empathy and genuineness must be high and used to convey understanding of the intern's difficulties, struggles, and sense of accomplishment.
5. Ideal supervisors recognize the personal strengths and abilities of student interns and know how to impart attitudes, behaviors, and practices to specific skill learning.
6. Student interns prefer supervisors who are flexible, amicable, and approachable and who model the qualities of genuineness and congruence.
7. Supervisors who emphasize interns' strengths rather than their deficiencies encourage them to reach for positive alternatives to unwanted practice behaviors.

Note. Adapted from "Evidence-Based Practices for Supervision," by B. Thomlison and K. Corcoran, 2008, in B. Thomlison and K. Corcoran (Eds.), *The Evidence-Based Internship: A Field Manual* (p. 103), New York, NY: Oxford University Press.

The Site Supervisor's Role in Giving Clinical Supervision

In their book on guidelines for internships, Grote and Hasl (2003) provided a brief description of clinical supervision. They explained that clinical supervision includes the following:

- Giving the intern constructive criticism, feedback and evaluation
- Establishing professional boundaries

- Conducting hands-on demonstrations and observation
- Lecturing on topics relevant to the particular setting or client population
- Providing opportunities for processing the intern's observations and learning (p. 15)

Austin (2013) offered a detailed description of the use of clinical supervision in RT. In his account, Austin discussed three roles of the clinical supervisor that site supervisors may apply when conducting clinical supervision with an intern supervisee. These are the *teaching role*, the *counselor role*, and the *consulting role*.

The teaching role includes the following:
- Observing the supervisee in clinical practice
- Identifying interventions to enhance the supervisee's performance
- Applying interventions through demonstrations, modeling, and other teaching techniques
- Explaining rationales that underlie interventions and clinical strategies
- Interpreting important events that occur during clinical supervision

Counseling role activities include the following:
- Exploring the supervisee's feelings about clinical and supervisory sessions
- Exploring the supervisee's feelings regarding specific techniques or interventions
- Facilitating self-exploration by the supervisee of worries or concerns regarding clinical sessions
- Helping the supervisee evaluate personal competencies and areas for growth
- Providing opportunities for the supervisee to discuss his or her effect on others and his or her use of defenses

Specific activities of the clinical supervisor in the consulting role include the following:
- Offering alternative interventions or conceptualizations for the supervisee to consider
- Encouraging brainstorming of strategies and interventions
- Discussing client problems, motivations, etc.
- Attempting to satisfy supervisee needs during the clinical supervision sessions
- Allowing the supervisee to control and structure the supervision session (Austin, 2013, pp. 394–395)

Austin (2013) explained that although clinical supervisors may assume all three roles, the roles are differentially employed:

Different roles are, of course, called for with various supervisees. For example, emerging supervisees (e.g., students and young staff) are likely to require the supervisor to take the teacher and counselor roles. More experienced supervisees (e.g., staff experienced in clinical practice) are apt to need the supervisor to fulfill the consultant role. (p. 395)

Site supervisors providing clinical supervision for student interns will likely largely assume a teaching role because of the need for students to learn and apply clinical skills. In many respects, site supervisors are educators in the field. Austin (2013) explained that interns, as emerging therapists, generally require the focus of clinical supervision to be on obtaining and refining clinical skills:

> These supervisees, therefore, respond positively to structured teaching methods such as completing assigned readings, attending didactic presentations, observing senior therapists conducting sessions, doing role playing, listening to suggestions for appropriate client interventions, and discussing the connection between theory and practice. Due to their typically high levels of anxiety, they also appreciate receiving support and reassurance from their supervisors. (p. 411)

Occasionally, the site supervisor providing clinical supervision will shift into the role of counselor. For instance, a normal concern that must be addressed is to offer student interns support in managing their natural anxiety about assuming the role of being a therapist. Other examples for assuming a counselor role include helping student interns explore their feelings about clinical and supervisory sessions or regarding specific techniques or interventions. The consulting role will most likely be assumed in the clinical supervision of interns toward the end of internships when students are functioning more independently and wish to seek consultation about their ideas about how to proceed with clients with whom they are working.

Clinical supervision is still an emerging program within RT, so a clinical supervision program to serve student interns may have to be established. The responsibility of establishing a clinical supervision program will likely be that of first-line managers once they have met with the RT staff to gain their support for such a program. Information on the process of establishing clinical supervision is found in Chapter 11, as well as in the chapter on clinical supervision in Austin's (2013) book. These chapters also provide a full description and explanation of clinical supervision.

Tasks to Be Completed Prior to the Arrival of Student Interns

A number of tasks must be completed prior to the arrival of student interns. Prior to receiving student interns, the first-line manager, in conjunction with the site supervisor and internship coordinator (should the agency have one), must ensure the agency internship manual is complete and has been approved by the agency administration. Once this document is in place, the site supervisor, again working closely with the first-line manager and/or internship coordinator, should develop and implement a marketing strategy to market the agency's internship program.

When applications are received, they must be reviewed and evaluated. This task may be completed by the site supervisor or by a selection committee that may include the first-line manager and/or internship coordinator. The students selected to be interviewed then normally complete a telephone or personal interview with the site supervisor. When a final selection is made (the agency may accept more than one intern), an agreement or contract is generally initiated with the college or university. This task is usually accomplished by the first-line manager or internship coordinator in concert with the agency administration. Finally, a formal letter of acceptance or denial is sent to students who interviewed. This letter will likely come from the first-line manager or internship coordinator. The letter of acceptance should name the site supervisor who will be working with the student intern.

Initial Responsibilities of the Site Supervisor With Each Intern

Boeve (2013) suggested that the site supervisor provide each student intern with a written guide to the internship that outlines agency requirements. She suggested that prior to their start dates students be sent the following:

- Orientation checklist
- Schedule for the first week
- Badge requirements
- Parking and other needed information
- A word of encouragement for the intern to contact the site supervisor with any questions or concerns

Orientation

Agencies almost always use the first two weeks of the internship to provide student interns with an orientation to the agency and the work environment. Following welcoming the students, taking them around to meet selected staff, and providing them with a general tour of the facility, the first day is devoted to routine procedures, such as gathering emergency contact information from the students; going over the orientation schedule; and reviewing the calendar for the internship, including dates of the midterm and final evaluations (Boeve, 2013).

During the initial orientation, an orientation checklist should be reviewed with the students that includes items such as obtaining agency identification badges and keys, the policy and procedure manuals for the agency, safety procedures, sick time and other absences, observation of other disciplines, computer use, and cell phone use. Each student should be given a desk or work space in which to organize the resource information received during the orientation (Boeve, 2013; Grote & Hasl, 2003). Such a work space should exist throughout the internship so students have a place to keep materials and to complete paperwork.

During the first week, the site supervisor should review the management structure of the agency with the intern. It is also advisable to provide a general orientation as to the purpose and organization of the overall program of the agency, as well as of the RT program. Information about the type and nature of clients served and outcomes expected to result from the clinical program should be included. A general review of the types of programs conducted by the RT staff should be provided, along with ways in which client assessments are conducted and outcomes are measured (e.g., assessment and evaluation instruments).

Additionally, during the first week, the site supervisor should meet with the intern to develop the personal objectives that the student will strive to obtain during the internship. This meeting may constitute the first regularly scheduled weekly meeting in which the intern will receive clinical supervision and serve as an opportunity for an initial discussion of the purpose and organization of clinical supervision.

Finally, from the beginning students should know specifically what they will be evaluated on and how the evaluation will be accomplished. Therefore, the site supervisor should go over the evaluation form with the student and explain how it will be administered so there are no surprises.

The second week of the orientation should largely be devoted to the RT program. This may include observing programs and shadowing and assisting staff, but should never involve the intern leading groups or seeing clients individually. Grote and Hasl (2003) suggested the following list of items to be accomplished during the second week:

- Review screening and assessment procedures.
- Learn procedures for documentation of treatment planning, evaluating client progress, and discharge planning.
- Review frequently treated diagnoses and clinical indications.
- Review program protocols/group descriptions.
- Shadow staff and observe assessments and interventions.
- Review client charts.
- Study agency's approved list of abbreviations.
- Discuss behavioral management techniques for motivating clients and managing disruptive behavior.
- Discuss the issue of professional boundaries between the intern and clients.
- Complete orientation to community resources.
- Review crisis intervention, emergency, safety, and code procedures.
- Learn and practice procedures for escorting, transporting, transferring, and lifting clients.
- Learn referral process.
- Discuss budget and fiscal resources.
- Discuss vehicle procedures.
- Learn about local professional organizations. (p. 17)

The Intern's Schedule Following the 2-Week Orientation

Grote and Hasl (2003) proposed a schedule that a site supervisor might set up for interns following the orientation. It progressively adds responsibilities including an ever increasing caseload. The sample performance schedule is presented in Table 10.3.

Of course, the intern schedule provided by Grote and Hasl (2003) is only an example of how an intern's schedule might be structured during an internship. The theme reflected in the sample schedule of Grote and Hasl of increasing the responsibilities of the intern continually, however, seems to be one that should be applied by all agencies with internship programs. Assignments (e.g., preparing a program protocol and visiting other agencies with RT programs) and a special project (e.g., preparing a resource manual for future interns and developing materials for RT month) were also reflected in the sample schedule. Such assignments and special projects are commonly included by agencies in the intern's schedule of activities. Each agency will have to determine the exact pattern to be followed, but all agencies should ensure that all aspects in the NCTRC (2014a) job analysis are covered during the internship.

Table 10.3

Research on Quality Internship Supervision

Week Three: (a) Adopt a caseload of one client; (b) Complete assessment; (c) Develop a treatment (i.e., intervention) plan; (d) Write progress notes; (e) Continue to observe treatment interventions; (f) Attend treatment team meetings.

Week Four: (a) Adopt a caseload of up to two clients; (b) Complete all documentation; (c) Co-plan and co-lead two assigned treatment groups or individual interventions; (d) Review treatment outcomes with supervisor; (e) Plan a recreation event or outing.

Week Five: (a) Adopt a caseload of up to three clients; (b) Arrange site visits to other RT programs; (c) Observe available medical procedures; (d) Co-lead three assigned groups or individual interventions; (e) Review agency and department quality performance improvement philosophy and plan; (f) Develop a plan for a special project.

By the End of Week Seven: (a) Adopt a caseload of up to five clients; (b) Lead one assigned group per day and individual interventions as necessary; (c) Meet with site supervisor to complete midterm evaluation.

By the End of Week Ten: (a) Adopt a caseload of up to eight clients; (b) Conduct family meeting or intervention to assess client progress or family patterns, or to discuss discharge planning; (c) Develop a new treatment group of at least six sessions, write a program protocol and evaluation procedure.

By the End of Week Twelve: (a) Adopt a caseload of a maximum of ten clients; (b) Complete all sessions of the new group and evaluate outcomes.

By the End of Week Fourteen: (a) Complete and present the special project; (b) Present a case study at the RT staff meeting.

Week Fifteen: (a) Complete all documentation for caseload clients; (b) Accomplish closure with clients and staff; (c) Turn in all agency supplies, books, keys, badges or other materials; (d) Obtain a copy of the site supervisor's certification; (e) Clarify the agency's procedures for obtaining employment references; (f) Meet with the site supervisor to complete final evaluation; (g) Complete evaluation of the agency's internship plan and site supervisor; (h) Complete evaluation of college/university internship program; (i) Turn in all required projects, papers and evaluations to the college or university.

Note. From *Guidelines for Internships in Therapeutic Recreation* (2nd ed., pp. 17–18), by K. A. Grote and M. A. Hasl, 2003, Alexandria, VA: American Therapeutic Recreation Association.

Gatekeeping Role of Agency Site Supervisor

In addition to the clinical supervision roles of teacher, counselor, and consultant, the site supervisor is also the gatekeeper. The recreational therapist conducting site supervision must take on the role of gatekeeper for the profession. Ethically, site supervisors need to take on the responsibility of monitoring and evaluating their supervisees' clinical abilities and personal qualities to determine if the supervisees should be allowed to enter the profession as clinicians. Specific areas that may be problematic include being hurtful to clients, boundary violations with clients or program standards, illegal behaviors, exhibiting significant psychiatric impairments, constantly lacking self-awareness, not adhering to codes of ethics, and demonstrating attitudes not conducive to working with clients (Corey, Haynes, Moulton, & Muratori, 2010; U.S. Department of Health and Human Services, 2009).

If a student should not be allowed to go forth to function as a clinician in the estimation of the site supervisor, the site supervisor is obligated to report this assessment to the student's university internship supervisor. Of course, the site supervisor is also obligated to apprise the student intern of the evaluation that he or she has not displayed behaviors that warrant entering the profession as a clinician.

The university internship supervisor must then determine how to proceed with the student. This could result in an action such as the student being asked to leave the RT professional preparation program or repeating the internship at another agency. If signs of significant problems are becoming apparent at time of the midterm evaluation, the site supervisor needs to inform the student intern and the university internship supervisor of these concerns so the student can make corrections or withdraw from the internship.

Thank goodness agency site supervisors rarely have to exercise their authority as gatekeepers, as the majority of student interns perform admirably. It is important, however, that site supervisors understand that they have an ethical obligation to serve as gatekeepers if the situation should arise.

Conclusion

The internship is the pinnacle of interns' professional preparation and the place where academia meets the "real world." It offers an opportunity for student interns to participate in a supportive, structured learning environment that allows them to acquire clinical skills and practical on-the-job training to prepare to assume responsibilities as RT professionals. In short, the overriding goal of the internship is to assist the student to think and act as a competent and effective recreational therapist.

It is a credit that agencies with internship programs see training as a part of their mission and are willing to invest time and resources in preparing emerging recreational therapists. Likewise, the efforts of recreational therapists who serve as site supervisors to provide students with enjoyable and worthwhile internships should be applauded.

References

Austin, D. R. (2013). *Therapeutic recreation processes and techniques: Evidence-based recreational therapy* (7th ed.). Urbana, IL: Sagamore.

Beck, T. M. (2013, October). *Using ATRA guidelines to facilitate student internships.* Presentation at the Illinois Recreation Therapy Association Conference, Alsip, IL.

Boeve, S. (2013, November). *Developing a quality student internship program for therapeutic recreation student interns.* Presentation at the Michigan Therapeutic Recreation Association Conference, Ypsilanti, MI.

Corey, G., Haynes, R., Moulton, P., & Muratori, M. (2010). *Clinical supervision in the helping professions: A practical guide* (2nd ed.). Alexandria, VA: American Counseling Association.

Grote, K. A., & Hasl, M. A. (2003). *Guidelines for internships in therapeutic recreation* (2nd ed.). Alexandria, VA: American Therapeutic Recreation Association.

National Council for Therapeutic Recreation Certification. (2014a). *Certification standards part II: NCTRC exam information.* New City, NY: Author.

National Council for Therapeutic Recreation Certification. (2014b). *NCTRC internship supervision guidelines for continuing education credit.* New City, NY: Author.

Nelson-Jones, R. (2002). *Essential counseling and therapy skills.* Thousand Oaks, CA: Sage.

Thomlison, B., & Corcoran, K. (2008). Evidence-based practices for supervision. In B. Thomlison & K. Corcoran (Eds.), *The evidence-based internship: A field manual* (pp. 97–126). New York, NY: Oxford University Press.

University of North Carolina at Wilmington. (2014). *Internship manual.* Retrieved from http://uncw.edu/oss/documents/SHAHS/Recreation%20Therapy/RTH%20498%20Internship%20Manual.pdf

U.S. Department of Health and Human Services. (2009). *Clinical supervision and professional development of the substance abuse counselor* (TIP 52). Rockville, MD: Author.

Chapter 11
Clinical Supervision

Objectives
- Define the term *clinical supervision.*
- Describe the status of clinical supervision in RT.
- Describe the purposes of clinical supervision.
- State why all levels of personnel doing RT should receive clinical supervision.
- Describe three major roles assumed by clinical supervisors.
- Differentiate between clinical supervision and administrative supervision.
- Delineate central principles of clinical supervision.
- List responsibilities of clinical supervisors.
- Describe how the clinical supervisor may be evaluated.
- List potential benefits for supervisees who receive clinical supervision.
- Describe steps in establishing a clinical supervision program.

Key Terms
- **Clinical supervision:** A program provided by a master clinician to supervisees that serves the dual purpose of helping supervisees to enhance clinical skills and of protecting client welfare.
- **Administrative supervision:** Administrative or managerial supervision is provided by a manager and focused on issues surrounding the supervisee as an employee and deals with concerns such as personnel matters and following the policies and procedures of the department in which the individual works.

Clinical supervision has the dual purpose of promoting the supervisee's professional development as a clinician and of protecting the welfare of clients (Aasheim, 2011; Austin, 2013). Thus, clinical supervision programs in recreational therapy (RT) help to ensure that practicing recreational therapists enhance their clinical skills and that clients receive quality care. As such, clinical supervision should be conceived to be essential to RT services. In fact, the authors of this text believe that receiving clinical supervision should be a necessity for the development of all recreational therapists and a right of every recreational therapist.

Yet clinical supervision is still an emerging area within RT (Austin, 2013). In the past, many RT departments have lacked clinical supervision programs and clinical supervisors generally gained their knowledge about doing clinical supervision from their personal experiences of having been supervisees when they were student interns or young practitioners. Such experiences were the only means to obtain skills in clinical supervision because of an absence of information in the RT literature and a lack of formal training opportunities.

Today, increasing attention is beginning to be given to clinical supervision within the RT literature. With the provision of this chapter, the authors hope to add to the literature on clinical supervision in RT by providing an introduction to basic concepts underlying clinical supervision, practical information on providing clinical supervision, and guidance for managers in establishing clinical supervision programs for practicing recreational therapists and student interns.

Clinical Supervision

As indicated, clinical supervision is provided by a clinical supervisor for a supervisee with the dual purposes of (a) helping the supervisee to develop and maintain clinical skills and (b) protecting client welfare by helping ensure clients are competently served. These purposes are clear in the definition of clinical supervision by Austin (2013):

> Clinical supervision then may be defined as a joint relationship in which the supervisor assists the supervisee to develop himself or herself in order to deliver the highest possible level of clinical service while promoting accountability in the agency's clinical program. (p. 388)

Austin further explained the process of clinical supervision:

> Skills related to the achievement of client objectives remain at the heart of clinical supervision. On occasion, however, clinical supervision involves issues related to teamwork or to maintaining positive relationships in working with other staff in order to conduct a successful clinical program. (p. 390)

Thus, the responsibility of clinical supervisors is to help supervisees gain and improve clinical skills, as well as to maintain the integrity of the agency's clinical program by assisting staff to carry out the clinical program at the highest possible level.

Clinical supervision clearly exists to benefit individuals performing clinical functions and to assist them in providing quality clinical services to clients. In contrast, Austin (2013), drawing from the work of Bishop (2007), stipulated what clinical supervision is *not* (see Table 11.1).

Table 11.1

Clinical Supervision Is NOT

- A management activity allowing for the overseeing of subordinates linked to the disciplinary process.
- Exclusively concerned with timekeeping, ranges of pay, and hours of duty.
- About having the supervisee's work controlled, directed, or managerially evaluated.
- A punitive or gratuitously negative experience for the supervisor.
- A continuous discussion of mistakes, failing, or errors on the part of the supervisee, without being balanced by a discussion or the supervisee's professional strengths and the positive aspects of his or her work.

Note. From *Therapeutic Recreation Processes and Techniques: Evidence-Based Recreational Therapy* (7th ed., p. 393), by D. R. Austin, 2013, Urbana, IL: Sagamore.

Every student intern in RT can certainly benefit from receiving clinical supervision because they are in the process of experiential learning to build their clinical skills. Site supervisors typically provide clinical supervision for student interns they supervise. But, as previously emphasized, clinical supervision is not limited to student interns. Young recreational therapists who, similar to student interns, are still developing their clinical skills can certainly benefit from receiving clinical supervision.

In fact, no matter their level, all clinicians need to receive clinical supervision. As clinicians develop, they become more competent and require less direction from their supervisors. Corey, Haynes, Moulton, and Muratori (2010) indicated that while promoting their supervisee's growth and development, clinical supervisors need to empower their supervisees to become increasingly independent so they learn the skills and awareness necessary to self-evaluate, or practice self-supervision. Competent clinicians should gain skills to be aware of the limits of their competency, monitor their own performance, and always place clients' welfare first so clients are not harmed.

> "Mistakes are guidelines and opportunities to learn how to do thing better."
>
> Collins Hasty

Nevertheless, every clinician still has needs that clinical supervision can assist them to meet. Even the most seasoned recreational therapist can benefit from clinical supervision. The clinical knowledge and practices of every therapist can be deepened and broadened because new concepts and practices are always becoming available and learning is a career-long enterprise. Additionally, a more seasoned recreational therapist may encounter problems with relationships with other staff that interfere with successfully conducting the clinical program, for which they may require counseling. Or they may confront difficult cases for which they can use consultation available through clinical supervision. Clinical supervisors assume the role of teacher or educator in the field, but they may also take on counseling or consulting roles depending on the needs of the supervisee (Austin, 2013). The three major roles of clinical supervisors are outlined in Table 11.2.

Table 11.2
Major Roles of Clinical Supervisors

Teaching Role Activities:

- Observing the supervisee in clinical practice.
- Identifying interventions to enhance the supervisee's performance.
- Applying interventions through demonstrations, modeling, and other teaching techniques.
- Explaining rationales that underlie interventions and clinical strategies.
- Interpreting important events that occur during clinical sessions.

Counselor Role Activities:

- Exploring the supervisee's feelings about clinical and supervisory sessions.
- Exploring the supervisee's feelings regarding specific techniques or interventions.
- Facilitating self-exploration by the supervisee of worries or concerns regarding clinical sessions.
- Helping the supervisee evaluate personal competencies and areas for growth.
- Providing opportunities for the supervisee to discuss his or her effect on others and his or her use of defenses.

Consulting Role Activities:

- Offering alternative interventions or conceptualizations for the supervisee to consider.
- Encouraging brainstorming of strategies and interventions.
- Discussing client problems, motivations, etc.
- Attempting to satisfy supervisee needs during clinical supervision sessions.
- Allowing the supervisee to control and structure the supervision session.

Note. From *Therapeutic Recreation Processes and Techniques: Evidence-Based Recreational Therapy* (7th ed., pp. 394–395), by D. R. Austin, 2013, Urbana, IL: Sagamore.

In addition to assuming the roles of teacher, counselor, and consultant in fulfilling their primary responsibilities of assisting supervisees to enhance their levels of clinical practice, clinical supervisors also take on the role of monitoring their supervisees' performance as gatekeepers for the profession to determine who should and should not be functioning as clinicians (Corey et al., 2010; U.S. Department of Health and Human Services, 2009). Ethically, clinical supervisors have the responsibility to monitor and evaluate their supervisees' therapeutic abilities and personal qualities to determine if they are competent to serve as clinicians. Personal characteristics of clinicians have been found to be highly related to client outcomes, so clinical supervisors must assess their supervisees' qualities such as insight, respect for others, empathy for clients, genuineness with clients, and concreteness to determine if their behaviors and attitudes are acceptable. Specific unacceptable behaviors include the following:

- Actions hurtful to clients
- Boundary violations with clients or program standards
- Illegal behaviors

- Displaying significant psychiatric impairments
- Constant lack of self-awareness
- Inability to adhere to professional codes of ethics
- Consistent demonstration of attitudes that are not conducive to working with the specific population of clients served by the agency, such as those with substance abuse problems (U.S. Department of Health and Human Services, 2009, p. 20)

Clinical Supervision and Administrative Supervision

Managers of RT units should be aware that there is a distinction between clinical supervision and administrative or managerial supervision. The focus of clinical supervision is on the supervisees' work in providing services to clients to achieve the therapeutic aims sought for and by clients. Administrative or managerial supervision, in contrast, deals with supervisees' responsibilities as employees to ensure they follow policies and procedures so the unit functions effectively and efficiently. Corey et al. (2010) clearly indicated the distinction between clinical supervision and managerial supervision: "*Clinical supervision* focuses on the work of the supervisee in providing services to clients" (p. 3) and "*administrative supervision* focuses on the issues surrounding the supervisee's role and responsibilities in the organization as an employee: personnel matters, timekeeping, documentation, and so forth" (p. 3).

Austin (2013) and Aasheim (2011) cautioned that clinical supervision and managerial supervision need to be kept separate and distinct. Austin wrote: "The authoritative nature of administrative supervision (with administrative power) simply gets in the way of establishing the cooperative, helping relationship that must exist as a part of clinical supervision" (p. 392). Aasheim explained:

> These supervisors who are both managerial and clinical supervisors are in a dual relationship with their supervisee/employee. In these cases, agency or administrative needs may take precedence above clinical focus and supervisee development, and the supervisor's two roles may be in direct opposition. For instance, clinical supervisors often make great efforts to ensure the supervisee feels safe and comfortable to discuss times of professional incompetence and needed development. However, supervisees may find it difficult to divulge professional weaknesses to their direct manager who has great control and influence over their ability to be promoted, given a raise or bonus, approved for vacation time, and the like. (p. 100)

The authors of this text believe that normally the same supervisor should not conduct clinical supervision and managerial supervision for the reasons provided by Austin (2013) and Aasheim (2011). Clinical supervision and managerial supervision are distinctive types of supervision that should remain separate if possible.

Central Principles of Clinical Supervision

The U.S. Department of Health and Human Services (2009) used a consensus panel to identify central principles of clinical supervision (pp. 5–6). The central principles of clinical supervision that follow have been drawn from that work and should be of interest to RT program managers:

1. *Clinical supervision is essential to all clinical programs.* Clinical supervision is a central organizing activity that integrates the program mission, goals, and treatment philosophy with clinical theory and evidence-based practices (EBPs).

2. *Clinical supervision enhances staff retention and morale.* Staff turnover and workforce development are major concerns, and clinical supervision is a primary means of improving workforce retention and job satisfaction.

3. *Every clinician, regardless of level of skill and experience, needs and has a right to clinical supervision. In addition, supervisors need and have a right to their own supervision.* Supervision needs to be tailored to the knowledge base, skills, experience, and assignment of each individual.

4. *Clinical supervision needs the full support of agency administrators.* An atmosphere of growth and openness within clinical supervision should be provided in an environment in which learning and professional development are valued and supported by the administration.

5. *The supervisory relationship is the crucible in which ethical practice is developed and reinforced.* The supervisor needs to model sound ethical and legal practices in the supervisory relationship. This is where ethical practice is translated from a concept to a set of behaviors.

6. *Clinical supervision is a skill in and of itself that has to be developed.* Not only do clinical supervisors need to be seasoned therapists with high levels of clinical competency, but they also need programs to increase their capacity to develop into good clinical supervisors.

7. *Clinical supervision may, in some situations, require balancing administrative and clinical supervision tasks.* When the same supervisor must provide administrative and clinical supervision, the person will likely feel caught between two roles. Administrators need to support the integration and differentiation of the two roles to promote the efficacy of the clinical supervisor in cases in which the two tasks cannot be kept separate and distinct.

8. *Culture and other contextual variables influence the supervision process; supervisors need to strive for cultural competency continually.* Cultural competence involves the supervisee's response to clients, the supervisor's response to the supervisee, and the program's response to the cultural needs of the diverse community it serves.

9. *Successful implementation of EBPs requires ongoing supervision.* Supervisors have a role in determining which specific EBPs are relevant for the organization's clients. Excellence in clinical supervision requires adherence to the EBP model.

10. *Supervisors have the responsibility to be gatekeepers for the profession.* Supervisors are responsible for maintaining professional standards, recognizing and addressing impairment, and safeguarding the welfare of clients. More than anyone else in an agency, supervisors can observe therapists' behaviors and respond promptly to potential problems, including counseling some individuals out of the field because they are ill suited to the profession. The gatekeeper function is especially important for site supervisors who act as evaluators for student interns prior to their entering the profession.

11. *Clinical supervision should involve direct observation methods.* Direct observation should be the standard in the field because it is one of the most effective ways of building skills, monitoring therapist performance, and ensuring quality care. Supervisors require training in methods of direct observation, and managers need to provide resources, such as one-way mirrors or video equipment, so direct observations can be employed.

Responsibilities of Clinical Supervisors

It is imperative that managers and clinical supervisors fully realize the responsibilities carried out by clinical supervisors, which are numerous. In fact, Corey et al. (2010) listed 14 responsibilities for clinical supervisors (pp. 29–36). Their work provides the basis for the discussion that follows. Clinical supervisors have the following responsibilities:

1. *Recognize that supervisors are ultimately responsible, both legally and ethically, for the actions of student interns under their supervision.* From legal and ethical perspectives, trainees are not expected to assume final responsibility for clients, so their supervisors are expected to take on decision-making responsibility and liability.

2. *Have knowledge of every case or client with whom the supervisee is working.* Supervisors must be familiar with each case of every supervisee and check on supervisees' progress with each. Of course, supervisors cannot be expected to know all details of each case, but should at least know the direction the case is being taken.

3. *Provide feedback and evaluation to the supervisee regardless of performance.* Supervisors need to provide formal and informal feedback and evaluation to supervisees on a regular basis. The task of supervisors is to tell supervisees how they are doing and their strengths and limitations as related to clinical practice.

4. *Monitor the actions and decisions of the supervisee.* An integral part of the work of supervisors is monitoring the actions and decisions of supervisees. One of the best means to monitoring supervisees, in addition to direct observation of supervisees working with clients, is to remain vigilant of what supervisees are reporting during supervisory sessions (e.g., how they make decisions or how they demonstrate self-awareness or a lack thereof).

5. *Document the supervisory sessions.* Careful documentation of supervisory sessions permits the tracking of clients and issues of supervisees and provides a history that supervisors can use in reviewing the supervisory relationship and following up on concerns. Maintaining good records also offers supervisors an excellent defense against criticism of the supervisory process or malpractice claims.

6. *Supervise only within the scope of the supervisor's expertise and refer out for additional supervision/consultation as necessary.* When issues present themselves that are outside of the supervisor's area of expertise, wise supervisors consult with colleagues regarding their availability to supervise the aspect of practice for which they do not feel competent.

7. *Provide the supervisee with due process information.* Corey et al. (2010) explained: "In supervision, due process includes providing supervisees with clear expectations for performance, outlining the procedures for handling adverse actions and disciplinary action, and explaining supervisees' rights to appeal such actions when performance expectations are not met" (p. 32). This is best accomplished at the beginning of the supervisory relationship before problems arise.

8. *Have a written contract between the supervisor and supervisee regarding the scope and expectations in supervision.* A written contract should be a simple and comprehensive document that provides a blueprint for a successful supervisory experience for both parties. A list of items that may appear in a contract follow, although in actual practice only items relevant to the situation will be used:
   * Purpose and goals of supervision
   * Logistics of supervision including frequency, duration, and structure of meetings
   * Roles and responsibilities of supervisor and supervisee
   * Guidelines about situations in which the supervisor expects to be consulted
   * Brief description of supervisor's background, experience, and areas of expertise
   * The model or methods of supervision to be used
   * Documentation responsibilities of supervisor and supervisee
   * Evaluation methods to be used including schedule, structure, format, and use
   * Feedback and evaluation plan including due process
   * Supervisee's commitment to follow all applicable agency policies, professional licensing statutes, and ethical standards
   * Supervisee's agreement to maintain healthy boundaries with clients
   * Supervisee's commitment to provide informed consent to clients
   * Reporting procedures for legal, ethical, and emergency situations
   * Confidentiality policy
   * A statement of responsibility regarding multicultural issues
   * Financial arrangements (if applicable) (Corey et al., 2010, p. 185)

9. *Monitor the personal development of the supervisee, as it affects clinical practice.* Addressing personal issues that affect supervisees' work with clients is a part of the supervisor–supervisee interaction. It is, however, important for supervisors to monitor personal issues that may affect supervisees' practice and to recommend actions as they are needed.

10. *Model effective problem-solving skills for the supervisee and help the supervisee develop problem-solving capabilities.* Modeling is an excellent means to teach problem-solving techniques, but it should always be used with the goal of assisting supervisees to develop their own problem-solving skills.

11. *Promote the supervisee's ethical knowledge and behavior.* Supervisors should acquaint supervisees with understandings of ethical codes and standards and how they apply to supervisees' work with clients. Modeling ethical behavior offers an excellent teaching method for supervisors.

12. *Promote the knowledge and skills required to understand and work effectively with clients' individual and cultural differences.* Supervisors need to help supervisees to understand how similarities and differences affect the dynamics between the supervisee and clients and the need for the supervisee to learn from clients about their cultures and how they may affect the therapeutic relationship.

13. *Educate supervisees about critical ethical issues.* Supervisees need to know about informed consent and its ongoing nature. They need to provide full, accurate, and complete information to clients. Supervisees must inform clients of limits to confidentiality. When working within managed care, supervisees must learn the limits of client insurance policies and make treatment plans with those in mind. They must make sure that they work within their scope of practice and competence as well as be certain they understand the plan in place to cover emergencies.

14. *Educate the supervisee in recognizing the importance of self-care and assist the supervisee in developing self-care strategies.* To carry out their responsibilities that inevitably bring about stress, supervisees need to develop and practice self-care habits. Therefore, supervisors should discuss with supervisees ways stress may be affecting their work and self-care means to manage stress.

Evaluation of Clinical Supervisors

Naturally, RT program managers need to consider how clinical supervisors should be evaluated. Evaluation data about the clinical supervisor's performance frequently come from instruments completed by supervisees. Often, universities supply their student interns with instruments on which to rate their supervisors. Agencies may also adopt rating forms for staff to rate their supervisors. Typically, such instruments contain brief statements (e.g., My supervisor and I have a positive rapport or I was taught therapeutic skills) to be rated by supervisees on a 5- or 7-point scale ranging from *strongly disagree* to *strongly agree*. Such an instrument is found in Appendix 10A of Corey et al.'s (2010) book on clinical supervision.

Corey et al. (2010) listed qualities on which supervisors can be evaluated:
- Availability
- Communication skills
- Cultural competence
- Ethical and legal knowledge
- Clinical and professional knowledge
- Professionalism
- Provision of useful feedback and evaluation
- Punctuality
- Responsiveness to supervisee's needs and ideas
- Resolution of issues/conflicts promptly and professionally
- Effective modeling for the supervisee
- Supervision of therapy
- Supportiveness
- Use of supervision interventions (p. 224)

Making a Case for Clinical Supervision With Administrators

Administrators wish to have a case made for establishing new services. It seems a strong rationale can be built for establishing a clinical supervision program. Support for clinical supervision within an allied health profession, such as RT, was made evident in a systematic literature review published in the *Journal of Allied Health* (Dawson, Phillips, & Leggat, 2013). Dawson et al. (2013) reported the following perceived benefits of clinical supervision for staff receiving supervision:

- Developing of clinical skills to support the quality and safety of patient interventions
- Promoting professional accountability
- Increasing clinical competence of supervisees
- Increasing well-being
- Building coping skills
- Increasing job satisfaction
- Increasing staff retention
- Reducing stress levels

Austin (2013) drew from several sources to develop an extensive list of the benefits staff derive from receiving clinical supervision. These appear in Table 11.3.

Table 11.3
Benefits of Clinical Supervision

- Reduced emotional exhaustion
- Reduced occupational stress
- Reduced sick leave
- Reduced burnout
- Reduced feelings of professional isolation
- Increased job satisfaction and staff morale
- Increased feelings of support
- Increased confidence
- Increased awareness of solutions in clinical problems
- Increased self-awareness
- Increased reflective practice
- Enhanced feelings of accomplishment
- Improved recruitment
- Improved retention

Note. From *Therapeutic Recreation Processes and Techniques: Evidence-Based Recreational Therapy* (7th ed., p. 390), by D. R. Austin, 2013, Urbana, IL: Sagamore.

An additional benefit of an RT clinical supervision program is ensuring the quality of the unit's clinical program. First, to initiate a clinical supervision program requires the services of an individual with the background to serve as a clinical supervisor. Typically, in RT clinical supervision, this is a senior-level recreational therapist who is a master clinician. Having such a person on staff ensures competent leadership for the clinical program. From their position, clinical supervisors serve to assist management by promoting quality improvement and fostering compliance with the agency's goals and policies. Furthermore, clinical supervisors serve as the liaison between the first-line manager and the RT clinical staff so staff needs can be interpreted to management.

Establishing a Clinical Supervision Program

Austin (2013) provided a description of how management may establish a clinical supervision program within an RT unit. It includes the following steps:

1. *Information sharing*: This step includes providing literature and meeting with staff to develop understanding of clinical supervision and then determining the level of interest of the staff and whether anyone has the clinical expertise to provide clinical supervision.
2. *Skills training:* The second step is to provide staff with training in giving and receiving clinical supervision. This may involve bringing in a consultant to conduct the training or having staff take university courses in clinical supervision.
3. *Deciding on the modalities:* Those establishing the clinical supervision program determine the structure for the program. For example, they may choose 60-minute one-on-one sessions (the modality typically employed with student interns) or group or peer supervision (a modality appropriate for seasoned clinicians).
4. *Pilot program being implemented*: The program is tested during this phase. Generally, three to six clinical supervision meetings should be held before the pilot program is evaluated.
5. *Establishing and monitoring the program:* Once the program has been tested, it needs to be put into place with a system set up to monitor its success. (pp. 414–415)

Modalities for Clinical Supervision

As mentioned in the third step in establishing a clinical supervision program, the modalities for clinical supervision will need to be considered and selected. There are two common modalities, or formats, for conducting clinical supervision. One is the weekly or biweekly face-to-face meeting of the supervisor and supervisee that typically lasts about an hour. The second is regularly scheduled group meetings. The group meeting format is sometimes employed when several clinicians are learning a new clinical skill. It is also used with advanced clinicians, who may consult with one another regarding their clinical work (Austin, 2013).

Management and staff developing RT clinical supervision programs, however, should be aware of additional ways to deliver clinical supervision. The one-on-one meeting in which a senior recreational therapist, who possesses advanced clinical skills, meets with the supervisee is the most traditional structure (and perhaps the most desirable approach), but it represents only one option among several.

In instances that a senior recreational therapist is not available to provide supervision, an expert from another discipline (e.g., psychology, social work) may be called upon to provide clinical supervision for recreational therapists. Other options are to have seasoned recreational therapists with similar experiences engage in one-on-one clinical supervision sessions with one another or gather for small group meetings. Often, these experienced staff use clinical supervision times to provide consultation to one another on difficult cases (Bishop, 2007). With the availability of technology, still additional options may present themselves. For example, in rural areas staff may be able to receive clinical supervision from someone in another location using a video chat, such as Skype. Regarding the use of such technology, Bishop (2007) observed: "Issues such as security and confidentiality will need to be carefully addressed here, but there is no good reason why, carefully thought out, electronic access to supervision should not be a great success" (p. 47).

Conclusion

To conclude this chapter, readers are reminded that the provision of clinical supervision with staff and interns is still an emerging area within RT. Those who wish to learn more about giving and receiving clinical supervision are encouraged to review Austin's (2013) chapter on clinical supervision in his book *Therapeutic Recreation Processes and Techniques: Evidence-Based Recreational Therapy.*

References

Aasheim, L. (2011). *Practical clinical supervision for counselors: An experiential guide.* New York, NY: Springer.

Austin, D. R. (2013). *Therapeutic recreation processes and techniques: Evidence-based recreational therapy* (7th ed.). Urbana, IL: Sagamore.

Bishop, V. (2007). *Clinical supervision in practice* (2nd ed.). New York, NY: Palgrave Macmillan.

Corey, G., Haynes, R., Moulton, P., & Muratori, M. (2010). *Clinical supervision in the helping professions* (2nd ed.). Alexandria, VA: American Counseling Association.

Dawson, M., Phillips, B., & Leggat, S. (2013). Clinical supervision for allied health professionals. *Journal of Allied Health, 42*(2), 65–73.

U.S. Department of Health and Human Services. (2009). *Clinical supervision and professional development of the substance abuse counselor* (TIP 52). Rockville, MD: Author.

Chapter 12
Volunteer Management

Objectives
- Define the term *volunteer*.
- Indicate possible agency requirements for volunteers.
- Explain the importance of training staff in working with volunteers.
- Indicate reasons why people volunteer.
- Explain why it is helpful to know why an individual wishes to volunteer.
- Describe means to recruit volunteers.
- Describe the selection and interviewing process.
- Describe examples of questions for interviewing volunteers.
- Identify possible areas to cover in a volunteer orientation program.
- Describe the three categories of services performed by volunteers (i.e., direct, supportive, and administrative).
- Identify items supervisors should consider when assigning tasks to volunteers.
- Identify potential areas of complaint by volunteers.
- Defend the statement that volunteers should be treated with the same respect as staff.
- State the importance of volunteer recognition.
- Name ways management can recognize staff for their support of the volunteer program.
- Identify means for data collection when evaluating a volunteer program.
- Contrast formative evaluation and summative evaluation.

Key Terms
- **Volunteer:** A person who spends time, unpaid, doing something to help others.
- **Formative evaluation:** A form of developmental evaluation that monitors and assesses ongoing processes to determine how successful a program is and if changes are required.
- **Summative evaluation:** A form of retrospective evaluation focused on the ultimate outcomes of a program at the end of a specific time.

Volunteers are unpaid individuals who give their time to help others. As such, volunteers offer first-line recreational therapy (RT) managers a unique and wonderful resource. Austin and Lee (2013) explained:

> Budget-conscious administrators may use volunteers to meet the needs of persons with disabilities while providing services under limited budgets. Volunteers offer a way to stretch an agency's resources. But volunteers supply far more than inexpensive labor in the absence of paid staff. They offer a wealth of diversity in backgrounds and skills that would rarely be available within regular staff. Volunteers also share a dedication to service. They can accomplish tasks that would be difficult or impossible without their efforts because of their diversity and dedication. (p. 267)

Because volunteers bring a diversity of backgrounds and abilities, they can assist an RT unit in many ways. For example, a retired university professor might help train other volunteers. A professional writer might assist with developing materials that describe the therapeutic offerings within the RT program or with constructing a website to interpret internship opportunities or volunteer opportunities within the RT program. A health and physical education teacher might consult with staff on establishing a weight reduction and fitness program. Volunteers who are good with their hands may have skills to use in maintaining and repairing recreational equipment. Of course, volunteers may have skills in a particular activity, such as yoga, horticulture, or aquatics, which may be applied in assisting recreational therapists in conducting activity programs.

Training Staff

First-line managers should recognize the many roles volunteers may take and the value of volunteers. However, it does not necessarily follow that staff will recognize the worth of the agency having volunteers. Therefore, wise managers train staff so they understand the contributions volunteers bring to the agency's program and how staff can foster positive relationships with volunteers. A way to begin to acquaint staff with the pluses of having volunteers is to meet with staff to allow them to consider how they may use volunteers effectively to enhance the agency's program. By doing so, staff will begin to see, in concrete ways, the advantages of volunteers assisting within the RT unit. Once staff understand the value of volunteers and commit to using volunteers, they need to learn how to build staff–volunteer relationships. Austin and Lee (2013) explained that establishing such relationships involves "knowing each volunteer by name; treating volunteers as colleagues by being welcoming and friendly with them; displaying interest in volunteers and what they are doing; and, in general, supporting the work of volunteers" (p. 269).

Being Familiar With Agency Requirements

Most healthcare organizations have volunteer requirements. These are basic stipulations to which all volunteers must subscribe and include items such as minimum age requirements (e.g., being at least 15 years old), background checks for volunteers over age 18, having PPD (purified protein derivative) tuberculosis screening testing, and having had seasonal flu shots. First-line managers should become acquainted with volunteer requirements in force at their agency or facility.

Why People Volunteer

People volunteer for many reasons. Reasons include a belief in the cause or a desire to help others. Some wish to meet new people. Others want to use their skills and abilities. A list of reasons why people volunteer is found in Table 12.1.

Table 12.1
Reasons Why People Volunteer

- Belief in the cause
- Personal satisfaction/feel good
- Meet new people
- Be part of community
- Build self-confidence
- Gain training and experiences
- Improve job prospects
- Use skills and abilities
- Satisfy spiritual obligations

- Make a difference/help people
- Enhance knowledge
- Share knowledge
- Pass time
- Follow family tradition
- Organization has helped them and they want to help others
- Need the support of the organization

Note. From *Recruiting and Retaining Volunteers* (p. 1), by M. A. Hashim, 2003, Montreal, Canada: World Federation of Hemophilia.

It is advantageous for the first-line manager to know why an individual wishes to volunteer, to help maintain the volunteer's interest. Individuals who get what they want out of their volunteer experience are more likely to wish to continue volunteering. Being aware of the reasons why individuals are volunteering is also valuable in knowing which tasks to assign them. If the tasks assigned to them meet their needs, they will be more likely to complete them and gain enjoyment from their efforts (Hashim, 2003).

> "Remember that the happiest people are not those getting more, but those giving more."
>
> H. Jackson Brown, Jr.

Planning

A step to take before recruiting volunteers is to complete planning so the RT unit is ready to accept and use volunteers. Of course, first-line managers initially need to secure the support of their superior. They likewise need to gain the support of the RT staff. Such planning offers staff the opportunity to express resistance to using volunteers and to develop a consensus of the value of volunteers in carrying out the program. A part of the discussion with staff should concern identifying tasks that volunteers may perform.

Once tasks have been identified, a detailed description of each needs to be prepared. Descriptions should include the objective, skills required, activities required, time required, frequency (e.g., weekly, monthly), volunteering location, to whom the volunteer reports, and expectations (e.g., performance criteria).

Additional areas for planning include (a) volunteer recruitment and screening, (b) training (e.g., orientation) to be provided, (c) supervision of volunteers, (d) volunteer evaluation and recognition, and (e) retaining volunteers (Hashim, 2003). Discussion of these areas follows.

Recruiting and Selecting Volunteers

Once the plan is in place, volunteers can then be recruited. When an agency is initiating a new volunteer program, it is best to start small until all policies and procedures have been tested.

Two avenues may be taken when recruiting volunteers. One is to recruit from the general public. A second is to recruit from those already acquainted with the agency (e.g., friends of staff or volunteers, people who have been affected by the health problem the agency addresses).

Whether the agency recruits from the general public or from people acquainted with the agency, a targeted recruitment approach may be employed in which volunteers who have specific skills or expertise are recruited. Carter and O'Morrow (2006) stipulated three categories of services performed by volunteers: direct, supportive, and administrative. Direct services involve the direct provision of programs to clients (e.g., conducting a reminiscence therapy program for clients). In support services, volunteers complement or supplement staff during group sessions (e.g., assist with an aquatic program). Administrative services do not directly involve clients (e.g., repairing equipment).

It is key that those recruiting volunteers know the specific needs of the RT unit so potential volunteers can be informed of specific tasks to be performed. Fritz (2014) suggested a targeted recruitment campaign in which the agency addresses the following questions before recruiting:

- What do we need?
- Who could provide this?
- How can we communicate with them?
- What would motivate them?

There are numerous methods to use when looking for volunteers. For instance, the recruiter (e.g., first-line manager, volunteer director) can make telephone calls; send e-mail messages; make presentations to clubs, organizations, or university classes; set up face-to-face meetings; attend volunteer fairs; post information on the agency's website; employ social media, such as Facebook; or use volunteer matching sites (e.g., Volunteers of America, Volunteering Solutions).

Following recruitment, the next step is volunteer selection. Volunteer selection involves three components according to Carter and O'Morrow (2006):

- Application and credential review and verification
- Candidate screening and interviewing
- Candidate disposition and documentation (p. 254)

Candidates for volunteer positions complete applications that include personal information in addition to credentials related to their competence. Personal information typically required includes contact information (personal and business addresses, e-mail address, phone number, emergency contact); employment and volunteer experiences (with addresses and references); credentials (specialized training or education); reason for volunteering along with commitment in terms of time and duration; previous RT experiences (e.g., setting, clientele, intervention); and job-related insurance, medical checkups, and police record verification.

Following the application review, candidates are screened and interviewed. The purposes of these processes are to match the volunteer with needed positions, to identify training needs, and to begin to orient the volunteer to the organization. Screening can be done by phone or in person. During this process, candidates are apprised of the mission and objectives of the agency and RT unit, operating parameters (e.g., time commitments, work schedules, out-of-pocket expenses), and volunteer needs. Applicants clarify how their qualifications relate to position openings. If there is a match between the applicant and needs of the RT unit, an interview follows. Interviews for administrative positions may be conducted by the first-line manager or volunteer director. For direct service or support service positions, RT staff are typically involved in the interviewing process. Interviews help the first-line manager and RT staff to determine not only if the applicant has needed skills, but also if the individual's character or disposition is a good fit with the clients being served, if the recreational therapists believe they can work with the individual, and if the person will enhance the program. Finally, during the interview, interviewees are given opportunities to ask questions, and interviewers gain permission from interviewees to check references, to conduct a police records check, and to contact former employers or supervisors (Carter & O'Morrow, 2006). Examples of interview questions to ask volunteers are listed in Table 12.2.

After the interview has been completed, the agency then decides whether the individual should become a volunteer. Whether or not the volunteer is accepted, a formal letter should be sent to all candidates informing them of the agency's decision. Carter and O'Morrow (2006) suggested: "Rejection letters to volunteers present other options, suggest needed training, encourage application at a later date, recommend trial placements, and/or cite reasons for incompatibility" (p. 261).

Table 12.2
Volunteer Interview Questions

General Questions

- Why are you interested in volunteering in our organization?
- Tell me about your work history.
- What do you do during your free time?
- Are you involved in organized activities, such as clubs?
- Tell me about your current and past volunteer experiences.
- What have you most enjoyed about your volunteer positions?
- How much time would you like to volunteer?

Leadership Skills

- Briefly talk about your experiences as they relate to this position.
- What skills and qualifications do you have that will help you for this position?
- Describe a leadership role you have held. What did you like about it? Dislike?
- What do you consider to be among your greatest strengths?
- What is your greatest weakness? What are you doing to improve it?
- Are there rewards that help you to keep motivated?

Human Relations Skills

- Why do you like helping others?
- What kind of people do you most enjoy working with?
- Being a volunteer, have you ever felt your work went unappreciated?
- Describe a time when you've been involved in a conflict with an individual or group. How did you handle the situation?
- How do you feel about working with people different from you, such as those with disabilities or of other racial or ethnic backgrounds?
- How do others view you as a role model?

Organizational Skills

- What record keeping experience have you had?
- Are you willing to attend orientation/training sessions to assist you as a volunteer?

Adaptability

- Describe a situation in which you didn't get your way or when you didn't agree with a decision. Was it stressful for you? How did you handle it?
- In what kind of environment do you thrive?

Dependability

- How do you handle a situation when you know that you are unable to complete an assignment or commitment?
- Do you have available transportation to get to your volunteer assignments?

Communication

- How comfortable are you in speaking in front of a group?
- What, in your opinion, makes you a good listener?

Note. Adapted from "Volunteer Interview Questions," n.d. (F:/com-serv/HUM-SERV/RSVP_NCVC/ Volunteer Management/Volunteer Interview Questions.doc) and "Volunteer Mock Interview," n.d. (https://mockquestions.com/position/Volunteer/interview/).

Volunteer Training

The first step in volunteer training is to orient volunteers before they begin their service. A good orientation program helps to ensure a smooth transition into volunteering and recognizes the importance of volunteers to the agency. Hashim (2003) explained:

> The purpose of orientation is to make them (i.e., volunteers) feel worthy and welcome, develop a positive perception of the organization, confirm they have made the right decision, build enthusiasm, ensure a mutual expectation of the task, and instill understanding of the dos and don'ts of the job. (p. 4)

Elements that may be included in an orientation program are listed in Table 12.3.

Table 12.3
Elements of an Orientation Program

- History and development of the organization
- Range of services provided by the organization
- Mission, vision, and goals
- Meeting key people in the organization
- Hours of operation
- Rules and policies (e.g., liability, consumer rights, parking, record keeping)
- Financial and promotional protocols
- Leadership principles
- Training and development
- Code of ethical conduct
- Volunteer boundaries and performance criteria
- Medical, health, and legal clearances
- Emergency procedures

Note. Adapted from *Effective Management in Therapeutic Recreation Services* (2nd ed., p. 262), by M. J. Carter and G. S. O'Morrow, 2006, State College, PA: Venture; *Recruiting and Retaining Volunteers* (p. 4), by M. A. Hashim, 2003, Montreal, Canada: World Federation of Hemophilia; and *Creative Management* (6th ed., p. 230), by R. G. Kraus and J. E. Curtis, 2000, Boston, MA: McGraw-Hill.

In addition to the orientation program, new volunteers should be provided training on their specific responsibilities. If several volunteers are assigned to the same or a similar task, group training sessions may be conducted. Throughout the volunteer experience, agencies typically provide continuing education for volunteers to ensure they have up-to-date information and to enhance their skills.

Volunteer Supervision

A hospital volunteer director once told one of the authors of this text: "There is no such thing as a bad volunteer. There are only volunteers out of place." Following this line of reasoning, it is imperative that supervisors closely monitor volunteers. If volunteers lack aptitude or interest for a particular job, they should be assigned to a job that better suits their skills and interests. Whether supervision is provided by the first-line manager or a recreational therapist, it is important that the supervisor realize the abilities and motives of volunteers and assign them to tasks that satisfy their personal abilities and motives.

According to Hashim (2003), when assigning tasks supervisors must ensure the following:

- Tasks are explained clearly
- Training is provided
- Volunteers understand how their task will benefit the cause
- Work is interesting and useful
- Success is attainable
- Guidance and feedback is provided
- Praise is given (p. 5)

Additionally, supervisors of volunteers need to remain vigilant of the work environment to prevent grievances by volunteers or to correct situations when problems arise. A number of areas of complaint by volunteers that may occur are listed in Table 12.4.

Table 12.4
Potential Areas of Complaint by Volunteers

• Poor role models	• Poor orientation
• Unclear task	• Little work or no work
• Boring task	• Lack of guidance
• No feedback on performance	• Little communication on the job
• No support	• No recognition
• Little sharing of information	• Financial promises not kept
• Little training	• Bossy attitude

Note. From *Recruiting and Retaining Volunteers* (p. 5), by M. A. Hashim, 2003, Montreal, Canada: World Federation of Hemophilia.

In sum, it is critical that volunteers are shown respect for the jobs they are doing and that they are recognized as being essential to the overall organization by their supervisor. A good rule to follow is to treat volunteers with the same respect as professional staff.

Volunteer Evaluation and Recognition

Understanding how to evaluate, motivate, and reward volunteers is a critical skill for first-line managers. Formative and summative evaluation should be completed with volunteers. Formative evaluation involves regular conferences (e.g., monthly) with volunteers to get feedback from them and to offer feedback to them on their performance and to praise them for their volunteer efforts. Summative evaluation is completed during annual reviews or during exit interviews, at which time the interviewer should find out why the person is ending their volunteering experience.

Should a volunteer be found to not be performing to the level required by the organization, the first step should be to determine the reason for the subpar performance. Perhaps corrective action can occur with the provision of further training. Or, as indicated previously, the volunteer may not be well suited for that job and need to be assigned an alternative task that better fits his or her desires and skills. As a last resort, a volunteer may have to be terminated. Termination is to be avoided because of possible negative repercussions on how the organization may be perceived by volunteers, but when it is necessary managers must follow the detailed procedures set by the organization to follow in cases of termination (Hurd, Barcelona, & Meldrum, 2008).

The majority of volunteers are hard working, responsible, and responsive to staff. These volunteers need to be recognized and rewarded for their contributions to the organization. Recognition makes volunteers feel appreciated for what they do and volunteers, like all people, want to feel appreciated and valued. Hashim (2003) wrote:

> It is very important for organizations to recognize the contributions of volunteers. How you provide recognition can range from a few words of praise to an award or other public acknowledgement. Whether personal or public, the type of recognition will depend on many factors including how long the volunteer has been involved, your organization's style and financial capacity, and the judgment of the volunteer coordinator. (p. 6)

Managers should also recognize staff for their support of the volunteer program, as the program would be destined for failure without staff being welcoming of and providing training and supervision for volunteers. Managers can formally recognize the efforts of staff through a number of means, including performance appraisals, letters of commendation for personnel files, and public acknowledgment of staff efforts before agency administrators. Managers can informally recognize staff efforts to enhance the volunteer program through means such as offering personal praise verbally or through a note or e-mail (Carter & O'Morrow, 2006).

Retaining Volunteers

Should volunteers be properly selected, trained, placed, supervised, and rewarded for their performance, they will likely remain with the organization. If they are happy and feel their efforts are meaningful and appreciated, they will be apt to remain long-term volunteers.

Bannon (1999) suggested that providing training is an especially valuable tool in retaining volunteers because the time and money the organization spends on training displays to volunteers the organization's commitment to the volunteers and sends them the message: "You are important to us – you count" (p. 340).

To ensure that volunteers experience success, it will be necessary to have a plan to evaluate the overall volunteer program. Such an evaluation plan should be developed when the volunteer program is initiated and should include formative and summative evaluation components. Formative evaluation is a form of developmental evaluation that monitors and assesses ongoing processes to determine how successful a program is and if changes are required. Summative evaluation is a form of retrospective evaluation focused on the ultimate outcomes of a program at the end of a specific time (e.g., annually).

Evaluation should include precise data collection on the number of volunteers and the number of volunteer hours. It should also encompass the systematic gathering of evaluation information from staff, volunteers, and clients. These data can be obtained through means such as individual conferences with staff and interviews with volunteers and clients (including exit interviews). Other means include having staff complete questionnaires on volunteer compliance with job descriptions and asking volunteers to complete surveys on the training and supervision they received (Carter & O'Morrow, 2006). Of course, the manager must assess the data derived from formative and summative evaluations of the volunteer program to initiate changes when necessary or to enhance strengths of the program. When making changes, managers, working with their staff, need to consider not only what has occurred in the past, but also future needs and opportunities (Bannon, 1999).

Summary

This chapter has covered major facets in establishing, conducting, and evaluating volunteer programs. Following a discussion of why people volunteer, components involved in conducting volunteer programs were covered. These included planning volunteer programs, recruiting and selecting volunteers, volunteer training, volunteer supervision, volunteer evaluation and recognition, retaining volunteers, and completing a systematic evaluation of the volunteer program. Key points for the first-line manager to consider in conducting a volunteer program are listed in Table 12.5.

Table 12.5
Key Points to Consider in a Volunteer Program

- Be systematic and comprehensive when you implement a volunteer program. Do not use the "shotgun approach." Do not just rush out and recruit a few volunteers and put them to work. Look at the big picture first and be sure you have the commitment necessary to run an effective volunteer program.

- Deal with paid staff attitudes and reservations about volunteers. Build a consensus on appropriate roles for volunteers in your organization.

- Develop and use effective volunteer application and evaluation procedures that will allow you to screen and accept only qualified candidates.

- Evaluate the volunteer's work performance. Resolve problems as quickly as possible.

- Review your program at least annually. Make sure that what you are doing is necessary and that the volunteer program fits the future needs and opportunity before you continue the program unchanged.

- Educate paid staff to the advantages of working with volunteers and reward them for effective collaboration.

- When possible, appeal personally to prospective volunteers by asking them face-to-face. Surveys indicate that the ideal way to approach volunteers is by personal contact.

- Establish high standards of conduct and expectations for your volunteer staff. Volunteers should feel as important as paid staff.

- Identify at least one prospect for each volunteer position. This matching process should involve two considerations: first, which job can best meet the needs and interests of the prospective volunteer, and second, which prospective volunteer can best fill the job.

- Do not always be in a rush. Let volunteers see you have time for them – they have time for you.

Note. From *911 Management* (pp. 340–341), by J. J. Bannon, 1999, Urbana, IL: Sagamore.

Conclusion

From the contents of this chapter, it should be clear that well-conducted volunteer programs can strengthen, extend, and enrich the provision of RT units within any agency. Therefore, wise managers put together a solid plan for the volunteer program and work closely with staff, volunteers, and clients to implement and evaluate all elements of the plan.

References

Austin, D. R., & Lee, Y. (2013). *Inclusive and special recreation* (6th ed.). Urbana, IL: Sagamore.

Bannon, J. J. (1999). *911 management.* Urbana, IL: Sagamore.

Carter, M. J., & O'Morrow, G. S. (2006). *Effective management in therapeutic recreation service* (2nd ed.). State College, PA: Venture.

Fritz, J. (2014). 3 ways to recruit volunteers for your nonprofit. Retrieved from http://nonprofit.about.com/od/volunteers/a/recruitvols.htm

Hashim, M. A. (2003). *Recruiting and retaining volunteers.* Montreal, Canada: World Federation of Hemophilia.

Hurd, A. R., Barcelona, R. J., & Meldrum, J. T. (2008). *Leisure services management.* Champaign, IL: Human Kinetics.

Volunteer interview questions. (n.d.). Retrieved from F:/com-serv/HUM-SERV/RSVP_NCVC/Volunteer Management/Volunteer Interview Questions.doc

Volunteer mock interview. (n.d.). Retrieved from https://mockquestions.com/position/Volunteer/interview/

Chapter 13

Managing Marketing

Objectives

- Define the term *marketing*.
- Explain what is meant by internal marketing.
- Explain what is meant by external marketing.
- Define advertising.
- Describe public relations.
- Explain what is meant by publicity.
- Describe personal selling.
- Outline the steps in developing an external marketing plan.
- Identify the four *P*s of external marketing.
- Identify strategies for recruiting volunteers.
- Discuss the responsibilities of recreational therapists to promote the profession.

Key Terms

- **Marketing:** "Marketing is how you reach those who need to know you're out there and will want to support you" (Winton & Hochstadt, 2011, p. 410).
- **Internal marketing:** An internal marketing program helps ensure employees are socialized into the organization, have the training they need to perform, and feel rewarded and appreciated within a system in which they are treated as professionals.
- **External marketing:** What is typically thought of when the term *marketing* is mentioned. Marketing to external publics outside of the organization.
- **Advertising:** "Any paid form of nonpersonal presentation and promotion of ideas, goods, or services by an identified sponsor" (Armstrong & Kotler, 2005, p. 399).
- **Public relations:** Public relations efforts provide ongoing means to project a positive image of an organization or profession.
- **Publicity:** "Publicity is communication in news story form about the organization, its products, or both, transmitted through a mass medium at no charge" (Pride et al., 2007, p. 427).
- **Marketing targets:** Individuals and groups that have or can have a relationship with the organization or profession being marketed (e.g., clients, families, other healthcare professionals).

The value of marketing has long been embraced by businesses, such as restaurants, retail shops, and banks. Recreational therapy (RT) has been slow to acknowledge, let alone embrace, marketing. Marketing therefore has not traditionally been an area of concern for RT professionals. This chapter is provided to help RT students and practitioners appreciate the need for marketing and introduce them to marketing principles.

Marketing

Marketing is about influencing behaviors of the agency's target group (Andreasen, 2012). Stated differently, "Marketing is how you reach those who need to know you're out there and will want to support you" (Winton & Hochstadt, 2011, p. 410). Marketing provides those in RT with a means to influence others' understandings of the nature and purpose of RT and to promote positive attitudes toward RT. Marketing therefore should be an area of concern for every first-line RT manager.

Within RT, managers should develop plans to market their RT unit to others within their organization (e.g., other units in hospitals or agencies) and externally beyond the confines of their organization (e.g., university students and community groups). But marketing is not a task for the RT manager to complete in isolation from staff. The RT manager should involve all staff in planning and conducting marketing programs.

Types of Marketing

The term *marketing* typically brings to mind efforts to reach those outside of the home agency or organization, which is termed *external marketing*. The marketing literature, however, indicates two types of marketing. In addition to external marketing, there is *internal marketing*.

> "Internal marketing is probably much more important than external marketing. That's even more true today than it's ever been."
>
> Tom Stewart

Internal Marketing

Internal marketing defined. In internal marketing, employees are the target group. Internal marketing is selling staff on the organization. It is about employee "buy-in" and "pride in." That is, internal marketing is directed toward employees believing in the organization and taking pride in being a part of the organization. Internal marketing also involves assisting employees to perform at high levels and having employees understand that they play a major role in the way that clients perceive the services provided. Ideally, internal marketing involves hiring and maintaining quality employees and motivating them to provide exceptional service to clients.

Providing an internal marketing program helps ensure employees are socialized into the organization, have the training they need to perform, and feel rewarded and appreciated within a system in which they are treated as professionals. The results of such a program produce employees who are satisfied with their jobs and are in positions to provide quality services. Through their resulting interactions with clients in providing quality services, employees bring about positive views of the organization and its services.

Internal marketing "is concerned with how organizational management should develop educational training, explicitly communicate organizational perspectives and create reward systems that improve employee service ability and satisfaction with their work" (Tsai & Wu, 2011, p. 2594). Thus, internal marketing offers a tool to prepare and motivate skilled staff to provide the highest levels of service to clients.

As indicated by Tsai and Wu (2011), internal marketing should "explicitly communicate organizational perspectives." A part of internal marketing therefore involves first-line RT managers establishing education and training programs to allow them to actively carry information from higher level managers to staff, to explain the organization's visions and the plans and strategies to achieve those visions. First-line managers additionally need to gather feedback from staff and send it to top-level managers. This permits higher level managers to consider additional perspectives and ensures employees know their voices are being heard. Also, sharing information about the organization's plans and strategies with employees heightens morale by making employees feel they are "in the know" about what is going on within their organization. Such communication helps employees feel included, which helps them to make positive emotional connections with the organization. Employees feel involved and a part of the organization. They connect with the organization through perceiving a common sense of purpose and identity. This allows them to feel good about the organization in which they view themselves playing a vital part and to take pride in their roles within the organization. When employees care about and believe in the organization, they are more prone to put forth their best efforts and have increased loyalty to the organization (Mitchell, 2002). Such affirming feelings lead to employees becoming "boosters" for the organization.

Another part of internal marketing is motivating employees by showing them that the organization is interested in them as individuals to perform at high levels. This can be accomplished by providing staff with professional development opportunities (e.g., workshops, short courses) as well as having a rewards program to reinforce staff for quality performances. There seems to be a natural reciprocity in that if the organization cares about employees and their performances, employees will care about the organization that is supportive of them. Thus, for an internal marketing program, the first-line manager needs to obtain opportunities for staff professional development and to acknowledge and reward staff who exhibit quality performances.

A final component in internal marketing is to educate employees to understand that they play a major role in the way that clients perceive the organization's services. Thus, first-line RT managers need to ensure their staff know that it is imperative to create client satisfaction and build client loyalty through their everyday interactions with clients. Corbin, Kelley, and Schwartz (2001) indicated means by which healthcare professionals may influence how clients view their services. For instance, client evaluations of the services often rest on the cleanliness of rooms, how polite staff were, and the appearance and demeanor of staff, regardless of whether the service produced the benefits they sought. Another healthcare area that affects client views is whether clients were active participants in their care. Actively participating with clinical staff in their treatment promotes positive feelings, loyalty, and cooperation with the clinical staff and the organization. Because recreational therapists regularly engage in partnerships with clients within therapeutic relationships or therapeutic alliances, they must realize the potential effects of these partnerships. It has been said that therapeutic relationships are at the heart of RT (Austin, 2011). If this is true (and many believe it to be true), partnerships with clients should be a critical concern for recreational therapists. Another related area is developing relationships with clients and offering meaningful interpersonal interactions. The fostering of relationships and the engagement with clients in interpersonal interactions, when accompanied with positive clinical outcomes, bring about intense feelings of loyalty in clients. It becomes vital that recreational therapists realize that the relationships they build with clients and their interactions with clients can produce strong feelings in clients. There is a final means by which healthcare professionals may influence how clients view their services: When clients are in positive moods, they tend to evaluate situations and events that occur within their healthcare more positively. This finding appears to have direct implications for recreational therapists, who often help clients to experience positive emotions.

The powerful effects that recreational therapists have on client views can be seen in the examples drawn from Corbin et al. (2001). For internal marketing, first-line RT managers should ensure that their recreational therapists realize the potential effect they can have on clients' impressions of the services and the organization as a whole.

Internal marketing as a foundation for external marketing. Internal marketing is a first priority in terms of marketing as it provides a foundation for external marketing. Armstrong and Kotler (2005) wrote: "Internal marketing must precede external marketing" (p. 251). If a sound internal marketing program is in place, employees are well prepared, have a grasp of the perspectives and approaches of the organization, and perceive they are working in a positive environment. This fosters self-pride in the employees for what they do and pride in being a part of a well-performing organization. The resulting high level of service produced as a result of a sound internal marketing program can then be marketed through the external marketing program.

> "By focusing on internal marketing, health care managers will gain a motivated staff composed of knowledgeable and prepared employees who feel embedded within and appreciated by the organization."
>
> (Masri, Oetjen, & Rotarius, 2011, p. 198)

External Marketing

External marketing is what is typically thought of when the term *marketing* is mentioned. External marketing is aimed at external publics outside of the organization. External marketing is also employed by professions, such as RT, to market themselves to target groups outside their profession, including elected officials and governmental agencies, as well as to the general public.

Advertising, public relations, publicity, and personal selling. Advertising, public relations, publicity, and personal selling are mechanisms used in external marketing promotions to reach marketing targets. *Advertising* is "any paid form of nonpersonal presentation and promotion of ideas, goods, or services by an identified sponsor" (Armstrong & Kotler, 2005, p. 399). *Public relations* (PR) comprises "a broad set of communication efforts used to create and maintain favorable relationships between an organization and its stakeholders" (Pride et al., 2007, p. 427). Thus, PR efforts provide ongoing means to project a positive image of an organization or profession. "*Publicity* is communication in news story form about the organization, its products, or both, transmitted through a mass medium at no charge" (Pride et al., 2007, p. 428). Press releases sent out to newspapers are an example. *Personal selling* is done through a number of means, including everyday interactions (with other healthcare professionals and the general public), speaking engagements (at conferences or to university classes), and face-to-face meetings (e.g., with elected officials or attendees at health fairs). *Marketing targets* include individuals and groups that have or can have a relationship with the organization or profession being marketed. Possible targets include clients, families, volunteers, other healthcare professionals (e.g., physicians, therapists), students, suppliers, administrators, government agencies, and elected officials.

Steps in developing an external marketing plan. The steps in developing an external marketing plan resemble the RT process (i.e., APIE process) of assessment, planning, implementation, and evaluation. The first step (assessment) is to analyze the market to determine marketing targets and to establish the objectives for the marketing program. It is important that the marketing objectives coincide with the aims and objectives of the organization. The second step (planning) is to create a marketing plan and decide which marketing strategies will be used to communicate with the target group or groups to achieve the marketing objectives. Consideration should be given to determining what strengths and obstacles exist. The third step (implementation) involves organizing functions to determine how the plan will be carried out, including the responsibilities and powers of the marketing organization. Elements include establishing and maintaining the budget, determining who will oversee the management of the plan, and identifying who will employ each strategy. The final step (evaluation) is to assess and redirect marketing strategies, considering whether goals need to be revised and strategies redirected (Richmond & Powers, 2009).

Four Ps of External Marketing

The marketing literature refers to the "four *P*s of external marketing": product, price, place, and promotion. The *Products* in RT are the services provided and the benefits derived. It is critical that recreational therapists have the skills and abilities to provide services that produce therapeutic outcomes. *Price* involves the cost of the services. In RT, costs are paid through a variety of mechanisms (e.g., government programs, direct charges, insurance). The *Place* is where the services are provided, which in RT includes a spectrum of settings, such as hospitals, clinics, schools, and home healthcare. During *Promotion,* the services and benefits, price, and place of the services are communicated. Means of communication include advertising, public relations, and personal selling (Fortenberry, 2010; Jacobs, 1998; Morley & Rennison, 2011; Penn & Penn, 1990; Richmond & Powers, 2009).

Marketing to Attract and Retain Volunteers

A particular area of marketing of concern to first-line RT managers is attracting and retaining volunteers who assist with the RT programs. The manager needs to be aware that internal marketing and external marketing are called for when designing volunteer marketing programs. Internal marketing is important because RT staff need to be assisted to develop an appreciation for volunteers so volunteers will be valued, welcomed, and provided with meaningful tasks. External marketing for volunteers involves two basic approaches. One is personal recruitment involving direct one-on-one interactions between staff and the potential volunteer. The best one-on-one recruitment occurs face-to-face rather than through telephone or e-mail. The second approach, nonpersonal recruitment, uses communications with potential volunteers. Here recruitment involves techniques such as making presentations to groups, sending press releases to newspapers, listing volunteer opportunities on websites, and posting flyers in public locations. Equally important to these means of recruiting volunteers is the means of retaining them once recruited. This entails the manager working with staff to implement a volunteer supervision program to enhance the volunteer experience and make sure volunteers know they are appreciated and valued (Wymer, Knowles, & Gomes, 2006).

About Promoting the Profession of Recreational Therapy

Although it is the responsibility of first-line managers to work with staff to develop and implement a marketing program for a particular unit, all recreational therapists should embrace the concept of marketing to promote their profession. It is the responsibility of every recreational therapist to make the marketing of RT a part of their everyday practices whether they are interacting with other healthcare professionals on the job, communicating with members of the general public, or working as a member of their professional association to promote the discipline of RT. February is a good time to provide a marketing drive about RT because it is the international therapeutic recreation/RT month. This month can provide substantial opportunities for celebration and increasing awareness.

Summary

Marketing has not gained a great deal of attention within RT. Today, however, recreational therapists and RT managers are beginning to realize the value of marketing.

It is important to understand internal marketing and external marketing. Although internal marketing is not what is usually thought of when thinking of marketing, it is a first priority in marketing because it provides a foundation for external marketing. Resting on internal marketing, external marketing involves following a systematic four-step process and employing the mechanisms of advertising, public relations, publicity, and personal selling. Another way to conceptualize external marketing is to consider the four *P*s of external marketing, which are product, price, place, and promotion.

Two specific areas for applying marketing principles are volunteer recruitment and the promotion of the RT profession. Marketing the RT profession is a responsibility of every recreational therapist.

References

Andreasen, A. R. (2012). Rethinking the relationship between social/nonprofit marketing and commercial marketing. *Journal of Public Policy & Marketing, 31*(1), 36–41.

Armstrong, G., & Kotler, P. (2005). *Marketing: An introduction* (7th ed.). Upper Saddle River, NJ: Pearson/Prentice Hall.

Austin, D. R. (2011). *Lessons learned: An open letter to recreational therapy students and practitioners.* Urbana, IL: Sagamore.

Corbin, C. L., Kelley, S. W., & Schwartz, R. W. (2001). Concepts in service marketing for healthcare professionals. *The American Journal of Surgery, 181,* 1–7.

Fortenberry, J. J. (2010). *Health care marketing: Tools and techniques* (3rd ed.). Boston, MA: Jones & Bartlett.

Jacobs, K. (1998). Innovation to action: Marketing occupational therapy. *The American Journal of Occupational Therapy, 52,* 618–620.

Masri, M. D., Oetien, D., & Rotarius, T. (2011). Internal marketing: Creating quality employee experiences in health care organizations. *Health Care Management, 30,* 196–204.

Mitchell, C. (2002, January). Selling the brand insider. *Harvard Business Review.* Retrieved from https://hbr.org/2002/01/selling-the-brand-inside

Morley, M., & Rennison, J. (2011). Marketing occupational therapy: Everybody's business. *British Journal of Occupational Therapy, 74,* 406–408.

Penn, B., & Penn, J. (1990). Marketing occupational therapy: Imperative for the future. *British Journal of Occupational Therapy, 53,* 64–66.

Pride, W., Elliott, G., Rundle-Thiele, S., Walker, D., Paladino, A., & Ferrell, D. (2007). *Marketing: Core concepts & applications.* Boston, MA: Houghton Mifflin.

Richmond, T., & Powers, D. (2009). *Business fundamentals for the rehabilitation profession* (3rd ed.). Thorofare, NJ: SLACK.

Tsai, Y., & Wu, S.-W. (2011). Using internal marketing to improve organizational commitment and service quality. *Journal of Advanced Nursing, 67,* 2593–2604.

Winton, J., & Hochstadt, Z. (2011). Nonprofit marketing. In D. R. Heyman (Ed.), *Nonprofit management 101: A complete and practical guide for leaders and professionals* (pp. 409–427). San Francisco, CA: Jossey-Bass.

Wymer, W., Knowles, P., & Gomes, R. (2006). *Nonprofit marketing.* Thousand Oaks, CA: Sage.

Chapter 14

Issues and Concerns for Managers

Objectives
- Define workplace politics.
- Describe negative workplace politics.
- Describe positive workplace politics.
- Describe means to smooth the transition into first-line management.
- Describe basic professional etiquette.
- Discuss how to work with your supervisor.
- Outline concepts of networking.
- Describe the dynamics of stress (e.g., causes, signs).
- Present guidelines managers may use to help reduce stress.
- Recognize the phenomenon of burnout (e.g., signs, stages).
- Discuss actions management can take to minimize burnout.
- Describe how managers can support research.
- Present the benefits of mentoring for the mentee and organization.
- Outline steps involved in establishing a mentorship program.

Key Terms
- **Workplace politics:** The way coworkers in an organization interact with each other in terms of the use or misuse of power and influence.
- **Negative workplace politics:** Produced by individuals who have the aim of furthering their own self-interests by using power and influence without regard for what happens to others or the organization.
- **Positive workplace politics:** Involves instances when a positive political act, carried out fairly and ethically by an individual, benefits not only the political person but also the entire organization.
- **Professional etiquette:** The way people handle themselves while interacting with others in professional situations.
- **Networking:** The cultivation of helpful relationships for the exchange of information and services among individuals.
- **Stress:** The nonspecific reaction that occurs when demands from threats in the environment exceed the individual's ability to deal with them.

- **Burnout:** The process that occurs when prolonged job stress produces a gradual loss of positive feelings about serving as a helping professional and may produce feelings of hopelessness, helplessness, and depression, which in turn may lead to negative outcomes, such as poor job performance, absenteeism, and high turnover.
- **Research:** "Research is defined as a systematic and well-planned process that allows the researcher to gather information about a phenomenon" (Van Puymbroeck, Negley, & Voelkl, 2015, p. 287).
- **Mentoring:** A professional relationship in which the mentor (an experienced person) assists another (the inexperienced mentee) in developing specific skills and knowledge that will enhance the less experienced person's professional and personal growth.

A number of issues and concerns are related to managing recreational therapy (RT) services. Unfortunately, within the RT literature many issues and concerns have not received the attention they deserve. For instance, the topic of workplace politics has generally been ignored. Nor has professional etiquette received the attention that might be expected, because of its importance in making impressions on others. Mentoring has received some attention, but coverage has lacked the specifics provided here for establishing mentoring programs. Other important areas that have likewise been largely neglected are covered in this chapter.

This chapter covers a variety of what should be prevalent issues and concerns for recreational therapists including the following:

- Workplace politics
- Transitioning to manager
- Professional etiquette
- Working with a supervisor
- Networking
- Stress
- Burnout
- Supporting research
- Mentoring

Workplace Politics

First-line managers often have to deal with what has been termed *workplace politics*. McConnell (2014) presented this description of workplace politics:

Politics, as commonly used and generally understood, is primarily the pursuit of power. However, the original meaning of the word was "to act in the service of society." Therefore it once meant a relatively high form of public service. But politics has been reinterpreted to mean primarily service to self, self-empowerment with what is usually a negative connotation. Often what winners call interpersonal relationships, losers call politics. Career failures can result from political as well as professional incompetence. Unwillingness to address the political components of a job has snuffed out many a promising career. Losers make no effort to find mentors or to build personal networks. They grow resentful toward their employers, their superiors, and their colleagues. Often, they become chronic complainers or shrill negativists.

He went on to write:

Corporate politics is gamesmanship, using forces other than good performance – and at times in addition to good performance – to improve one's stance in an organization. This includes trying to influence superiors and gain a competitive edge over one's peers. If your political script is a positive one, you play the game fairly and ethically.

Finally, McConnell explained:

At the other end of the scale politics is selfish, unethical, or illegal. At the other end political behavior supplements professional competency. It is often beneficial not only to the political person, but also for his or her subordinates, superiors, team-mates, and employer. (p. 624)

> "The person who says 'I'm not political' is in great danger. Only the fittest will survive, and the fittest will be the ones who understand their office's politics."
>
> Jean Hollands

Negative Workplace Politics for Managers to Avoid

First-line managers should not take part in political games. Instead, they need to build the trust of staff. Trust is built when mutual respect exists between the manager and staff. Managers who treat staff equitably build trust. And if seen by staff as supporting them, they will be perceived in an even more positive light.

On the other hand, workplace politics can be destructive when managers focus on making personal gains. In negative workplace politics, managers use others and abuse power, putting their interests first at the expense of others and the organization. Power corrupts when it is employed for self-serving interests. Thus, wise managers avoid self-serving actions that can negatively influence the organization's functions. McConnell (2014) listed behaviors that can gain managers disfavor by staff:

- Stealing ideas or credit from others
- Excluding others from meetings or information to gain personal advantage by keeping certain people uninformed
- Eliminating or downgrading the jobs of employees they dislike or distrust
- Assigning unpleasant tasks
- Delegating work that places delegates at risk or that prevents them from handling their regular work
- Pitting one employee against another

- Giving unfair or false performance appraisals
- Not hiring employees who could be threatening to them (pp. 625–626)

Managers should avoid establishing circumstances that can foster staff discontent. McConnell (2014), citing work by Terrell (1989), provided a list of behaviors by managers that produce negative politics:

- Lack of clear organizational goals or lack of communications of the goals
- Autocratic or bureaucratic leadership
- Multiple layers of management (the more layers, the more politics)
- Little upward communication
- Frequent changes
- Controversial management shifts of power
- Poor relationships between workers and managers (p. 625)

The Need for Managers to Understand Workplace Politics

Even though negative workplace politics can be disruptive to the organization and distasteful to individual employees, it occurs in almost every organization. Even if managers dislike dealing with negative workplace politics, they need to understand it because more likely than not, they will have to deal with it. Becoming knowledgeable of the dynamics related to workplace politics will also allow managers to understand that positive workplace politics can also occur within organizations, with beneficial results.

Thus, managers should not avoid workplace politics. In fact, managers need to be proactive in developing the political savvy to comprehend social interactions in the workplace and to use these understandings in ways that will enable those in the workplace to achieve the organization's goals, rather than disrupting the work of the organization.

Understanding involves learning to be alert to political games that staff or colleagues may play when they attempt to manipulate the system for their own benefit. Political games by staff and colleagues may include the following negative workplace political behaviors:

- Taking advantage of being indispensable
- Abusing friendships
- Probing for weaknesses of others and revealing those weaknesses
- Undermining operations or new services
- Starting unfounded rumors or providing misleading information
- Creating crises or discord
- Displaying undue emotional distress to achieve selfish gains
- Discrediting teammates in public or undermining them in private
- Intimidating new employees and provoking sensitive people
- Invoking the names of high-level managers to get their way
- Currying the favor of those who outrank them to advance their own agendas
- "Forgetting" promises
- Passing the buck

- Procrastinating
- Saying what they don't mean (McConnell, 2014, pp. 625–626)

Another part of grasping the dynamics of workplace politics is understanding the workings of informal groups (e.g., cliques, social relationships) within the organization. By doing so, managers develop knowledge about where power and influence lay. According to one source (Mind Tools, 2014), to understand social networks managers need to consider the following:

- Who gets along with whom?
- Are there groups or cliques that have formed?
- Who is involved in interpersonal conflict?
- Who has the most trouble getting along with others?
- What is the basis for the interrelationship? Friendship, respect, manipulation?
- How does the influence flow between the parties? (Understand the Informal Network section, para. 1)

Positive Workplace Politics

Still another understanding that managers must keep in mind is that although self-serving negative workplace politics are disrupting to meeting the organization's goals, staff can and will engage in positive workplace politics to further their interests without harming others. For example, to gain support for an initiative that may help the organization, an employee may take their idea to others in the organization who hold informal power and influence. By so doing, the individual engages colleagues by giving them opportunities to provide input that will help them to buy into the idea, ultimately leading to garnering their support. Once the idea has the support of influential staff, it can be brought to management as an idea endorsed by staff and not just the individual who initiated the idea (Shimmler, 2009). McConnell (2014) termed such an instance a positive political act played fairly and ethically that benefits not only the political person but also the entire organization.

Similarly, like an individual staff member, managers can employ positive workplace politics. If carried out fairly and ethically, positive workplace politics can be used by managers to build support for an idea or to initiate change by gaining backing for the innovation from staff members who possess informal power and influence. With such ability to mobilize staff, the manager is displaying managerial leadership because leadership requires building coalitions by bringing staff members together to embrace an idea or change.

Final Word on Workplace Politics and Recreational Therapy First-Line Managers

In sum, workplace politics exists to some degree in all organizations, including RT services. It can be used to harm or advance an organization depending on whether individuals use power and influence for their own self-interests or for the benefit of the organization. It behooves first-line RT managers to gain understandings of workplace politics so (a) they do not fall into the trap of employing negative workplace politics,

(b) they recognize negative workplace politics among staff, and (c) they gain insights about how positive workplace politics can be used to benefit the RT program.

Transitioning to Manager

What actions can recreational therapists use to ease the transition into first-line management positions? Roepe (2002) suggested: "The first step in being a successful manager is having self-confidence. This in turn helps you gain the trust and respect of staff and peers" (p. 1). She went on to suggest that new managers remind themselves that being hired for the position indicates this trust and respect is already present and the agency administration believes in them, otherwise they would not have been put in a supervisory position.

> Something to think about:
>   "By working faithfully eight hours a day you may
> eventually get to be boss and work twelve hours a day."
>
>   Robert Frost

Roepe (2002) also suggested what new managers should do initially upon starting their new position. She suggested that managers map out a daily plan for the first day and ensuing weeks. Among tasks for the first day, managers should (a) arrive at least 15–20 minutes prior to the normal start of the day; (b) introduce themselves to everyone (e.g., recreational therapists, assistants, secretaries, nurses, MDs) and, as they do, take the initiative, not wait to be introduced, and finally, shake everyone's hand and memorize their names; (c) be visible during change of shifts; and (d) tour the facility to master its layout.

Roepe (2002) suggested that during the first week managers (a) make it a point to be conspicuous in the department throughout the day; (b) continue introductions as new people enter the department; (c) take ownership of the office (e.g., making it a comfortable space for themselves by putting out personal items, arranging the furniture in accord with their personality and leadership style); (d) become comfortable with the reporting structure (e.g., meeting formally or informally with their supervisor at least twice a day for the first week); and (e) learn key players by introducing themselves to people with whom they will work in the future, such as human resources and risk management personnel (p. 3).

Roepe (2002) stated the single most important thing new managers can do the first week:

Get out and get known. Colleagues will decide "who" you are in the first 60 days. Resist the temptation to hide in the office, because, in reality, there is probably a lot of initial work to do. One survey said a common reason managers fail in a new position is not building good relationships with peers and staff. (pp. 3–4)

The second week, according to Roepe (2002), should be used to learn about the routines of the department, to begin to assess the staff (e.g., their strengths and limitations), to meet other managers within the agency, and to remain in close contact with their supervisor. By the end of the third week, Roepe stipulated a formal department staff meeting be held so staff learn about the values and expectations of the manager. At this meeting, she suggested that managers (a) do most of the talking to share their vision and acceptable behaviors for the department; (b) keep focused on the future, not allowing staff to whine about "but we've always done it this way"; (c) talk about their leadership style and explain their office policies, such as open door or hours; and (d) share the management job description to give a clear picture of what the administration expects of the new manager (p. 5).

McConnell (2014) developed a list of ideas that can be used by recreational therapists who wish to launch successful supervisory careers. These means provide the best chance that the transition into a first-line management position will go smoothly and are listed in Table 14.1.

Table 14.1
Tips to Launching a Successful Supervisory Career

- Know what is expected of you. Be thoroughly familiar with all aspects of your job description.
- Hold regular one-to-one meetings with each employee. Group meetings, although necessary are not enough; each employee deserves your undivided attention from time to time – and not just when criticism is necessary.
- Work to build relationships and establish a personal network.
- Learn to trust your intuition more than you ever had to before you became a supervisor.
- Remain available to help others; become a great listener.
- Be sensitive to the feelings, needs, and desires of the people who report to you.
- Keep your people as fully informed as possible.
- Maintain high ethical and moral standards; be a model of integrity.
- Be willing to ask for help when needed and to ask questions.
- Join professional organizations serving your field and attend their meetings.
- Maintain an active self-education program, recognizing that the supervisor who does not continue to learn will steadily fall behind.
- Insist on good performance, and acknowledge and reward it.
- Remain calm under stress; avoid shouting and pouting.
- Display self-confidence at all times.
- Remain fair; always keep your conduct free from favoritism or discrimination.
- Defend your employees from hostile people and tormentors.
- Display the courage to make unpopular decisions and see them through.

Note. From *Umiker's Management Skills for the New Health Care Supervisor* (6th ed., pp. 14–15), by C. R. McConnell, 2014, Burlington, MA: Jones & Bartlett Learning.

Professional Etiquette

Professional etiquette deals with the way people handle themselves while interacting with others in professional situations. Areas of concern within professional etiquette are far ranging, from how individuals dress, to meeting and greeting others, to manners while dining. The use of proper etiquette is important because it presents a favorable impression of the individual, the individual's organization, and even the individual's profession.

On the other hand, problems with professional etiquette can produce negative outcomes. Bannon (1999) wrote that within an agency "without proper etiquette, clients, coworkers, and employees may be offended by certain behaviors or may receive an undesirable message about the organization" (p. 365). The effect of the absence of proper etiquette, however, can certainly extend outside of the agency. For example, recreational therapists who do not know how to conduct themselves at conferences they attend with other healthcare professionals may leave undesirable impressions not only about themselves but also about recreational therapists in general, and this can negatively influence attitudes toward all those in the RT profession.

Making Introductions

It is important to handle introductions well. The first rule of thumb in making introductions is naming the person with the higher ranking (i.e., most important, oldest) first. For example, "Professor Smith, I would like to introduce you to my roommate, Sally Jones." In an agency, the introduction might be, "Dr. Brown, I'd like to introduce to you our new RT intern, Jim White" (Martin, 2014).

Bannon (1999) elaborated on other rules of thumb for making introductions:

Often when making introductions, it is difficult to know how to address someone being introduced or refer to someone being spoken about. The best advice, when in doubt, is to ask the person what she feels most comfortable with. Someone named Charles may prefer to be called Charlie. Showing sensitivity by asking beforehand is far better than making an introduction and being incorrect. Following others employees' leads when it comes to proper titles is also acceptable. When referring to executives, it is almost always safe to assume the use of last names, unless told otherwise. When dealing with subordinates or equals, it is often common to use first names. (pp. 366–367)

Meeting Etiquette

Etiquette needs to be followed during meetings as well. The most important etiquette for meetings is to not be tardy for a meeting. Being late signals that the other person's time is not important. As a matter of professional courtesy, the individual who is late should call to explain the circumstances if they cannot avoid being late for a meeting and apologize for the lateness. Meeting etiquette also indicates that it is important to come to the meeting well prepared so the meeting is productive. If unprepared, it is best to reschedule the meeting (Bannon, 1999).

Telephone and Media Etiquette

The first rule of thumb in telephone etiquette is that phone calls should be answered in a professional, friendly, and courteous manner with the focus on the person calling. A second rule is to return calls in a timely manner. Not returning calls in a timely fashion signals that the person who called is not important enough to make an effort to call them back in a timely way.

An important area for consideration is the appropriate use of cell phones and other technologies while at work. Texting, using Facebook, and using other social media is not appropriate while at work. Unless agency policies encourage the use of cell phones, consider leaving your cell phone in your car or in your office so that you are not tempted to use it during the day. Also, be familiar with HIPAA regulations and take care to never violate them by posting patient pictures on your personal sites or without their consent.

Dressing for Success

Most important in selecting the right attire is knowing what is acceptable within the workplace. Generally speaking, the correct attire for the recreational therapist should be appropriate for the aspect of the job being accomplished. Certainly conducting a fitness class in the gym requires a different type of dress than that called for when meeting with a supervisor. Consistency is called for in terms of accessories, piercings, and tattoos, however. Accessories should generally be kept at a minimum and piercings and tattoos should be hidden if possible while on the job (Neter, 2014). Casual business dress has been widely accepted for recreational therapists attending conferences and workshops. In all situations, recreational therapists should be clean looking and well groomed.

Dining Etiquette

The area of dining etiquette is perhaps the most troubling for most individuals. Rules of thumb can be helpful to those unsure of themselves while dining. A number of these are found in Tables 14.2 and 14.3.

Table 14.2
Nine Dos When Dining

1. Once seated, unfold your napkin and use it for occasionally wiping your lips or fingers. At the end of dinner, leave the napkin tidily on the place setting. Should you leave the table (e.g., to go to a buffet), place your napkin on the seat of your chair, not on the table.
2. It is good dinner table etiquette to serve the lady sitting to the right of the host first, then the other ladies in a clockwise direction, and last the gentlemen.
3. Hold the knife and fork with the handles in the palm of the hand, forefinger on top, and thumb underneath.
4. While eating, you may rest the knife and fork on either side of the plate between mouthfuls. When you have finished eating, place them side by side in the center of the plate.
5. If the food presented to you is not to your liking, it is polite to at least make some attempt to eat a small amount of it. At the very least, cut it up a little and move it around the plate!
6. It is acceptable to leave some food to one side of your plate if you feel as if you have eaten enough. On the other hand, do not attempt to leave your plate so clean that it looks as if you have not eaten in days!
7. Desserts may be eaten with either a spoon or a fork. Use a fork alone if it is a cake or pastry-style sweet. If there is a fork placed horizontally in front of your plate, it is a dessert fork.
8. Always make a point of thanking the host and hostess for their hospitality before leaving.
9. It is good dinner table etiquette to send a personal thank-you note to the host and hostess shortly afterward.

Note. Adapted from "The Basic Essentials of Dinner Table Etiquette," 2013 (http://www.gourmet-food-revolution.com/dinner-table-etiquette.html).

Table 14.3

Ten Don'ts While Dining

1. Never start eating before a signal from the host to do so.
2. Forks should not be turned over unless being used for eating peas, sweetcorn kernels, rice or other similar foods. In which case, it should be transferred to the right hand. However, at a casual buffet, or barbecue it is quite acceptable to eat with just a fork.
3. It is not generally regarded as good dinner table etiquette to use one's bread for dipping into soups or mopping up sauces.
4. Loud eating noises such as slurping and burping are very impolite. The number one sin of dinner table etiquette!
5. Talking with one's mouth full is not only unpleasant to watch, but could also lead to choking! Definitely not a good idea!
6. Don't stretch across the table crossing other guests to reach food, wine or condiments. Instead ask a guest sitting close to pass the item to you.
7. Good dinner table etiquette sometimes involves a degree of diplomacy when it comes to the host's choice of food and wine! Even if you feel that you can do better, don't ever offer your criticism. If you feel unable to pay any compliments, at least remain silent on the subject.
8. Picking teeth (unless toothpicks are provided) or licking fingers are very unattractive! The only exception to the latter is when eating meat or poultry on the bone (such as chicken legs or ribs). In which case, a finger bowl or wipes should be provided.
9. Drinking too much wine can be very embarrassing! Where a different wine is served with each course, it is quite acceptable to not finish each glass.
10. Don't forget to make polite conversation with those guests around you. Dinner parties are not just about the food, they are intended to be a sociable occasion.

Note. From "The Basic Essentials of Dinner Table Etiquette," 2013 (http://www.gourmet-food-revolution.com/dinner-table-etiquette.html).

First-line managers should keep in mind that they need to conform to the rules of etiquette not only to make a good personal impression but also to represent the agency well. Additionally, first-line managers who employ proper etiquette set a good example for staff, who can then model their behaviors. Staff who have difficulties with etiquette need to be provided with training so they know how to conduct themselves properly in professional social situations.

Working With Your Supervisor

McConnell (2014) wrote: "Communication is by far the most important management skill" (p. 510). Certainly first-line managers maintaining regular and clear communication with their supervisor is a key to their success.

Most first-line managers probably find it easier to communicate with their staff than with their supervisor. Even so, the duty of first-line managers is to keep their supervisor informed of the department's climate and activities (Dunn, 2002).

> "It's always better to deliver the news yourself rather than allow your boss to be surprised."
>
> Mary Cheney

In communications with supervisors, it is desirable to know their preferences. Some will prefer a spoken message either face-to-face or through a telephone call. Others want everything to come to them in written form. Sullivan (2012) indicated that, even considering the supervisor's preferences, a combination of spoken and written communication typically works best:

> Usually some combination [of written and spoken communication] is used. Even if you have a brief meeting about a relatively small request, it is a good idea to follow up with an e-mail, detailing your ideas and the plans to which you both agreed. Sometimes the procedure works in reverse. If you provide the supervisor with a written proposal prior to a meeting, both of you will be familiar with the idea to start. In the latter case, careful preparation of the written material is essential. (p. 124)

Additionally, it is helpful to keep in mind the supervisor's frame of mind. Sullivan (2012) stated:

> One aspect of managing upward is to understand the supervisor's position from her or his frame of reference. This will make it easier to propose solutions and ideas that the supervisor will accept. Understand that a supervisor is a person with even more responsibility and pressure. Learn about the supervisor from a personal perspective: What pressures, both personal and professional, does the supervisor face? How does the supervisor respond to stress? What previous experiences are liable to affect today's issues? This assessment will allow you to identify ways to help your supervisor with his or her job and for your supervisor to help you with yours. (p. 124)

Nobody likes to hear about problems, and supervisors are no different. Nevertheless, sometimes first-line managers need to take problems to their supervisor, whose job it is to help them solve problems. So managers should not hide problems from their supervisor, hoping the problems will go away. It is better to seek out the supervisor. Sullivan (2012) suggested:

> Go to your supervisor with a goal to problem solve together. Have some ideas about solving the problem in hand if you can but do not be so wedded to them that you are unable to listen to your supervisor's ideas. Keep an open mind. Use the following steps to take a problem to your supervisor:
> - Find an appropriate time to discuss a problem, scheduling an appointment if necessary.
> - State the problem succinctly and explain why it is interfering with work.
> - Listen to your supervisor's response and provide more information if needed.
> - If you agree on a solution, offer to do your part to solve it. If you cannot discover an agreeable solution, schedule a follow-up meeting or decide to gather more information.
> - Schedule a follow-up appointment.

By solving the problem together and, if necessary, by taking active steps together, you and your supervisor are more likely to accept the decision and be committed to it. Setting a specific follow-up date can prevent a solution from being delayed or forgotten. (p. 125)

Within the management literature, there are excellent tips on how to work with supervisors. Kelly (2008) provided one series of tips (see Table 14.4).

Table 14.4

Tips for Maintaining a Good Relationship With Your Boss

Know your boss':

- Goals and objectives
- Pressures
- Strengths, weaknesses, and blind spots
- Working style

Understand your own:

- Objectives
- Pressures
- Strengths and weaknesses
- Working style
- Predisposition toward dependence on authority figures

Develop a relationship that:

- Meets both your objectives and styles
- Keeps your boss informed
- Is based on dependability and honesty
- Selectively uses your boss' time and resources

Note. From *Nursing Leadership & Management* (2nd ed., p. 200), by P. Kelly, 2008, Clifton Park, NY: Thomson Delmar Learning.

Sullivan (2012) also offered a series of tips for working with supervisors. These are listed in Table 14.5.

Table 14.5

Rules for Managing Your Boss

- Give immediate positive feedback for good things that the supervisor does; positive feedback is a welcome change.
- Never let your supervisor be surprised; keep her or him informed.
- Always tell the truth.
- Find ways to compensate for weaknesses of your supervisor. Fill in weak areas tactfully. Volunteer to do something the supervisor dislikes doing.
- Be your own publicist. Don't brag, but keep your supervisor informed of what you achieve.
- Keep aware of your supervisor's achievements and acknowledge them.
- If your supervisor asks you to do something, do it well and ahead of the deadline if possible. If appropriate, add some of your own suggestions.
- Establish a positive relationship with the supervisor's assistant.

Note. From *Effective Leadership and Management in Nursing* (8th ed., p. 124), by E. J. Sullivan, 2012, Boston, MA: Pearson.

Networking

Zimmermann (2002) provided this brief definition of networking: "Networking is the process of aligning oneself with others to obtain information, ideas, advice, power, and influence" (p. 61). The old (and generally true) cliché is, "It's not what you know but who you know that counts."

McConnell (2014) listed a number of benefits of networking:

- Technical, professional, legal, or financial advice
- Advance information about trends, new projects, or organizational changes
- Opinions on proposals, ideas, speeches, or reports
- Moral support
- Mentoring or counseling help
- Learning about job opportunities
- Becoming aware of the availability of job candidates
- Soliciting recommendations or support
- Sharing experiences, both successes and failures (p. 628)

The more managers form coalitions and alliances, both within and outside the organization, the more power and political clout they will possess from having the support of others, rather than going it alone (Marquis & Huston, 2009). McConnell (2014) identified a number of potential participants with whom to network:

- *Colleagues and coworkers* who work with you in committees or other work groups
- *Former teachers* under whom you have studied
- *Vendors* with whom you do business
- *Community associates* who are fellow members of your various organizations
- *"Gatekeepers"* who can provide access to important people, services, or knowledge
- *Counterparts* at other organizations in the community that are similar to yours
- *Family members* who can have numerous contacts in their own personal networks (p. 628)

McConnell only indirectly identifies a prime group with whom recreational therapists tend to network. This is members of professional societies to which they belong, such as the American Therapeutic Recreation Association (ATRA) or the Canadian Therapeutic Recreation Association (CTRA). It is important for managers to reach out to make themselves available and visible to others. Establishing contacts at professional conferences and symposia, such as those sponsored by ATRA or CTRA, is a good way to build national networks. Similarly, going to state, province, and local meetings provides an effective means to building networks. An excellent means of networking is RecreationalTherapynet (maintained by Oklahoma State University), where those on the electronic mailing list can post messages on topics such as position vacancies, advice on establishing programs or locating resources, or information to support evidence-based practice.

A final useful piece of information for any first-line manager is McConnell's (2014) list of characteristics of successful networkers (see Table 14.6).

Table 14.6

Characteristics of Successful Networkers

- They know how to interact with people; they ask good questions and listen attentively.
- They keep in touch with their contacts.
- They are active joiners.
- They circulate at parties and meetings and introduce themselves rather than waiting for someone else to do the honors.
- They are cordial and courteous to all but selective about the people with whom they develop special rapport.
- They use coffee breaks and lunch times to chat with different people.
- They volunteer for committees and other group functions.
- They teach, coach, and mentor.
- They serve as officers in social and professional organizations.
- They go out of their way to establish relationships with newcomers.
- They share clippings, reports, articles, and other information.
- They send out many thank-you notes, and they remember birthdays and other special occasions.
- They express their appreciation for favors in special ways.

Note. From *Umiker's Management Skills for the New Health Care Supervisor* (6th ed., pp. 629–630), by C. R. McConnell, 2014, Burlington, MA: Jones & Bartlett Learning.

Stress

This segment of the chapter discusses stress, a phenomenon that recreational therapists and other helping professionals face on the job. The objective of this discussion is to help students and professionals identify stressors and be able to recognize the effects stress may produce, as well as to identify ways in which managers can help to minimize feelings of distress among staff.

> "Stress: The confusion created when one's mind overrides the body's basic desire to choke the living daylights out of some jerk who desperately deserves it."
>
> Author Unknown

Stress Defined

But what is meant by stress? Joyful events sometimes produce eustress or positive stress. The concern here, however, is negative stress or distress. Here stress is perceived as the nonspecific reaction that occurs when demands from stressors in the environment exceed the individual's ability to deal with them. Or, as defined by Yoder-Wise (2007), "stress is the uncomfortable gap between how we would like our life to be and how it actually is" (p. 532). Sullivan (2012) explained:

A balance must exist between stress and the capability to handle it. When the degree of stress is equal to the degree of ability to accommodate it, the organism is in a state of equilibrium. Normal wear and tear occur, but sustained damage does not. When the degree of stress is greater than the available coping mechanisms, the individual experiences negative aspects of stress. The situation is often described metaphorically through such statements as "carrying a load on one's shoulders" or "bearing a heavy burden." This often leads to physiological and psychological problems for the person and poor performance for the organization. (p. 317)

Stress on the job involves physical and emotional reactions that occur when job requirements exceed the employee's abilities to deal with demands placed on him or her. Two sources of stressors cause job-related stress: external (working conditions) and internal (individual factors).

External Causes of Stress

Staff have little control over a number of factors within their work environments, including the following:

- *Work environment in general:* rotating shifts, uncomfortable or noisy surroundings, lack of equipment, equipment failures, and safety concerns (e.g., infection in healthcare institutions).
- *The job itself:* heavy workload, inadequate training or experience for job assigned, inadequate staffing, mandatory overtime, time pressures, dealing with death, organizational and procedural changes, and job insecurity.
- *Staff relationships:* harassment, threats, personality conflicts, difficult clients or client families, competition between and among staff and departments.
- *Hierarchical factors:* a lack of goals, mission, or objectives; confusing or difficult policies; policies imposed by administrators; and lack of support from management.
- *Poor leadership:* poor communication, top-down communications, lack of opportunity for staff to make input, favoritism, discrimination, insufficient authority to fulfill responsibilities, nitpicking, role ambiguity, and unclear responsibilities.
- *Outside factors:* family, financial, legal, or health concerns. (McConnell, 2014; Sullivan, 2012; Yoder-Wise, 2007)

Internal Causes of Stress

Internal causes of stress come from within and may multiply external factors. Internal factors include the following:

- *Lack of confidence or self-esteem:* due to a lack of competence or experience.
- *Health problems:* from decreased immunity or frequent illnesses.
- *Lifestyle choices:* inadequate exercise, poor diet, inadequate sleep, cigarette smoking, and a lack of leisure enjoyment affect the amount of stress felt.
- *Irrational thinking:* feeling powerlessness, unrealistic assumptions, unrealistic goals or aspirations, and making virtues into evils (e.g., perfectionism or excessive emotional involvements with clients).
- *Negative thinking:* pessimistic thinking, self-criticism, or negative self-talk.
- *Unrealistic thinking:* taking things personally, all-or-nothing thinking, exaggerating, overanalyzing situations, or rigid thinking.

- *Values and actions clash:* Valuing family, but neglecting them because of work pressures.
- *Heightened emotions:* Strong negative emotions, such as fear, guilt, anger, or resentment (with or without real cause), cause heavy strain on the individual and the ability to function optimally. (McConnell, 2014; Yoder-Wise, 2007)

Management Sets the Tone

McConnell (2014) indicated that managers can profoundly affect staff:

One of the most common reasons for employees voluntarily leaving their jobs, sometimes but not always cited during exit interviews, is the style of the employee's immediate supervisor. The supervisor who continually pushes employees, who is quick to dispense criticism but rarely offers praise, who assigns and delegates task after task heedless of overloading employees, and who insists on setting impossibly tight deadlines, is invariably creating stress among the employees. (pp. 593–594)

From the comments of McConnell (2014), supervisors clearly play critical roles in the levels of stress experienced by employees who work under them. Therefore, it is clear that managers need to think about how they are affecting staff and how to minimize employee stress.

Actions by Managers to Reduce Stress

One action that managers may take to reduce stress is to consider the following questions posed by Sullivan (2012):
- Is role ambiguity or conflict creating stress?
- Can the manager help clarify individual staff members' roles, thereby reducing the conflict of ambiguity?
- Is the manager using an appropriate leadership style?
- Does the manager need to clarify a staff member's goals and eliminate barriers that are interfering with goal attainment? Involving staff in decision making is one way to identify and reduce such stress.
- Is the stress due to feelings of low self-worth?
- Would additional training or education help reduce the stress?
- Would recognizing and reinforcing positive behaviors and accomplishments reduce stress?
- Can other sources of support, such as the work group, help the individual deal with stress?
- Is an employee assistance program with counseling services available in the organization? (p. 321)

A second strategy managers may take involves hiring, orienting, training practices, and providing a supportive work environment. The first consideration should be in hiring employees who have a good fit with the demands of the job so they are not overwhelmed by what they are asked to do. New hires should also receive well-designed orientation programs so they know what is expected on the job. In addition, managers should never excessively control staff, but instead should strive to help staff feel empowered to do their jobs and support staff. Supporting staff should include fostering upward and downward communications, allowing staff to express concerns and frustrations, encouraging them to set realistic goals, helping to build work teams to provide social support for staff, reinforcing their positive behaviors by reviewing past successes, and referring them to professional counselors when warranted. Other practical actions managers can take are to ensure staff take breaks and to modify assignments or work schedules when needed (McConnell, 2014; Sullivan, 2012).

A third area for managers to consider to reduce stress in the workplace is to develop department stress management programs. McConnell (2014) suggested the following:

- Encourage staff to establish support groups in which participants can speak freely about their work demands since social support received from the group can serve as a buffer to stress.
- Establish wellness and disease prevention programs. Included may be programs covering conflict resolution, exercise, relaxation and meditation techniques, and talks by dietitians and health experts.

Burnout

Burnout was first acknowledged in the literature in the 1970s (Morse et al., 2012). Freudenberger (1975) originated the term *burnout,* which he used to describe the emotional and physical exhaustion healthcare professionals experienced in the workplace. Unfortunately, burnout is a phenomenon that continues to exist today at a high rate of prevalence (Jenaro, Flores, & Arias, 2007) and is a serious problem for individuals and organizations (Rupert, Stevanovic, & Hunley, 2009). The unchecked escalation of stress on the job may cause staff to burn out, a condition that can be debilitating to individuals and organizations.

Early burnout researcher Cherniss (1980) defined burnout as "a process in which the professional's attitudes and behavior change in negative ways in response to job strain" (p. 5). Cherniss' contemporaries Edelwich and Brodsky (1980) stated burnout involved a "progressive loss of idealism, energy, purpose, and concern as a result of conditions at work" (p. 14). More recently, prominent burnout researchers Maslach, Schaufeli, and Leiter (2001) defined burnout as a "prolonged response to chronic emotional and interpersonal stressors on the job" (p. 398).

Within the RT literature, Austin (2011) wrote:

Burnout occurs when the prolonged mental stress of the job results in a gradual loss of positive feelings about serving as a helping professional. Positive feelings are replaced by negative attitudes and behaviors. Burnout may result in an employee who has blunted emotions, lacks motivation for the job, and quits caring about clients. At its extreme, burnout may even produce feelings of hopelessness, helplessness, and depression. (p. 64)

A Distinction Between Stress and Burnout

Smith, Jaffe-Gill, Segal, and Segal (2007) drew a helpful distinction between stress and burnout:

Burnout may be the result of unrelenting stress, but it isn't the same as too much stress. Stress, by and large, involves *too much;* too many pressures that demand too much of you physically and psychologically. Stressed people can still imagine, though, that if they can just get everything under control, they'll feel better.

In contrast, burnout is about *not enough.* Austin (2013) explained:

Being burned out means feeling empty, devoid of motivation, and beyond caring. People experiencing burnout often don't see any hope of positive change in their situations. If excessive stress is like drowning in responsibilities, burnout is being all dried up. (p. 244)

Candidates for Burnout

The RT manager must understand that only good, caring staff burn out. Those who don't care, and are only on the job for their salary, never burn out, but simply rust out over time. Burnout expert Vikesland (2006) wrote: "The employees most likely to develop burnout are your best employees. Your superstar employees are more likely to feel burnout because they usually put more of themselves into their jobs, spend more time at work, and take work more seriously and personally."

> "It's better to burnout than it is to rust."
>
> Neil Young

According to the Mayo Clinic (2006), those prone to burnout (a) identify so strongly with work they lack a reasonable balance between work and their personal lives; (b) try to be everything to everyone; (c) work in a helping profession, such as healthcare, where their roles are generally defined as "givers," a requirement that may not always result in a sense of reward and satisfaction; and/or (d) have feelings of boredom and stasis because job responsibilities or duties are monotonous.

Signs and Symptoms of Burnout

RT managers need to know signs and symptoms of burnout so they can identify staff at risk for burnout. Patrick (1981) identified objective and subjective signs of burnout. *Objective manifestations* of burnout include the following:

- Overtime work increases as it becomes more difficult to get work accomplished during normal hours.
- Rest breaks and lunch are skipped to get work done.
- Vacations are delayed or canceled.
- People lose their sense of humor, often being overly serious and, perhaps, effectively flat.
- Physical fatigue occurs.
- People become more irritable.
- Susceptibility to illness increases.

- Physical complaints of muscle tension, headaches, low back pain, and gastro-intestinal irritability increase.
- Social withdrawal occurs in the form of pulling away from coworkers, peers, and family or taking part in life activities but without true participation.
- Job performance declines, as reflected in absenteeism, tardiness, use of sick days, accidents, and decreased efficiency and productivity.
- Self-medication begins or increases. (pp. 18–22)

Subjective manifestations of burnout include the following:
- Emotional exhaustion occurs as people experience emotional emptiness and drained inner resources.
- Self-esteem declines.
- People feel trapped in their jobs.
- Emotional withdrawal occurs.
- Depression commonly appears.
- People experience increasing difficulty receiving support from others.
- Boredom and apathy occur.
- Helpers shift from understanding clients to blaming client for their dysfunctions.
- Feelings of frustration increase.
- Feelings of anger appear.
- Feelings of aloneness and isolation occur. (pp. 23–29)

Burnout Stages

Individuals typically pass through stages when burning out. Using Maslach's (1982) stage model, Austin and Voelkl (1986) described three phases during the process of burnout. The initial phase begins when an individual experiences emotional exhaustion or a lack of energy to face another day. The second phase involves a reduction in contact with clients and the treatment of clients in a depersonalized fashion. Finally, in the third phase individuals experience a sense of reduced personal accomplishment and become apathetic. When people become apathetic, they are burned out, at which time their prospects for positive change are greatly reduced (Baird, 2002).

Management Has Responsibility to Combat Burnout

Burnout experts Maslach and Leiter (2005) emphasized the responsibility that those in the workplace must take to combat burnout:

Burnout is not a problem of individuals but of the social environment in which they work. Workplaces shape how people interact with one another and how they carry out their jobs. When the workplace does not recognize the human side of work, and there are major mismatches between the nature of the job and the nature of people, there will be great risk of burnout. A good understanding of burnout, its dynamics, and what to do to overcome it is therefore an essential part of staying true to the pursuit of a noble cause, and keeping the flame of compassion and dedication burning brightly.

Maslach and Leiter (1997, 2005) went beyond this statement to specify that organizations must be involved in preventing and reducing burnout in the workplace. Furthermore, they presented a concrete means by which organizations may combat burnout by making efforts to reduce the negatives and to increase the positives in the work environment. They called for a five-step approach for employee and management cooperation in addressing burnout:

- *Step one.* An individual must take the lead. One employee must prompt a work group to organize to consider the problem of burnout.
- *Step two:* Group momentum needs to follow. A group in the workplace must then get involved to work to maintain the momentum for change.
- *Step three:* The organization must become involved. The agency or organization must become involved because solutions cannot be implemented in a vacuum.
- *Step four:* Assessment and action need to follow. Areas to assess are: (1) employee workloads (too much work, not enough resources); (2) feelings of choice and control (micromanagement, lack of influence, accountability without power); (3) the recognition and reward system (not enough pay, acknowledgement, or satisfaction); (4) the sense of community or social support or lack thereof (isolation, conflict, disrespect); (5) employee treatment in terms of fairness, respect, and justice (discrimination, favoritism); and (6) work related values (ethical conflicts, meaningless tasks).
- *Step five:* It is an ongoing process. Fighting burnout is a continual process that is ever evolving within the organization.

The fourth step may be enlarged to include two additional categories identified by Ilhan, Durukan, Taner, Maral, and Bumin (2007): (a) physical conditions of the workplace (e.g., provision of technological devices, such as computers) and (b) dissatisfaction with relations with colleagues and supervisors (e.g., level of social support offered). The fourth step seems to be the key to the process because from it can come the identification of mismatches between individuals and the workplace that need to be addressed. Once these are identified, specific solutions can be implemented to help employees avoid burnout.

Clinical Supervision Can Combat Burnout

A vehicle in the continuing efforts to combat burnout among staff is the clinical supervision program that should be provided to staff in RT units (see Chapter 11 for a discussion of clinical supervision). The RT unit's clinical supervision program can assist staff with potential problems with burnout in several ways according to the U.S. Department of Health and Human Services (2009).

First, the clinical supervisor can normalize therapists' reactions to stress in the workplace by explaining that feeling stressed is a natural part of being a helping professional who is caring and compassionate and not an individual failing or pathology. Second, the clinical supervisor can emphasize self-care to supervisees and assist them to develop self-care strategies that will help them to cope with stress. Third, the clinical supervisor can assist staff in understanding what brings them peace and joy by asking them to address questions such as the following: Why are you in this field?

What gives you meaning and purpose at work? When all is said and done, when you have seen your last client, how do you want to be remembered? What do you want said about you as a therapist? Fourth, the clinical supervisor can help staff to identify what is happening within the organization that creates workplace stress and learn how to address the situation. Fifth, as the liaison with management, the clinical supervisor can provide support for staff by advocating for changes in the organization when appropriate. Sixth, the clinical supervisor can assist staff in making lifestyle changes to reconnect with those in their social support network (e.g., family, friends, mentors) to build emotional resilience. Helping supervisees to minimize or eliminate what-ifs and negative self-talk is a seventh action the clinical supervisor can employ with staff to reduce stress. An eighth way the clinical supervisor can be useful in combating stress and burnout among staff is helping them to improve their work environment by adhering to scheduled time off, maintaining a personal lunch time, setting reasonable deadlines, and keeping work away from personal time. Number nine on the list of how the clinical supervisor can help staff deal with stress is to educate them about positive work habits, such as basic organization, time management, and being a contributing member of a work team. Finally, the clinical supervisor can direct staff toward recognizing positive aspects in their lives by asking them, "When was the last time you had fun?" or asking them to construct a list of for what they are grateful in their job or to list five accomplishments they have had in their professional life.

Supporting Research

Research is another word for the systematic gathering of information. Writing about research and RT, Van Puymbroeck, Negley, and Voelkl (2015) provided a more specific definition of research: "Research is defined as a systematic and well-planned process that allows the researcher to gather information about a phenomenon" (p. 287).

RT managers should strive to create a culture in which staff do not reply on their old ways but instead absorb and integrate new research-based ideas and concepts into their practices, as well as actively support the conduct of research. Managers can provide in-service training so staff recognize the importance of research. Training can assist staff in how to integrate it into their practice through basing their interventions and approaches on research findings and engaging in the conduct of field-based research by either cooperating with researchers (e.g., allowing access to clients, conducting interventions with researchers) or being directly involved in research by collaborating with researchers in the design, implementation, analysis, and publication of research.

Evidence-Based Practice

Melnyk, Fineout-Overholt, Giggleman, and Cruz (2010) described evidence-based practice (EBP): "Evidence-based practice is a problem-solving approach to the delivery of health care that integrates the best evidence from well-designed studies (i.e., external evidence) with a clinician's expertise and a patient's preferences and values" (p. 302). Thus, EBP is an approach within which practitioners base their practices on the best available research evidence while considering their own clinical expertise and the preferences of clients. Healthcare professionals have embraced the EBP approach.

Thus, it is incumbent on managers of RT units to inform staff that EBP has become the standard in health professions and to provide training to enable staff to adopt EPB.

How Do Practitioners Stay Informed on Current Research?

Practitioners may stay informed on current research in a number of ways. Scholarly publications (e.g., *American Journal of Recreation Therapy, Therapeutic Recreation Journal, Annual in Therapeutic Recreation*) offer research articles that recreational therapists may read. Textbooks that review research are another means for practitioners to keep up with research findings. An example is Austin's (2013) *Therapeutic Recreation Processes and Techniques: Evidence-Based Recreational Therapy,* in which research findings supporting evidence-based practice may be found. Finally, recreational therapists may attend research presentations at national conferences, such as those of ATRA and CTRA.

It behooves the RT manager to provide as many means as possible for staff to keep up on research. One action the manager may take is having the organization subscribe to research publications and purchase books for a professional library for the unit. The manager may also serve as a role model by attending research sessions at professional meetings and making sure budget is available for staff to attend conferences.

Mentoring

Mentoring is a professional relationship in which the mentor (an experienced person) assists another (the inexperienced mentee) in developing specific skills and knowledge that will enhance the less experienced person's professional and personal growth. Porter-O'Grady and Malloch (2013) offered this formal definition of mentoring: "Mentoring is the process of a more accomplished person assisting others to develop expertise and learn new skills based on the mentor's personal, untapped wisdom, reinforcing their self-confidence, supporting real-life situations, and sharing personal experiences when appropriate" (p. 393). Ellis and Hartley (2009) explained: "A **mentor** is an individual who actively supports the development and growth of another person—the **mentee**." They went on to state: "Typically the **mentoring** relationship is a one-on-one experience that covers a significant time period—perhaps 5 to 10 years" (p. 251).

The mentoring relationship between the mentor and mentee is either formal or informal and typically involves a senior mentor and a junior protégé. Usually the mentor is outside the mentee's chain of supervision.

The mentor offers insights into issues and approaches the mentee otherwise might not consider. The mentor also gives honest (positive and negative) feedback to the mentee that stretches the individual, to enhance growth that can produce feelings of empowerment and self-confidence for the mentee (Ellis & Hartley, 2009).

The purposes of mentoring for mentees have been further delineated by Ellis and Hartley (2009):

- Gaining insights as to how to function initially in a new role by learning how to organize his or her activities and set priorities by considering the aspects involved in situations to develop the most productive behaviors. Developing productive behaviors provides for growth and feelings of accomplishment.

- Being able to be introduced to those in the organization who may assist them in their growth and development, and ultimately in their advancement within the organization.
- Being supported by an individual (the mentor) who can advocate or serve as a "cheerleader" for the mentee. (p. 252)

> "A mentor is someone who allows you to see the hope inside yourself."
>
> Oprah Winfrey

Mentoring programs are established in organizations for a number of reasons, including the following provided by the U.S. Office of Personnel Management (2008):

- Mentoring is a part of the onboarding process that helps new personnel settle into the organization.
- It enhances skills by enabling experienced, highly competent staff to pass on their expertise to newcomers who need to acquire specified skills.
- It establishes professional identity by teaching younger staff what it means to be a professional in the working environment.
- It helps employees plan, develop, and manage their careers and assists them to be more responsible as self-directed learners.
- It encourages the development of leadership competencies on the part of the mentee through learning by the example provided by the mentor.
- It bridges the gap between theory and practice, as the mentee gains knowledge and hands-on experience under a competent mentor.
- It helps mentees comprehend the values, vision, and mission of the organization and come to understand the organization's culture.
- It influences employee retention by showing employees in a tangible way that they are valued and thought to be included in the organization's future.
- It enhances recruitment by the mentoring program being offered as an additional incentive to prospective employees. (p. 3)

RT managers who set up mentoring programs can profit from a list of elements provided by the U.S. Office of Personnel Management (2008) and cited by that agency as having proven effective in establishing mentoring programs:

1. *Conduct needs assessment.* To build a case for mentoring, a needs assessment is a first step. Needs assessments can be accomplished by using online or paper surveys, focus groups, and interviews with staff. Additional assessment information can be drawn from secondary data, such as retirement trends, attrition rates, succession plans, and performance ratings. The following are example questions that may be included in a survey, in focus groups, or in interviews:
   - If the agency were to develop and implement a formal mentoring program, how would you benefit?
   - Would you participate as a protégé?
   - Are you available as a mentor?

- What specific knowledge, skills, and abilities do you look for in a mentor and/or protégé?
- What activities would you like to see implemented in a mentoring program?
- Do you believe the agency encourages a mentoring culture?
- Do you currently receive any type of mentoring? If so, are you receiving any benefits from the mentoring relationship?
- Do you have access to mentors in this agency?

2. *Develop a mentoring program road map:* A road map should include a case for it, project plan, and implementation plan. It should also include needs assessment findings, key milestones expected, and the program description. The following should be included in the program description: (a) the goals of the mentoring program, (b) success factors and desired outcomes, (c) targeted populations (e.g., new employees), (d) duration of the program, (e) how the agency plans to market and recruit mentors and mentees, (f) benefits to mentors and mentees, (g) benefits to the agency, (h) budget, (i) the process to match mentors and mentees, (j) outline of the orientation session, (k) types of materials provided to mentors and mentees, and (l) potential mentoring and career development activities.

3. *Gain top management support and commitment:* A formal mentoring program will succeed only if senior leadership supports it and makes it a part of the learning culture, so it is critical to gain support from higher level management. It is best if a senior leader champions the mentoring program.

4. *Commit a program coordinator:* Successful mentoring programs have a program coordinator. The coordinator oversees the entire mentoring program from working with the steering committee or working group, to creating the road map, to carrying out the plan, to assisting with problems that may occur. In the case of an RT unit, the program coordinator may be the unit manager.

5. *Create a steering committee or working group:* A steering committee or working group should be formed to establish the goals and objectives for the mentoring program and to set their roles and responsibilities, which should include how program evaluation is to be conducted.

6. *Develop a recruitment and marketing strategy:* A good marketing strategy will help in recruiting mentors and mentees.

7. *Match mentors and mentees:* It is suggested that the mentees review the bios of possible mentors and indicate their top choices. Following this, the program manager matches the mentees with one of their top choices. Of course, occasionally mentoring relationships do not work and the mentee should be matched with another more suitable mentor.

8. *Conduct an orientation program:* The orientation is a means for mentors and mentees to get acquainted and begin working toward a mentoring action plan.

9. *Develop an instruction guide for mentors and mentees:* This instruction guide should (a) define a mentoring relationship, (b) make clear roles and expectations, (c) recommend topics to cover at mentoring meetings, (d) present other ideas to enhance the mentoring relationship, (e) highlight the time commit-

ments for mentors and mentees, (f) highlight qualities a mentor and mentee should have before beginning the relationship or should work to improve during the relationship, (g) list critical skills or competencies for a successful mentoring relationship, and (h) explain a successful mentoring relationship depends on the commitment to the relationship and the participants understanding their roles.

10. *Develop an instruction guide for supervisors:* Without the support of their supervisor, the mentor and mentee may not be able to accomplish their goals. The instruction guide for supervisors should include (a) time commitments from mentors and mentees, (b) benefits to the mentor and mentee, (c) benefits to the supervisor, and (d) the role of the supervisor during the program.

11. *Conduct a pilot:* The mentorship program should be piloted before the full-blown mentoring program is implemented. Feedback on how the pilot program is going can be gained through the use of evaluation forms, surveys, interviews, focus groups, and observations. Then senior leadership should approve proposed changes before they are implemented.

12. *Develop a mentoring agreement:* Agencies can allow mentors and mentees to develop their own mentoring agreements or a standardized one can be used. Any agreement form should include (a) the roles, responsibilities, and expectations during the program for the mentor and mentee; (b) an action plan with a completion date; (c) the number of times the mentor and mentee will meet; (d) a confidentiality clause; (e) termination of agreement rules; and (f) signatures of the mentor and mentee.

13. *Develop a mentoring action plan:* The mentee should develop a personal action plan or individual development plan that includes goals and objectives, learning activities to reach goals and objectives, and desired outcomes.

14. *Provide a list of topics to discuss:* To assist mentors and mentees, the program coordinator can suggest topics to discuss during mentoring meetings. Examples include managing conflicts, career progression, networking, managing office politics, time management, leadership development, and work–life balance.

15. *Provide development activities:* Examples of development activities include career development seminars, training activities that provide techniques to maintain effective mentoring relationships, networking events, and guest speakers.

16. *Conduct an evaluation:* Evaluations should be conducted throughout the program by mentors, mentees, and supervisors. If the mentoring program has a time frame, at least one evaluation should be conducted at the midpoint of the program and another at the end.

17. *Conduct an end-of-program graduation/recognition ceremony:* Senior leaders should be invited to speak at the ceremony, and awards, such as certificates, can be presented to mentors and mentees. (pp. 9–14)

Astute RT managers notices the similarity between a mentoring program and a clinical supervision program. If a good clinical supervision program exists within an RT unit, it can achieve many of the goals of a mentoring program, so parts of a mentoring program may be redundant.

Conclusion

The issues and concerns covered in this chapter are meant to supplement the fundamental information needed by first-line RT managers. Accordingly, some issues and concerns will be seen by students and faculty as more important than others because of the curriculum provided by a particular professional preparation program. For example, some issues and concerns may be covered in other RT courses or in related courses. Thus, instructors will naturally select specific issues and concerns from those in this chapter to emphasize within an RT seminar or course. Students may find certain issues and concerns particularly interesting because they did not understand the content when they first encountered it or because they simply need to reinforce prior learning.

References

Austin, D. R. (2011). *Lessons learned: An open letter to recreational therapy students and practitioners.* Urbana, IL: Sagamore.

Austin, D. R. (2013). *Therapeutic recreation processes and techniques: Evidence-based recreational therapy* (7th ed.). Urbana, IL: Sagamore.

Austin, D. R., & Voelkl, J. E. (1986). Effects of social support and locus of control on camp staff burnout. *Camping Magazine, 58*(5), 18–21.

Baird, B. N. (2002). *The internship, practicum, and field placement handbook* (3rd ed.). Upper Saddle River, NJ: Prentice Hall.

Bannon, J. J. (1999). *911 management.* Urbana, IL: Sagamore.

Cherniss, C. (1980). *Professional burnout in human service organizations.* New York, NY: Praeger.

Dunn, R. (2002). *Haimann's healthcare management* (7th ed.). Chicago, IL: Health Administration Press.

Edelwich, J., & Brodsky, A. (1980). *Burn-out: Stages of disillusionment in the helping professions.* New York, NY: Human Services Press.

Ellis, J. R., & Hartley, C. L. (2009). *Managing and coordinating nursing care* (5th ed.). Philadelphia, PA: Wolters Kluwer/Lippincott Williams & Wilkins.

Freudenberger, H. (1975). The staff burnout syndrome in alternative institutions. *Psychotherapy: Theory, Research, and Practice, 12,* 73–83.

Ilhan, M. N., Durukan, E., Taner, E., Maral, I., & Bumin, M. A. (2007). Burnout and its correlates among nursing staff: Questionnaire survey. *Journal of Advanced Nursing, 61*(1), 100–106.

Jenaro, C., Flores, N., & Arias, B. (2007). Burnout and coping in human service practitioners. *Professional Psychology: Research and Practice, 38*(1), 80–87.

Kelly, P. (2008). *Nursing leadership & management* (2nd ed.). Clifton Park, NY: Delmar Cengage Learning.

Luebbert, P. P. (1989). The elusive menace of office politics. *Training, 26*(5), 48–54.

Marquis, B. L., & Huston, C. J. (2009). *Leadership roles and management functions in nursing* (6th ed.). Philadelphia, PA: Wolters Kluwer/ Lippincott Williams & Wilkins.

Martin, P. (2014). Proper etiquette for introductions. Retrieved from http://www.ehow.com/way_5220691_etiquette-proper-introductions.html

Maslach, C. (1982). *Burnout: The cost of caring.* Englewood Cliffs, NJ: Prentice Hall.

Maslach, C., & Leiter, M. P. (2005). Reversing burnout: How to rekindle your passion for your work. *Stanford Social Innovation Review.* Retrieved from http://ssir.org/articles/entry/reversing_burnout

Maslach, C., & Leiter, M. P. (1997). *The truth about burnout: How organizations cause personal stress and what to do about it.* San Francisco, CA: Jossey-Bass.

Maslach, C., Schaufeli, W., & Leiter, M. (2001). Job burnout. *Annual Review of Psychology, 52,* 397–422.

Mayo Clinic. (2006). Job burnout: Know the signs and symptoms. Retrieved from http://www.majoclinic.com/print/burnout/WL00062/METHOD=print

McConnell, C. R. (2014). *Umiker's management skills for the new health care supervisor* (6th ed.). Burlington, MA: Jones & Bartlett Learning.

Melnyk, B. M., Fineout-Overholt, E., Giggleman, M., & Cruz, R. (2010). Correlates among cognitive beliefs, EMP implementation, organizational culture, cohesion, and job satisfaction in evidence-based practice mentors form a community hospital system. *Nursing Outlook, 58,* 301–308.

Mind Tools. (2014). Dealing with office politics. Retrieved from http://www.mindtools.com/pages/article/newCDV_85.htm

Morse, G., Salyers, M. P., Rollins, A. L., Monroe-DeVita, M., & Pfahler, C. (2012). Burnout in mental health services: A review of the problem and its remediation. *Administrative and Policy in Mental Health, 39,* 341–352.

Neter, B. (2014). Professional dress etiquette. Retrieved from http://www.livestrong.com/article/65932-professional-dress-etiquette/

Patrick, R. K. S. (1981). *Health care worker burnout: What is it, what to do about it.* Chicago, IL: An Inquiry Book.

Porter-O'Grady, T., & Malloch, K. (2013). *Leadership in nursing practice.* Burlington, MA: Jones & Bartlett Learning.

Roepe, L. J. (2002). Beginning the new role. In P. G. Zimmermann (Ed.), *Nursing management secrets* (pp. 1–6). Philadelphia, PA: Hanley & Belfus.

Rupert, P. A., Stevanovic, P., & Hunley, H. A. (2009). Work–family conflict and burnout among practicing psychologists. *Professional Psychology: Research and Practice, 40*(1), 54–61.

Shimmler, J. K. (2009). The positive side of workplace politics. Retrieved from http://www.womenonbusiness.com/the-positive-side-of-workplace-politics/

Smith, M., Jaffe-Gill, E., Segal, J., & Segal, R. (2007). Preventing burnout: Signs, symptoms, and strategies to avoid it. Retrieved from http://www.helpguide.org/mental/burnout_signs_symptoms.htm

Sullivan, E. J. (2012). *Effective leadership and management in nursing* (8th ed.) Boston, MA: Pearson.

Terrell, R. D. (1989). The elusive menace of office politics. *Training, 26*(5), 48–54.

U.S. Department of Health and Human Services. (2009). *Clinical supervision and professional development of the substance abuse counselor* (TIP 52). Rockville, MD: Author.

Van Puymbroeck, M., Negley, S. K., & Voelkl, J. E. (2015). Management, consultation, and research. In D. R. Austin, M. E. Crawford, B. P. McCormick, & M. Van Puymbroeck (Eds.), *Recreational therapy: An introduction* (4th ed., pp. 281–291). Urbana, IL: Sagamore.

U.S. Office of Personnel Management. (2008). *Best practices: Mentoring.* Washington, DC: Author.

Vikesland, G. (2006). Employee burnout. Retrieved from http://www.employer-employee.com/Burnout.html

Whitehead, D. K., Weiss, S. A., & Tappen, R. M. (2007). *Essential of nursing leadership and management* (4th ed.). Philadelphia, PA: F. A. Davis.

Winton, J., & Hochstadt, Z. (2011). Nonprofit marketing. In D. R. Heyman (Ed.), *Nonprofit marketing 101: A complete and practical guide for leaders and professionals* (pp. 409–427). San Francisco, CA: Jossey-Bass.

Yoder-Wise, P. S. (2007). *Leading and managing in nursing* (4th ed.). St. Louis, MO: Mosby Elsevier.

Zimmermann, P. G. (2002). *Nursing management secrets.* Philadelphia, PA: Hanley & Belfus.

Index